A N N E
BOLEYN

500 YEARS
OF LIES

ANNE BOLEYN

500 YEARS OF LIES

HAYLEY NOLAN

Little
a

Published by Little A, New York

www.apub.com

Amazon, the Amazon logo, and Little A are trademarks of Amazon.com, Inc., or its affiliates.

ISBN-13: 9781542041126
ISBN-10: 1542041120

Cover design by James Jones

Printed in the United States of America

*This book is dedicated to
every powerful woman
whose truth has ever been
suppressed and censored.*

*It is also dedicated to every person
who has had a hand in that censorship.
Sit down. It's over.*

INTRODUCTION

CAN YOU HANDLE THE TRUTH?

This is not a love story. I hate to be the one to break the news, but epic love stories don't end with one partner decapitating the other. The more we normalise and romanticise this notion the deeper down the great rabbit hole of self-deception we go.

If you're coming to Anne's story fresh, let me fill you in on what you've missed.

We've been sold a lie. All these years. It's been one vamped-up story after another in a desperate bid to keep the ever-growing legend of Anne Boleyn alive. But the lies don't add up. So many of the stories that have been spun just don't make sense – in the media and movies, but even more shockingly, in the hallowed history books by those we've come to trust. I'm angry and you should be too. Anne Boleyn has been wrongly vilified for five hundred years, her truth silenced and suppressed, with no one revealing the full, uncensored evidence of this complex, convoluted and contradictory story. Until now.

After four years of rigorous and exhaustive research, the archives have begrudgingly revealed that, contrary to popular belief, Anne Boleyn was *not* the smarmy and smug, cold-hearted scheming seductress we've so often been assured she was, in everything from sixteenth-century propaganda to modern-day mass-market history. Nor was she the ruthless mistress with lofty yet empty ambition, as she is repeatedly dismissed as being in the Tudor biographies. In fact, all these 'versions' of Anne's character clash spectacularly with the few fragments of evidence we actually have regarding her life: facts that rarely see the light of day because, to the irritation of writers the world over, they somewhat ruin the pantomime villain caricature they feel is necessary to sex up their dastardly Tudor plot.

Of course, the age-old story you'll be familiar with, straight from the trusted wisdom of some distinguished historical sage, goes something like this: Anne and her father scheme to place her in the king's path, whereupon she oozes sexuality, her wit and foreign charm seducing the hapless Henry VIII. Then, being the devious mastermind that she is, Anne plays a blinder, telling the king that she won't be his mistress. Oh no, if he wants her . . . he'll have to divorce his queen and marry her.

And for what?

For mindless power and selfish gain, of course; Tudor villains don't need any more motivation than that.

But there are several years of vital information – either brushed over, dismissed or downright ignored – that happen to ruin that entire theory. For why does anyone want power? So they can sit on a throne contemplating inwardly how powerful they are? No! Power is used to put policies in place and implement change. So what deceitful plans did the power-hungry Anne Boleyn enforce as queen? Surely this is where every theory regarding her true character either gains merit or falls flat? Indeed, it does, and as you will discover within the pages of this new analysis, every single one of Anne's royal missions had charity, education or religion at the heart of it. A true sign of a terrible trollop, if ever I saw one.

The level of censorship that has taken place over the last five centuries – and is still alive and well today, I hasten to add – will shock, disturb and baffle in equal measure. Well, I'm afraid I can't help you with the shock (perhaps try a sip of brandy), but I can help with the confusion by providing a groundbreaking re-examination of Anne Boleyn and her entire relationship with Henry VIII – one that for the first time pieces their story together realistically, reflecting the true people we have hard evidence that they were, providing light-bulb moments for the questions historians have, so far, only managed to provide absurd and illogical answers to. As a result, I've found myself tackling the first Tudor biography that mixes historical fact with psychological analysis; this, I've discovered, is vital to finally understanding the two Tudor monarchs with whom society has had a mild obsession for several centuries now.

Already I can hear the academic reader guffawing at such a statement: *we only deal with facts and evidence here, Ms Nolan!*

Well, sure, if we're talking about a study on the interaction of robots. But if we want to understand the *human beings* that were Anne Boleyn and Henry VIII, complete with all their seemingly irrational decisions and nonsensical actions, then we must also take into account the one thing historians tend to dismiss, and that is the screwed-up enigma of the human psyche. I mean, let's face it, no one makes the monumental decision to divorce a queen, start an international war, relentlessly pursue an annulment for seven years and fight to change the religion of an entire country without little things like emotions coming into play. Or an alarming lack of emotion, as you will come to see in the case of Henry VIII.

Which is why you should question anyone – historian or not – who tells you that true love can end in decapitation. When similar acts of violence are carried out as terrorism around the world today they are met with an appropriate level of horror and disgust, but throw in a Tudor king and queen and suddenly it's the most tragic love story of all time. Often it's presented to us so subtly that we don't even realise it's a love story we are being sold; it's the biographer who tells the tale of a passionate king fighting to marry his forbidden mistress, the researcher who calls Henry's correspondence 'love letters', the historian who credits the religious reformation to 'the lovers who changed history', or the news article that cites England's break from Rome as the grandest romantic gesture a man ever made for a woman.

However, we need to ask ourselves what the more logical truth is: that all-consuming true love can end with a man cutting his soulmate's head off because she apparently broke his heart? Or that the two were never in love in the first place and there was something else powering their dysfunctional relationship?

For indeed there was, and if ever there was a moment in history for the truth to finally be revealed, that time is now. Our bullshit meter is at capacity. Our tolerance for being lied to, manipulated and treated as the gullible consumers who will lap up anything has well and truly hit its limit. And so, as a consequence, I'm here to introduce a woman you're unlikely to have met before. This isn't a woman you'll recognise from the commercial or academic history that is readily available, where Anne is repeatedly relegated to the subplot role of 'love interest' or 'opportunistic wife'. But worry not, for this is a woman I guarantee you will grow to respect and admire, because a funny thing happened in uncovering the truth, and that is that Anne Boleyn's story has now become more relatable and inspiring to the modern reader than we could have ever predicted.

Ah yes, for who could fail to be inspired by that classic tale of the systematic suppression of a strong and powerful woman who tried to take on a corrupt establishment?

I'm afraid I can provide no whimsical escapism here, so please leave any expectations of outdated Tudor folklore at the front door. This is no fairy tale and Anne Boleyn was no heartless villain. Yet equally, I'm not here to paint her as the fantasy princess – as though these are the only two categories available for women in history!

Anne was real. She lived and existed just like every one of us. Her personality wasn't written to fit plot points; that means she was complex, with contradicting character traits that cause biographers in need of a neatly packaged page-turner to leave out the vital parts that don't make sense and somewhat ruin their narrative. Anne's story wasn't created for entertainment purposes, which is perhaps why it's been so heavily rewritten over the years. But as tempting as it might be, let's be careful not to describe this analysis as a 'new take', a 'retelling' or 'reinvention' of Anne Boleyn and instead call it what it really is: an exposé of the truth.

The problem is, history is written by the winners. The story the world was told of Anne Boleyn in the sixteenth century was carefully stage-managed by those who killed her, so is there any wonder that what has filtered down is a warped and perverted version? This great legend has now been passed on from generation to generation, evolving along the way. Snippets of her story were told by those who knew her best, but the majority has been told by the people who hated her the most. Of course, the centuries that followed Anne's death were hardly known for their level-headed rationality, so they were unlikely to question the standard spin. Why would they even want to, when they had tabloid tales of witchcraft and incest to tell?

As for how the lies have survived in the twenty-first century, I blame lazy writers not bothering to venture beyond surface-level research, a disturbing spate of sexist historians with outdated interpretations of the actions of women, and a need for Anne to fit the caricature of the 'scheming seductress' within the whole 'six wives' gimmick that it's become.

Divorced, beheaded, died; divorced, beheaded, survived . . .

What a delightful way to trivialise thirty-eight years of collective trauma, misery and murder into a memorable playground ditty. But believe me when I say that Anne being 'one of six' is the least interesting thing about her. So, it's time to rescue her from the restraints of a fictional character description as *Wife Number Two*, remove her from the 'six wives' line-up and let her stand on her own. *Women aren't numbers!*

You may or may not be surprised to hear the main problem encountered over the past five centuries is that most historians simply aren't as impartial as they are meant to be, and neither are the historical sources from which we all work. Be it due to the political climate of that era, social beliefs of that generation, or a whole host of other personal agendas, what the reader gets to see is rarely the unembellished truth. Of course, in the modern world, we also have to contend with the fact that the media can legally rewrite Anne's life in books, movies and TV shows – the means by which the wider public consume history nowadays. Here they declare it 'historical fiction', safe in the knowledge that the reader and viewer will assume the only 'fictional' aspects will be the imagined scenes and dialogue, never suspecting for a minute that what writers are actually doing is changing the entire timeline and facts of Anne's life, rendering her whole story a fabrication.

Yet even those rare gems, the few non-sensationalist academic biographies, somehow manage to overlook the most vital evidence about Anne's life. This is where I have come to realise, with fiction or non-fiction, often it's not what a writer says but what they miss out that can do the most damage when trying to uncover who Anne Boleyn really was, what drove her and why she made the decisions she did.

This censorship is a real issue and it starts with Anne's Tudor peers. One of the most comprehensive accounts of life at the court of Henry VIII was written by the Spanish ambassador, Eustace Chapuys. God bless this man's attention to detail and ability to ramble or we would never be in possession, as we are, of the intricate knowledge of life and politics during Anne's reign. However, rather frustratingly, his reports are deeply biased in favour of the king's first wife, Queen Katherine of Aragon, whose family Chapuys was working for. Of course, none of the reports written by Anne's enemies were ever going to be an impartial reflection of true events, and if they were the only accounts history had to go by, the truth would have died along with Anne. But they're not, and that's where we discover a disturbing double standard.

We have the writings of a range of sixteenth-century historians from in and around the Tudor court, including John Foxe, who reported stories from Anne's household employees, George Wyatt, who provided a unique insider family account, not to mention Anne's own chaplain William Latymer and theologian Alexander Alesius, who both knew her personally, and worked directly with her in the crucial months leading up to her murder. Yet these reports continue to be dismissed to this day as merely trying to gain favour with Anne's daughter, Elizabeth I, during her later reign. Of course, they did themselves a disservice by glossing over every negative in order to paint Anne as an angelic martyr devoid of any human fault. But equally, her enemies would gloss over the overwhelming good, and paint her in a singularly one-dimensional bad light. Yet their negative propaganda is not similarly dismissed as 'biased and unreliable', and this is where the shocking censorship begins.

This lack of objectivity was, perhaps, understandable when writers were so close to events in the sixteenth century, but modern researchers and writers, with their apparent impartiality, should surely now see all these accounts for what they were: wade through the propaganda – negative and positive – in order to piece together a story reflective of the truth. You'd hope they would. You'd trust they would. Alas, they don't, and I have discovered it increasingly rare to find a neutral historical Tudor biography.

A famous female historian recently illustrated this point in a succinct tweet, admitting she is on #TeamAragon, demonstrating somewhat depressingly that we have been pitting women against each other in divorce for the past five centuries and we're not about to stop now.

So, may I take this moment to assure the reader that I have approached this biography with an ambitious attempt at unbiased neutrality, strictly regulating my work to avoid being in favour of one person over another – admittedly, a difficult task when the whole book is centred around arguing Anne's case against the lies! Even so, my vow has been never to deviate into sympathiser, apologist or martyrdom territory. Hence, in order to present the most honest and objective account of Anne's life, this new analysis has incorporated it all: the good, the bad and the censored. Because, as you'll see, it's only when we fuse the contrasting sixteenth-century reports that we are at last met with a fully rounded, fallibly flawed Anne Boleyn who starts to resemble something close to a human being.

Of course, I am fully aware that the world holds many clashing opinions on the life and character of one of Britain's most controversial queens – expressing everything from hate to indifference, admiration to pity; not to mention the restless and growing community worldwide who suspect she has been terribly maligned, but are just not yet privy to the evidence that proves it. Try as I might, I'm afraid it will be impossible to address each person's individual assumptions and beliefs in this correctional biography. Instead, I can only endeavour to highlight the manipulation of the facts and revelation of the truth – or at least the closest we will ever get to it with the evidence that remains.

I don't know why it's taken this long for vital research to come into the mainstream, or why the task of Tudor whistle-blower has fallen to me, but it's a challenge I'm ready to take on. The sheer thrill I've experienced in piecing it all together, the moments of sudden realisation when the penny dropped and it all started to fall into place, excited me more than any sexed-up version of the story ever has.

Bit by bit, the one-dimensional portrayal of the ruthlessly ambitious Anne Boleyn who wanted power for power's sake was replaced by a real-life person I could finally understand. Sometimes you'll want to shout at her from behind the page for being so self-destructive; behold, here is a woman who had more foot-in-mouth moments than Bridget Jones. You'll cheer for her. You'll cry for her. You'll grimace as she plays the situation *so* wrong, storming inevitably into the plot of her own murder.

Don't worry, the truth you're about to read is still worthy of a thousand books and movies. But better than most soap operas, you can't make this stuff up. Well, as we're about to see, over the past five centuries they *have* tried, but the lies aren't nearly as exciting as the truth.

Anne's final words in her scaffold speech heartbreakingly declared, 'If any person will meddle of my cause, I require thee to judge the best.'

Well, I have judged the best and to Anne I say, like for her, the time has passed for staying silent. The world in which we live now requires us to stand up for the truth and fight for what's right, because, disturbingly, the twenty-first century is starting to mirror Anne's own era; so we need to know what really went down in order to ensure we never repeat it again.

We are the people, and together we have a power that is stronger than those who want to manipulate us. As historian Professor Timothy Snyder says, 'To abandon facts is to abandon freedom.'[1] It starts with knowledge. It starts with the truth. It starts here.

So, if you want to know the story behind the shocking censorship of a woman whose power to do good was considered so threatening she was killed, and her reputation systematically ruined over the years, then read on!

#TheTruthWillOut

CHAPTER 1

The Part They Don't Tell You

For most people, Anne Boleyn simply appeared at the Tudor court one day, an ice-hearted villain, ready to smarm and smirk her way into history. Yet there is an incredibly valid reason writers tend to brush over Anne's early life, and that's because it contradicts and spectacularly ruins the whole 'scheming seductress' image we've been repeatedly fed.

However, these aren't just the revelations that have come to light in recent decades of a strict upbringing at the hands of several pious, powerhouse European monarchs – although this was indeed a long overdue, truthful counterargument to sixteenth-century propaganda that had Anne practically raised as a courtesan in the sex-driven boudoirs of the French courts. Not that even this admission of virtue would cause modern historians to stop and question how such an honourable upbringing could produce a depraved schemer who would soon stalk the halls of the Tudor court. In fact, it only served to add a delicious new element to their juicy story: that of the *good girl gone bad*.

But no, as it turns out, Anne's childhood was more monumental than the mere fact that she was nurtured in the royal courts of the Low Countries and France; for she grew up in the pulsating heart of the religious Reformation. This meant that far from simply attending a finishing school that churned out well-bred young ladies brought up to honour and obey, Anne was taught instead to fight back against the questionable authority of Rome by the very activists who kick-started the Reformation.

This 'fierce intelligence' Anne was later said to possess was not used to outwit and bring down petty rivals at the royal court, but to join a war that was brewing across the whole of Europe. This was the rousing religious climate in which Anne thrived and became a passionate fighter for those who had not been afforded the same privileges in life as she; those who had not yet understood that they were being suppressed by what many saw as the all-dominating authority of the Church.

It's only when we delve into Anne's world during the vital years in which she entered adulthood – the people she grew up with, the court influences and hot topics debated daily – that we can truly grasp how laughable it is to say that she returned to England an unscrupulous temptress whose sole aim in life was to be flirty, frivolous and to frolic with kings.

Of course, even when taking her story back to the innocent years of her childhood, we have to wade through an onslaught of eye-roll-inducing lies. The obvious one we should get out of the way first is that Anne was banished abroad as punishment in adulthood. Contrary to what has been depicted in recent novels and movies, she was in fact sent on a prestigious placement as a child.

However, it would appear this lie wasn't plucked entirely out of thin air and was inspired by sixteenth-century propagandist Nicholas Sander. One of his stories is that Anne was sent away to France after her father caught her in bed with both the family butler and chaplain at her childhood home of Hever Castle in Kent. Anne was only fifteen years old when this illicit debauchery was meant to have taken place, following which we're supposed to believe that her father sent his disgraced daughter to one of the most distinguished courts in Europe, that of Archduchess Margaret of Austria, which Thomas Boleyn frequented as a special envoy representing the king of England.

Of course.

It makes perfect sense to risk Anne continuing her alleged sexual exploits in the legendary imperial court, where she could bring shame on not just the Boleyn family and the English monarchy, but her new mistress, Archduchess Margaret, daughter of the Holy Roman Emperor Maximilian I, governess of the Low Countries, who was charged with overseeing the education of her nephew, the future King Charles V of Spain.[2]

Need I really point out the improbability of this claim? Not likely. Particularly as we'd have to also overlook the fact that Anne had been living in France for two years by the time this scandal was meant to have taken place back in England. Ah.

In reality, Anne was sent to Margaret of Austria at around the age of twelve, following her father's first diplomatic mission at her court, where it's said the pair struck up a friendship of mutual respect. This resulted in the offer for Anne to finish her education there in 1513. Boleyn family expert and historian Dr Lauren Mackay states in her doctoral study of Anne's father, Thomas, that securing such an illustrious placement for his daughter reveals a great deal about his relationship with his middle child: not only in that he sought out such a placement, but trusted she would conduct herself well and bring honour to the Boleyn family.[3]

Margaret even wrote to Thomas: 'I find [Anne] so bright and pleasant for her young age that I am more beholden to you for sending her to me than you are to me.'[4]

This note proves what an asset Anne was considered to be and the incredible impression she made on the royals and nobles of Europe within mere months of her arrival.

So, no sign of her hooking up with the mail man, then.

It has to be said, this education was seen as a highly radical move in itself. While it was the norm for boys in the Tudor era to be given tutors and sent to university, girls of Anne's social standing were merely expected to be taught at home by their mothers. Here they would specialise in household chores, while simultaneously tackling heavyweight subjects such as embroidery, music and dancing.[5]

Anne's placement also supports the argument for her year of birth being 1501, not 1507, as some have suggested, with the generally accepted age to serve abroad being twelve. But more to the point, a letter Anne sent home to her father where she spoke of being a 'worthy woman when I come to court' is written with the intelligence of a young teen, not a six-year-old.[6]

Though it has been widely acknowledged that Anne's French education was responsible for the more radical belief system that would carry her through life, the impact this first year abroad at the Habsburg Imperial Court would have had is often overlooked. Even to just take a look at the works Margaret of Austria promoted within the court library shows us the intellectual, religious and cultural interests Anne was exposed to. Among them were names that are still studied in universities to this day, including philosophers Aristotle and Boethius, the Renaissance humanist Boccaccio as well as the incredibly progressive work of Christine de Pizan, who became infamous for challenging misogyny and stereotypical views of women in the late medieval era.[7]

In addition to the books they read, Margaret's court was well known for accepting some of the most enlightened thinkers of Europe, including the humanist priest and theologian Erasmus of Rotterdam, who would go on to be commissioned later in life by Anne's father.

So it was here, in this extraordinary setting, that Anne would spend over a year following a strict regime of study and courtly etiquette at the hands of an inspirational and powerful female ruler. But even that short time was filled with drama.

It was some time around 1514 that rumours began to swirl that Anne's mistress, Margaret of Austria, was set to marry King Henry VIII's closest companion, the infamous Charles Brandon. The couple had seen each other regularly in the autumn of 1513, at approximately the time of Anne's arrival.

Historians revel in playing up the importance of the moment when Henry and Anne most likely set eyes on each other for the first time, at the iconic Tudor summit that was the Field of the Cloth of Gold in 1520. *This was the first time she saw the man who would become her husband!* Talk about romanticising history. You mean, *this was the first time she laid eyes on the man who would murder her?*

But as historian Steven Gunn confirms, Anne would have met the king many years earlier, because Henry VIII and Charles Brandon visited the court of Margaret of Austria together during the time of Brandon and Margaret's courtship, if we can even call it that.

So realistically *this* is more likely to have been the moment and the setting in which a young Anne Boleyn first saw her future killer.[8] But what did she make of him? Was she besotted? In awe of the two men? Probably not. In fact, the events that unfolded were likely to cement Anne's lifelong disdain for the king's best friend and fuel a feud that would one day destroy her.

It started when Margaret and her ladies were summoned to celebrate the victory of her father the emperor and Henry VIII at Tournai, in September 1513. Drunk on high spirits and no doubt copious amounts of wine, Charles Brandon appears to have taken the game of courtly love too far when, egged on by a boisterous Henry, he proposed to Archduchess Margaret.

To confirm their 'engagement' and as a token of their love, Brandon then took a ring from her. But clearly feeling the joke had run its course, Margaret was quick to ask for it back; at which point Brandon refused, no doubt thinking the whole thing was *totally hilare*. But the situation soon got out of hand – as most drunken proposals tend to do. She called him a thief; people in London started taking bets on a wedding; her father, the emperor, was shocked to say the least, and Margaret began threatening death to those who continued to spread the story.

All in all, this was not the best first impression for Anne Boleyn to have of Henry VIII, but it most certainly would have fixed her low opinion of Charles Brandon.[9]

By the final months of 1514, Anne's French was so accomplished that she was requested to join the court of the new French queen, Henry VIII's sister Mary Tudor. Yes, on the advice of Henry's chief minister, Cardinal Wolsey, England and France were to settle their political differences with a marital alliance between Henry's younger sister and the old and ailing King Louis XII of France.[10] She was eighteen. He was fifty-two. I believe this is what they call 'taking one for the team'.

However, the royal request for Anne to move to France caused friction between her father, Thomas, and his old friend the archduchess of Austria, as Mary Tudor was breaking her betrothal to Margaret's nephew Charles V in order to marry their rival over in France. Boleyn biographer Eric Ives gives this as the reason for a gap between the request for Anne to join the French court and official records of her eventual arrival, suspecting the archduchess might have held on to her for a while just to spite them.[11] But for his part, Thomas was honest with Margaret, saying he 'could not, nor did not know how to refuse' the request.[12]

This meant that, although Mary Tudor arrived in France and married the French king in October 1514, we don't have evidence of Anne's arrival until January 1515. So consequently, she spent hardly any time serving the new French queen, Mary, for after a mere eighty-two days of marriage, King Louis died on 1 January.

Louis's daughter, the fifteen-year-old Claude, was poised to take her father's place on the throne; however, due to the delightfully sexist sixteenth-century French laws, her new husband, Francis, became the reigning monarch. Claude was henceforth relegated to baby-making machine, apparently a fair trade-off back then. 'Twas indeed a great time to be alive.

But eager to not let Mary Tudor's short-lived reign stunt his daughter's education, Thomas Boleyn pulled a few strings in order for Anne to remain as lady-in-waiting to the new Queen Claude – not that this was a hard sell, coming straight from the tutelage of the Imperial Court in Mechelen and being the same age, Anne was no doubt seen as the ideal companion for the young queen.

Some historians have tried to argue that when Anne moved on to serve the wife of the notorious womaniser King Francis I, she most definitely must have been corrupted; that, as French historian Brantôme once said, no one leaves the infamous French court chaste,[13] and that this is how Anne became the sultry seductress the world has come to know.

However, if we look closely into the time Anne spent in France, we discover that she lived an extremely sheltered existence and was never exposed to the legendary shenanigans for which the court was well known. In fact, far from joining a court of debauchery, when Anne entered the service of the French royal family in the early months of 1515 it was a sad and subdued time.

When Claude's father, King Louis, married Mary Tudor, it had been a mere nine months since Claude's mother had passed away. Fifteen-year-old Claude was so distraught that she cried throughout her own wedding ceremony to her twenty-one-year-old husband, Francis, on 18 May 1514. The court at the Château Royal de Blois was still in mourning when Francis's sister Marguerite d'Angoulême joined them, taking on the role of big sister to Claude and her younger sister Renée.[14] To add to Claude's misery, several days after her wedding her new husband left for Paris to be with his mistress for two months.[15]

As Queen Claude began her spate of obligatory pregnancies, she spent more and more time retired within the castle at Blois, accompanied by Anne Boleyn and her other ladies-in-waiting, living what sounds to have been a pretty dull life of seclusion.

Tudor historian Elizabeth Norton confirms that Queen Claude was renowned for her piety and keeping her household apart from that of her scandalous husband.[16] It's well known among Anne's more serious biographers that in this household, she was educated in a strict code of conduct and the highest moral standards. Claude was known for being reserved and retiring. She rarely made public appearances, which was why it was said her husband's sister, Marguerite d'Angoulême, was queen in all but name, performing most of the duties usually required of Claude. Even when attending the legendary Field of the Cloth of Gold it was Claude's mother-in-law, Louise of Savoy, and sister-in-law, Marguerite, along with her husband's official mistress, who stepped in to perform Claude's duties at the event.[17] Vitally, what this demonstrates is that as lady-in-waiting, Anne was given rare opportunity for the life of smut and corruption she was meant to have led in her early years in France.

Now, the reason for Claude's isolation was less to do with social anxiety and more to do with illness. She was never a healthy girl to begin with, walking with a limp from a young age, and she soon found herself crippled with continual pregnancies, giving birth to seven children in eight years. That's a lot of time to be pregnant and confined to bed rest. So, what did Anne Boleyn and her fellow ladies do during those months Claude was being 'churched' alone?

After careful discussions with the Château Royal de Blois, where Anne and Claude spent the majority of their time, it's thought likely that Anne would have been put to work in the retinue of other members of the royal household. But who?

Well, let us consider the evidence: two decades later, in 1535, Anne would write to Marguerite d'Angoulême saying that her 'greatest wish, next to having a son, was to see you again'[18] – quite the statement for someone she had known only at a distance. Similarly, in 1534, when Henry VIII wanted to get out of a meeting with Francis I, Anne was the one who sent a message to Marguerite via her brother, George Boleyn, that she was, in fact, pregnant and needed Henry by her side, so could they possibly postpone. Pretty intimate information to be sharing with someone she barely knew. It's certainly not the kind of excuse you would give another politician – which the royals of Europe essentially were in the sixteenth century – if schedules had to be changed. It is these glimpses into the obvious intimacy of the two women's friendship that indicates it was most likely that, during Claude's bouts of sickness and pregnancy, Anne and the other ladies-in-waiting were placed in the unofficial service of Marguerite.[19] This explains why Francis I referred to Anne Boleyn as Claude's lady rather than his sister's, because, officially, that was the role she was contracted to do.[20]

Yet, if you are an avid reader of Tudor biographies you will be aware that this friendship is something many have set out to discredit. But why do historians feel it so necessary to prove, or more to the point *disprove*, that Anne was close to Marguerite during her time in France? Because Marguerite was a renowned reformist and a huge supporter of France's leader of religious reform, Jacques Lefèvre d'Étaples. So, of course, such a strong, religious upbringing for the young Anne Boleyn does not, I repeat *not*, fit in with the slutty, scheming seductress image we have of her. It works much better for historical writers on #TeamAragon if Anne was involved in the immoral depravity that we are repeatedly told was rife at the French court.

But even if we don't take into account the likelihood of Anne directly serving Marguerite, with the latter seen as the 'unofficial queen', it's inescapable that all courtiers would have been hugely impacted by this powerhouse ruler. So, what did this mean for the religious climate at court?

Marguerite was only twenty-two, yet already known to be 'learned and witty'. She called herself the 'prime minister of the poor', something you'll come to see Anne Boleyn could equally have called herself later in life. Marguerite was a woman of high moral standards; even though she was in an infamously unhappy marriage, she apparently never took a lover, when it was all the rage in sixteenth-century Europe.[21] She was to fill the French court at Blois over the years with religious activists who would go on to be major players in the rebellion against the Catholic Church. These were the very people with whom Anne Boleyn would have been interacting on a daily basis and found herself inspired and influenced by.

In 1515, following the deaths of Queen Claude's parents, their *valet de chambre*, the poet Jean Marot, moved into the household of Francis I along with his son, Clément.

Clément Marot would go on to become the renowned French reformist who controversially translated the Psalms. Interestingly, he moved into the new royal household at the same time as Anne, and together the two became immersed in court life. The fact that when Clément was later accused of heresy he was offered royal protection by Anne Boleyn, it's clear she was not just aware of his work but cared deeply about him, indicating she knew him on a personal level from her childhood in France.[22] But one might question how they could have become so closely acquainted when working in the separate households of the king and queen. Quite. Which is why it's intriguing to learn that Clément moved into the service of Marguerite d'Angoulême as her valet in 1518, with her becoming his patron the following year,[23] suggesting that the obvious time frame Anne would have got to know Clément was during her stints serving Marguerite.

Whenever Clément Marot's time at Blois is discussed, it's implied that it was he, as an avid reformer, who ran around court radicalising all those he came into contact with. But in actual fact, it appears it was the other way around; it was here that Clément first came into contact with the evangelical ideas that would drive the course of his life. This confirms one vital thing for us: that the French court was a hotbed for reformist ideology. And if it was to have this impact on Clément, then what effect would it have on Anne Boleyn?

Alas, despite the clear evangelical influence of Anne's French childhood home, some historians have tried to skirt around this by pointing out that we only have evidence of Marguerite's own interest in religious reform from mid-1521, when she started writing letters to the reformist Bishop Guillaume Briçonnet; and that this being a mere six months before Anne left court, it could not have had the profound effect we presume.

But in fact, European historians suspect it was Marguerite who, in 1515, encouraged her brother, Francis I, to make Briçonnet the bishop of Meaux in the first place: a post that would see him create the Circle of Meaux, an infamous group of French reformists including Jacques Lefèvre d'Étaples, France's leader of the Reformation.[24]

Indeed, religious reform is something that Marguerite would have been debating with the scholars and theologians of the court for years before her letters to Briçonnet began. The Cholakian biography states that it was as early as 1516, when Marguerite was on an expedition with the royal court, that she began to show early signs of being unhappy with the Church and was actively trying to reform its ways. During the trip she called in on badly run convents that were home to nuns surviving on insufficient funds. This was where she came across a pregnant nun who revealed a monk had seduced her, and at another had stopped a nun from self-harming as penance for her sins.[25]

But guesswork is not required here, as we have evidence that Marguerite's interest in reform had an impact on young Anne Boleyn's childhood more than is ever revealed, with Marguerite's letters to Briçonnet showing she was actively working on converting the whole French court to this new underground religion.

The explosive letters exchanged between Marguerite and the man who would become her confidant and counsellor date from 12 June 1521 to 18 November 1524. So sensitive were the contents that she only entrusted a few close allies to deliver them, one being Clément Marot. During this correspondence Marguerite wrote excitedly to Briçonnet telling him, 'My sister-in-law, my dear sister is quite of our opinion.' Marguerite's biographer, Mary F. Robinson, believes she could only have been talking about Queen Claude.

There is the possibility that the 'sister-in-law' Marguerite speaks of could have been Françoise, the sister of her husband Charles, duke of Alençon. However, considering Marguerite's main aim was to convert the king, her excitement at getting his wife, Queen Claude, on side would make more sense than her husband's sister, who had no power to help the Reformation whatsoever. Her victory there would certainly not have been worthy of writing with celebratory news to Briçonnet. Nor would it have prompted Jacques Lefèvre d'Étaples to write to congratulate Marguerite, as he did, on her good work.[26]

Briçonnet was ecstatic that the 'true fire which since long has been lodged in your heart, [is now] in that of the King and Madame', again confirming that this had long been an issue of importance for Marguerite, not a burning new religious query that suddenly began to eat away at her only months before Anne left court.

Marguerite later responds, 'Madame has begun to read in the Holy Scriptures. You know the confidence that she and the King place in you.'[27]

So, you see, the detail of this correspondence proves to us that Marguerite had long been questioning the Church. Not only that, but she had been recruiting at court for her religious cause. To that end, it makes perfect sense for her to try and influence the young daughter of the English ambassador who, one day, would be returning to the royal Tudor court of England, where she would be able to spread the word of their new religious fight.

Mackay points out that when Thomas Boleyn joined his daughter at the Château Royal de Blois for almost two years, from November 1518 to March 1520, he found numerous evangelical and humanist priests preaching the reform message, to which, at this stage, Francis I and his sister, Marguerite, were sympathetic. This was a court that was at the forefront of the reformist development. So it's unrealistic to think that Anne lived among these progressive thinkers, was educated alongside them and socialised with them, without them influencing her and enlightening her as to the revolution that was tearing through Europe.

Oh, but wait, what was that you say? Anne's father joined her in France?

Oh yes, as if a strict, religious upbringing at the hands of France's leading reformists wasn't enough to keep Anne in check during her years abroad, then her father living with her for nearly two years as an ambassador for King Henry VIII ought to do it!

Sorry, what was that? No one's told you that before?

No, of course they haven't. I mean, how could she have been running riot, learning sordid French tricks at the court, if she was the respectable daughter of the royal ambassador representing the king of England? Once again, we have the pesky facts ruining the slutty narrative.

In 1518, Thomas Boleyn joined his daughter at the Château Royal de Blois, during which time he became so highly respected by the royal family that he was invited by Louise of Savoy to personally socialise with Queen Claude herself. Similarly, it would be during those intense years abroad, when Thomas and Anne were each other's only immediate family, that father and daughter would have really bonded, becoming closer than ever before.

Thomas's role negotiating diplomatic relations between England and France was such a delicate one that it was of utmost importance that the whole Boleyn family represented king and country with grace and dignity. So where did that leave the 'great and infamous whore' Mary Boleyn – Anne's sister, who, history will tell you, was banished from the French court following an illicit affair with the new French king?

The original source of the Mary Boleyn/Francis I affair rumours is a single letter written by the pope's official representative, Pio, Bishop of Faenza, on 10 March 1536. The fact it was sent mere months before Anne's death, when the anti-Boleyn slur campaign was in full swing, should tell us all we need to know about its reliability, but here we go nevertheless. Pio wrote:

> Francis said that 'that woman' [Anne Boleyn] pretended to have miscarried of a son [her last miscarriage before her death] not being really with child, and, to keep up the deceit, would allow no one to attend on her but her sister, whom the French king knew [supposedly in the biblical sense, having slept with] in France to be a great prostitute and infamous above all.[28]

Considering that two months later, this same man would write that Anne had been arrested with her whole family, including mother and father,[29] should again highlight the fact that Pio's reports are to be taken with a pinch of salt and dash of seasoning.

The only problem with his Mary Boleyn claim – which has built in momentum and infamy with historians ever since it was written – is that she has been recorded as having spent a grand total of seven months in France before returning home to England, along with Mary Tudor, at the end of April 1515. Mary first arrived with the royal party from England in October 1514, ahead of her sister Anne's arrival, and was not one of the ladies who were kept on to serve Queen Claude after the death of the French king in January.

It was during the transitional, crossover period of the monarchs that both Anne and Mary Boleyn would have spent the obligatory forty days of mourning locked away with Mary Tudor, a precautionary move to check Louis's widow was not pregnant with his heir before King Francis

I and Queen Claude took over the throne. Mary Boleyn left with the English party in April once the all-clear was given.

For two of her months in the French court, January and February, Francis was away from Blois in Rheims and Paris for his coronation;[30] then we have the forty days spent in isolation with Mary Tudor. So, if these accusations of Mary Boleyn's string of torrid affairs are true, this must have been some record achievement, with the young girl treating sex as an Olympic sport during the five short months she and Francis were actually in court at the same time. This, in order for them to not only hook up, but for Mary to stand out to Francis as a particularly depraved sexual beast. That's if Bishop Pio did indeed mean Francis knew Mary in the biblical sense; after all, he said he 'knew her to be a great prostitute', not that he simply 'knew her', implying that he had slept with Mary himself.

After all, if this had been the case, it would certainly beg the question as to quite *why* her sister, Anne, would have been allowed to serve Queen Claude, if Mary had been having it away with her husband. Come to think of it, if Mary Boleyn had earned herself a sordid reputation and been disgraced, would she really have been taken on to serve Queen Katherine of Aragon back in England in 1519? More to the point, would Mary have realistically been allowed to marry the king of England's cousin and member of the exclusive privy chamber, William Carey, in 1520? This was two years *before* she was to begin an affair with Henry VIII, so not something we can dismiss as a reward for being the king's mistress, as many have claimed over the years.

So, you see, when you consult the facts and not the gossip, the idea that Mary Boleyn ever had an affair with the king of France, or indeed anyone at the French court, starts to look less and less likely. But if you came here for sex and scandal, worry not, for as I say, it appears she *did* have an affair with Henry VIII, and all the juicy gossip there is yet to come.

Well, thank God for that!

Can't have a Boleyn biography without at least one affair, can we?

◆ ◆ ◆

The religious revolution that was brewing during Anne's years in France was inescapable. It was at the forefront of everyone's mind, and everyone had an opinion. It would divide not just the country but the whole of Europe.

In 2017 we marked the 500th anniversary of the Reformation. Yes, it's been five hundred years of war, death and sacrifice over exactly *how* we pray for love, peace and forgiveness. Oh, the irony. But you may note that Henry VIII didn't break from Rome in 1517. Indeed, he did not, and that's because the sixteenth century experienced two very different reformations that often get muddied and mixed into one.

1517 was to be the year of sixteenth-century whistle-blower Martin Luther's infamous war with the pope that created a religious storm and made fighters out of the most unlikely of people. You want to know what was Anne Boleyn's driving force? What made her the ballsy, driven and unapologetic fighter she grew up to be? Then it's vital we take a look at the religious climate of her youth that she was to rebel against.

Like their rulers, the people of England and Europe lived for Catholicism and all its so-called 'superstitions' that these new reformists were opposed to. People would wake in the night to pray, suffer treacherous pilgrimages to have their prayers answered and wear hair shirts in penance for their sins. English reformer and Bible translator William Tyndale complained of the relentless tolling of bells from dusk till dawn by friars and nuns who 'vex themselves, night and day, and take pains for God's sake'.[31]

It's difficult in this day and age to convey how deeply religious the sixteenth century was, and how seriously the people took all these rituals. Yet to understand it, we have to remember just how grim the Tudor times truly were. The mortality rate was high and life expectancy was low; disease could unexpectedly wipe out whole communities within days, and public executions were a normal part of daily life. Death wasn't something that would eventually creep up many decades later, but was ever looming ominously overhead. For the nation, faith was more than saying prayers by rote; it was a vital connection to an afterlife that not only promised salvation beyond the dour realities of the world around them, but one they might have to face in the not-too-distant future.

So, believe me when I say it was no joke that there were charms to recite during childbirth to make sure babies were born without complications, certain incantations were said to halt bleeding, and fevers could be stopped in their tracks by 'casting of the heart', which is not an 80s pop song but apparently some sort of magical process.[32] It was said that a prayer to St Apollonia would cure toothache, and oats offered to the statue of St Wilgefortis apparently rid women of unwanted husbands.[33] There were 'dismal days' on which weddings and travel were to be avoided at all costs;[34] and when high winds once hit the steeple of St Alkmund's Church, there was talk that Satan himself had left scratches on the bell.[35]

It's all too easy to mock now, but sixteenth-century folk had a true fear of God, and apparently some priests were all too happy to take full advantage of it. But by 1517 the people had finally had enough. You see, the backlash that was to come with the Reformation wasn't against God or even initially the Catholic faith – it was against a number of people who ran the Church at the time.

The storm finally broke in October 1517, when Martin Luther accidentally released hell by posting his now infamous *Ninety-Five Theses*. However, this was not on the door of Wittenberg's Castle Church, as we've been told, and I say 'accidentally' because it was never intended to be the war cry it became.

Now, if a *Ninety-Five Theses* sounds like quite a heavy tome to pin anywhere, let me explain that it was actually a one-page document, a sort of *Ninety-Five Dos and Don'ts* of how Luther believed the Catholic Church should be run. For the uproar it caused you would have thought he had condemned the pope to the fiery pits of purgatory, but in actual fact it listed simple notes such as: 'Only God can give salvation and forgiveness, not a priest. Penitence must be accompanied by a suitable change in lifestyle. An indulgence will not save a man; people are being deceived by indulgences.'

Now, indulgences were pardons for sins that were being sold by the Catholic Church.

Yep, you could buy a pardon for your sin. Pay for salvation, not pray for it.

Early modern humanist Erasmus famously mocked those who 'enjoy deluding themselves with imaginary pardons for their sins' in his satire *In Praise of Folly*.[36] To illustrate this point, in 1519 Frederick the Wise catalogued over five thousand supposed holy relics at Castle Church in Wittenberg, which you could pay to be in the presence of.[37] It was said the saints in heaven would listen more attentively to prayers made close to these holy relics.[38] And let's just say that the authenticity of some of them was somewhat questionable – this, in particular, is an issue we will see Anne Boleyn personally fighting against during her time as queen.

Yes, depending on which relics you prayed in front of, you earned a certain number of days' suspension from your sins. In 1513, Castle Church was offering forty-two thousand years' worth of cancelled sins in the afterlife – that's if you could perform all the devotions for their five thousand or so relics.[39]

Sounds great. Where do I pay?!

Safe to say, indulgences were quite the money-spinner for the Church. So, when Martin Luther and his fellow reformists suddenly called them out and tried to regulate or put a stop to them altogether, you can imagine the Church wouldn't have been all too happy about it.

The money from the sale of indulgences and access to holy relics at Castle Church largely paid for the establishment of the university in 1502, at which Martin Luther also taught. So, there is something to be said for the money going to good use. In England and Europe, money raised from the sale of indulgences was often ploughed back into the local community to build roads and bridges, so you could see it as some sort of religious tax. Indeed, people who bought into these indulgences sometimes did so just to support local projects, not necessarily to 'save their soul'.

But that wasn't so much the issue; after all, there is such a thing as free will. No, it was more the lies the preachers were telling their congregations in order to get them to pay up, playing on their fears of damnation in the afterlife. Indulgences even had a slogan: 'As soon as the coin in the coffer rings, at once the soul to heaven springs!'

Ah yes, so that was the other issue the new evangelicals had with indulgences: the promise that a priest could forgive your sins.

Reformists were firmly of the belief that no man on earth could guarantee your salvation. Only God could forgive. Not even the pope could save you, who, the people had been told, was the only figure of authority who could grant complete forgiveness for sins – meaning if he deemed you worthy, you could skip purgatory altogether and go straight to heaven.

Another area where these bothersome evangelicals were demanding reform, and one Anne Boleyn was to be heavily involved with in her lifetime, was how the Bible should be read; they claimed it should be available in all languages for everyone to read and understand. This was as opposed to hearing it only in Latin from a priest. Given that the majority of people couldn't understand Latin, this made the language barrier in daily Mass somewhat tricky. Yet the pope was adamant that Latin was the official language of the Church and the only language the Bible should be read in. However, he clearly flunked religious education in school, as that's not quite the case.

The Old Testament was originally written in Hebrew, and the New Testament in Greek. It was only from there that they were both translated into Latin. But, unable to understand it, the majority had no idea what was being preached to them; so the reformists wanted this changed in order for the people to have a more meaningful connection with God's word. These may sound like pretty reasonable requests now, but in 1517 they were radical and dangerous thoughts.

But why would the Church be so scared of the people reading the Bible in their own language?

Some claimed it was so the priests could have more power over them. This way they could twist the scripture to suit their own agenda regarding the sale of indulgences and exactly who was responsible for a soul's forgiveness. After all, if the people didn't understand what was written in the Bible, they couldn't challenge what they were being told.

Martin Luther wasn't the first to speak out or question the Church about all of this. Nor did the poor bloke intend to be the spokesperson and international hate figure for the Reformation. On 31 October 1517, rather than posting his *Ninety-Five Theses* on the door of Castle Church, as has been reported for the past five hundred years, Martin Luther sent it to the Bishop of Mainz for approval. It was accompanied by a very polite letter drawing the bishop's attention to the shocking sermons of controversial indulgence preacher Johann Tetzel, for the 'insanity' of claiming that the latest indulgence he was selling was so powerful it could even forgive a sinner who had violated the Virgin Mary![40]

Ah. Right. Tad blasphemous.

But Luther ran into problems due to the fact that his *Ninety-Five Theses* was intentionally provocative. It was purposefully written and designed to stir up academic debate at the university where he taught. Years later Luther would say of his gutsy letter: 'I did not yet see the great abomination of the Pope but only the crass abuses' and that his intention was not 'to attack the Pope, but to oppose the blasphemous statements of the noisy declaimers', meaning the indulgence preachers.[41] Either way, I'm sure he didn't expect the Bishop of Mainz to forward the thesis directly to the pope. Nor did Luther expect such an overwhelming reaction from the people.

After university staff posted his *Ninety-Five Theses* around the city of Wittenberg to advertise the upcoming debate (historian Peter Marshall believes it was more likely *they* who posted it on the church door bulletin board), Luther went viral. He was shocked to find his argument was spread 'throughout the whole of Germany in a fortnight', and by spring the next year it had reached the rest of Europe.

Henry VIII got his hands on the controversial thesis when Erasmus sent a copy to Thomas More,[42] who was acting at the time as, among other things, Henry's secretary, interpreter, chief diplomat and adviser.

Reformists at the French court would have been abuzz with news of this gutsy priest who was daring to stand up and challenge the pope. There is no doubt that Anne would have followed the story just as intently as everyone else. Whether you were for or against Luther, you could not have failed to hear about him. And there were plenty who were against him, with Henry VIII fast becoming one of Luther's most famous critics. As the increasingly volatile situation developed, the king of England was kept up to date with secret coded letters via his right-hand man, Cardinal Wolsey.

The people's army of rebel 'Lutherans' grew so fast in Europe that by June 1518 the pope was forced to react. He authorised a judgement saying that, 'Whoever says regarding indulgences that the Roman church cannot do what it de facto does, is a heretic.'[43]

This wasn't just a threat against Luther but all reformists who took issue with indulgences, making it incredibly dangerous for the likes of Anne Boleyn and Marguerite d'Angoulême to go on to support such radical thinking. A line had been drawn in the sand.

The pope's judgement also stated, quite incredibly, that his authority was greater than that of the Bible.

Tensions continued to build, but by 1520 Luther had well and truly had enough. He had been accused of being a heretic, ripped to pieces by every high-profile figure in the land, and so he fought back by publishing three pamphlets that put his little *Ninety-Five Theses* to shame. Here he called for German nobility to reform the Church, incredulously declaring that four of the seven sacraments had been invented. It was at this point that the pope issued a papal decree, in June, threatening to excommunicate Luther if he didn't abandon his entire belief system immediately. I couldn't help but laugh out loud when I learned that this meek friar, who had at first set out to get papal approval for his unassuming university debate and didn't want to upset anyone, on 20 December 1520 threw the pope's threat on to a bonfire outside Wittenberg's Elster Gate, to the rapturous cheers of his supporters.[44]

Perhaps caught up in the adrenaline rush of rebellion, Luther then published the jauntily titled 'Assertion of All the Articles Condemned by the Last Bull of Antichrist'.

Needless to say, the pope confirmed Luther's excommunication in January 1521.

Like all his new fellow reformists, Luther was scared but defiant. Sometimes, in order to cover our fear, the human psyche will have us play up the bravado even more, which certainly seems to have been the case here, and is something we will see in Anne Boleyn many a time, too.

And so, you see, *this* was the explosive religious climate in which Anne was being raised in Europe. After seven years of a radical religious upbringing, in which she was taught to question the authority of those she had been conditioned to follow blindly, and made aware of how she and the people were being manipulated and taken advantage of, like most of her generation she was ready to join the crusade: fight *with* the people *for* the people in order to reconnect with the undiluted doctrine.

It was then, at this crucial moment, that Anne is meant to have returned to England and magically morphed into a ruthless, morally corrupt, scheming seductress for no apparent reason whatsoever.

CHAPTER 2

BANISHED FROM COURT: WHAT REALLY HAPPENED

In December 1521 Anne was summoned home to England. Some have attributed this timing to the war that was brewing between England and France,[45] but in truth a marriage match was being arranged for her with a courtier named James Butler.[46] This marriage was meant to kill two birds with one stone. Firstly, it would unite two sides of Anne's family who were at loggerheads over the title of the earl of Ormond. Secondly, Wolsey needed a ploy to keep James, who was a valuable courtier in his own household, in London rather than him being sent back home to Ireland.

In a letter to the king, Wolsey says: 'On my return I will talk with you how to bring about the marriage between [Butler's] son and Sir Thomas Boleyn's daughter, which will be a good pretext for delaying to send his son over [to Ireland].'[47]

Who says romance is dead, eh?

So, while this match was being negotiated, Anne Boleyn at last made her debut at the Tudor court of King Henry VIII.

Anne's personality is said to have stood out in court because she actually possessed one. She was said to have been a fan of lively conversation at a time when to give a simple smile was considered the height of intelligence. No wonder historians accuse her of shamelessly flirting with every man she encountered; she was probably the first woman who talked back and held eye contact when a coy glance to the side was all the fashion.

One historian recently described Anne as having 'brazen self-confidence'.[48]

Brazen, you say? How very dare she? If Anne was living in the modern world today, I suppose she would be one of those presumptuous women who speak up in the boardroom with an opinion of her own. So *very* brazen!

Now she was back in England, far from her focus solely being on how to have an uninterrupted stream of banquets and balls, as it's often said, fresh from her powerful and progressive education in France among reformists and royalty, Anne would have been ready to make a difference in the world. And indeed, it's said she made a splash from the start. People would speak of how she dazzled with a natural charm, impeccable manners, social grace and witty repartee. Even George Cavendish, a firm member of the later anti-Boleyn faction, admits that when Anne joined the court to serve Katherine of Aragon her 'excellent gesture and behaviour did excel all others'.[49] Frankly, this is a missed opportunity from Cavendish to paint her as the flirty whore from hell, but he provides his readers with a startlingly honest recollection of her. Needless to say, this is one report from Cavendish that rarely sees the light of day in the popular history books.

As we've seen, during her time in France Anne had learned all about the state of religion, and the girl certainly had an opinion about it. Here was a lady of the court who was not scared of taking on the men in a theological debate. As part of Marguerite d'Angoulême's court she had been taught to be literate, accomplished, intelligent and, lest we forget, in possession of that infamous *brazen self-confidence*. So, you see, it would have been impossible for Anne to return to the English court and play the meek and mild submissive.

Yet we have to realise that although she was joining her family at court, with her older sister, Mary, in the service of Katherine of Aragon and younger brother, George, in the king's prestigious privy chamber, Anne was also joining a strange new world of cliques and factions where she was viewed as a foreigner.

Now, while Anne is regularly described as arriving at court with enviable French sophistications, the reality of sixteenth-century London, as J. J. Scarisbrick points out, was that the English held a deep-rooted antipathy towards the French. As unsavoury as this thought is, it got to the point where, on 1 May 1517, a racist mob took to the streets of London attacking all foreigners, including the Spanish and Portuguese, causing hundreds of locals to end up imprisoned in the Tower. Katherine of Aragon, to her great credit, intervened to appeal for leniency against the xenophobes who had abused her countrymen.[50]

But one thing this tells us is that the French influence in Anne's life would have been something that marked her out in a not particularly positive way at court. Following her arrival, she couldn't have failed to notice the animosity felt by the English towards her childhood home. So while she may have appeared confident and knew how to hold a conversation, she probably would have been desperate to fit in and be accepted by these new people.

Alas, there was one way in which courtiers of every rank bonded, and that was via the sporting act that has now gone down in history as courtly love; this is basically an over-romanticised way of saying that they loved to flirt. The men would endeavour to outdo each other with acts of chivalry to woo the women, who in turn played along, writing poems and riddles back and forth.

What can I say? They didn't have TV back then so they had to make their own entertainment. But it was all incredibly sanitised and proper;

they exchanged rings, not bodily fluids, as most at court were married or betrothed to others. But this was just an innocent way to kick back and have a few bants after the daily toil of serving king and country. No one took it too seriously.

No one, that is, except the past five centuries' worth of historians who have since pored over every jaunty poem in existence that Anne Boleyn may or may not have written, searching for any hint that she was a wanton vixen who lured men in with a saucy iambic pentameter.

Now, of all the relentless accusations of illicit affairs that have plagued Anne from adolescence to adulthood, there is one that has really gained momentum over the centuries, and that is her supposed dalliance with Thomas Wyatt. Popular history has reduced him to a simple court poet, but he was also a diplomat and ambassador to Rome. Wyatt was supposedly good-looking and wealthy, hence quite the catch. He was also married, and had been for ten years; so if Anne was as smart as she appears to have been, it makes absolutely no sense for her to have risked her honour and respectability for a quick roll in the hay with a married man with whom she had no future. Even when she accepted Henry VIII, he was separated and in the process of getting his marriage annulled.

Of course, that's not to say that Wyatt didn't fall head over heels with Anne and try his luck.

Boys will be boys, eh?

As his grandson George explains in one of Anne Boleyn's first sixteenth-century biographies, her 'witty and graceful speech' had Wyatt utterly smitten. However, the vital part we must take away from this insider family account is Anne's response to his unwanted advances, with his grandson conceding that upon 'finding him to be then married . . . rejected all his speech of love'.[51]

Now, it's certainly not improbable that Anne played along in the etiquette of courtly love and flirted with the good-looking Wyatt. Indeed, we have a few poems and ditties they apparently wrote to each other, which, of course, certain historians have taken to be hard evidence of a full-blown sexual affair.[52] (For the benefit of the jury I am inserting an 'eye roll' emoji right here.) But Wyatt's grandson hits the nail on the head when he confirms in his biography that Anne 'was not likely to cast her eye upon one who had been married ten years'.[53] I rest my case.

Of course, Anne was meant to have achieved this alleged feat in mass seduction during her early years in England and France while, according to some sources, looking like a three-armed hunchbacked deformed crone.

So let's just clear up the sixth-finger rumour once and for all, shall we?

The fact is that Anne's mere presence at the royal court meant there was no way she could have had an extra finger, welts on her face and wens on her chin,[54] as has been reported over the years, because noticeable birthmarks or any kind of deformity in the sixteenth century were interpreted as the 'devil's mark' and signs of being a witch.[55] So, while this explains why the slurs about Anne's appearance became part of the great legend following her death, it's the very extremity of these supposed disfigurements that makes it impossible for them to be true or she would never have been allowed in high society, let alone the queen's household and the king's bed.

Henry VIII was extremely superstitious – we're talking about the man who would cross himself at the sound of thunder and interpret any inclement weather as a sign from God. So, do we really think he would have been cool about his lover having an extra digit?[56]

George Wyatt addressed the sixth-finger rumour directly, stating that while, no, there *was* none, Anne simply appeared to have 'some little show of a nail'[57] on the side of her finger. But he went on to explain it was so small that it could be easily covered by her other fingertip. So whatever the anomaly was, realistically this has to be the extent of any deformity in such superstitious times, when people lived in fear of any signs of the devil, witchcraft or the occult. It also means you need to seriously question the reliability and motivation of any modern-day historian who implies the presence of a sixth finger in order to complete the picture of Anne Boleyn the Evil Witch who swept into court on her broomstick and cast a spell on the lovesick Henry VIII.

But I have something controversial to admit: I really couldn't care less what Anne Boleyn looked like. I harbour not even a morbid curiosity. Those who hated her say she was ugly; those who loved her say she was pretty, as though any of it matters as to the person she was and what she achieved in her lifetime. The only thing these contrasting reports succeed in proving is that society has had an obsession with beauty since time began.

The Venetian ambassador said she 'is not the most handsomest woman in the world. She is of middling stature, swarthy complexion, long neck, wide mouth and bosom not much raised.'[58]

Oh, you old charmer!

Catholic propagandist Nicholas Sander later reported Anne to have had jaundice, a projecting tooth, the obligatory sixth finger on her right hand and a large wen under her chin. But then, in contrast to the insults, he describes her as 'rather tall of stature' and somewhat bafflingly concludes 'she was handsome to look at'.[59]

The French diplomat Lancelot de Carles, who was never a big fan of Anne's, surprisingly goes against the trend of hostile sources in saying she was beautiful and 'of elegant feature'.[60]

However, I don't need Anne to have been a stunning beauty devoid of all human imperfection, and neither should you. She had far too much else going for her. She was a kick-ass young woman, so I couldn't care less if she was 'goggle-eyed'[61] or 'reasonably good-looking'.[62] The only reason I address her looks here at all is because, as we've seen, the accusations actually have a much more sinister meaning, with every imperfection being an apparent sign she had been 'marred by the devil'. So it seems only right we put those myths to rest once and for all.[63]

Alas, though those early days of courtly love were jolly good fun and all, while everyone else around her grew up, got married and became serious courtiers, Anne Boleyn has never been allowed to escape this flirty reputation from her early years at court, even as she matured and focused her energy on more important issues of the day.

Historian Maria Dowling points out that: 'Traditionally [Anne] is pictured at the centre of a circle of brilliant gentlemen-poets who were devoted to the pursuit of courtly love and other frivolous matters.' [64]

Yes, as though there weren't more pressing concerns to be thinking about. While all of Europe was in religious upheaval, some writers will have you believe the royal courts were solely focused on shagging. You'll be relieved to hear that this was not quite the case.

As it turns out, all evidence points towards Anne coming back to England with a revolution building inside her. Like a lot of her young European contemporaries, she would have been inspired by Martin Luther's ongoing battle with the pope, which had begun to seep into England by the summer of 1521.[65] Now that the injustices had been brought to light, Anne would have been ready to join the cause herself and make a difference. But what could she do? Where was she needed?

One thing was for sure, if Anne wanted to do anything for the evangelical cause, she would need a voice. She needed to be in a position of power, and for most Tudor women, who weren't allowed to climb the ranks of Parliament, this came in the form of a marriage alliance. If Anne was going to have the clout she required to help this so-called reformation that was rousing a new generation of activists then she needed the protection of a powerful title. Unfortunately, that wasn't going to come from James Butler, whose father was still locked in a battle with Anne's own father over the title of the earl of Ormond.

So, when she caught the eye of the strapping and single Henry Percy, who was the direct heir to the earldom of Northumberland, it's not surprising that this would be a marriage she would want to pursue. Percy was a much better match than Butler, who, in time, did indeed spend years back home in Ireland and would have likely taken Anne with him. It's always implied that Anne chased Percy down so she could live a meaningless life of luxury, but as the evidence we are soon to uncover shows, she had other plans in mind. As the wife of a genuine, legitimate earl, just think of the difference she could make in the world.

However, if Anne and Percy wanted to be together, not only would she have to perform a Houdini-style escape from Wolsey's marriage negotiations for her to Butler, but they also had to tackle the small matter of Henry Percy's own betrothal to Mary Talbot. That's not even taking into account the fact that both marriages had already been personally approved by the king of England.

But young and headstrong, Percy and Anne were swept up in the romance of it all, for she had found herself that rarity in sixteenth-century England: a smart marriage match and alliance with a man she was not only attracted to, but who was equally as dedicated and smitten with her. So, throwing caution to the wind, the two did something highly controversial that would cause an uproar in court and come back to haunt them many times over the years: they attempted to arrange their own marriage match.

You thought I was going to say ran off, got married and consummated their illicit affair, didn't you?

Not that I'd blame you. So much has been made of the whole Henry Percy debacle over the centuries. So many sordid rumours are thrown around in the history books and documentaries that during my research I kept expecting to come across some damning evidence of the two having had a forbidden sexual relationship; or perhaps a secret elopement so that their parents had no choice but to accept their union. Just *something* terrible, as it was dredged up during Anne's imprisonment and has been used ever since as a scandal that irrevocably proves she was a vixen of moral depravity.

But though Tudor biographer George Cavendish claims Percy and Anne signed a binding pre-contract,[66] the king's men never found any proof of this in all their years at court. Evidence of an illicit marriage or pre-contract would have been a godsend when later annulling her marriage to the king. The fact that they even felt the need to interrogate Percy on the subject around the time of Anne's trial speaks volumes. Surely, if they already knew Percy had been pre-contracted back when it supposedly happened, they wouldn't need him to confess to anything, because they would have already had an admission of guilt in 1523 when the couple were trying to marry.

So, what *did* they do?

Well, the bare facts are pretty straightforward. Anne and Henry Percy wanted to be married, but his father disapproved, as he didn't think she was of a high enough social ranking to marry his son. The Percys and Talbots had been in marriage negotiations since 1516, and for good reason;[67] Mary Talbot's father was the fourth earl of Shrewsbury, lord lieutenant of the North and a trusted courtier of Henry VIII.

And who was this Anne Boleyn? Her great-grandfather Geoffrey Boleyn was a merchant who became the lord mayor of London in 1457, where he was later knighted. It was due to Geoffrey's son William marrying Margaret Butler that the Boleyns had the Butler connection and an earldom in the family themselves. It was Margaret's father who became the earl of Ormond, making Anne the great-granddaughter of an earl.

Nevertheless, this did not carry the same weight as 'daughter of an earl', which is what Mary Talbot was. Even though Anne's father was an esteemed royal diplomat and her mother, Elizabeth Howard, was the daughter of the earl of Surrey, this connection was still not good enough. Sorry, love.[68]

There was also such a thing as courtly etiquette; one did not gazump a husband or wife while marriage negotiations were ongoing. So, the happy task of warning Percy off his plans with Anne fell to the king's adviser Thomas Wolsey.[69] You see, not only were Percy and Butler both members of staff in Wolsey's own household – *can we have a #Awkward?* – but Wolsey was also good friends with Mary Talbot's father. So, as well as taking orders from the king to stop Percy and Anne ruining a powerful alliance between two high-profile families, Wolsey was also looking out for his friend, who didn't want to see his daughter Mary essentially ditched at the altar.

Wolsey's gentleman usher, George Cavendish, reports in his biography that Wolsey gave Percy a public slap on the wrist in front of all his staff, explaining that the king had already arranged a match for Anne. However, it is at this point that Wolsey is meant to have confided in the group of men that the king wanted Anne for himself.

Oh, but shhhh, they had to keep it a secret, as no one knew, least of all Anne.[70]

Do you even need me to point out how unrealistic this was? Firstly, *as if* Wolsey would just announce the king's supposed top secret to his entire workforce, even if it were true. Secondly, the James Butler marriage to Anne was still in negotiations, so it's highly likely that *this* was the match the king had in mind for her. And then, of course, there was the trifling matter of Henry VIII being in the midst of a relationship with Anne's sister, Mary, at the time of the Henry Percy debacle in 1523.

But what we have to realise here is that Henry VIII didn't end his relationship with Mary and begin to pursue her sister until 1525. So, are we meant to believe the king put a stop to Anne's marriage attempt in 1523, then played coy for two years before finally plucking up the courage to make a move? Henry was many things, but a cautious and slow mover he was not. Alas, the timing simply doesn't add up for us to credit the king's desire for Anne as his motivation behind putting a stop to her attempted match with Percy.

But either way, I think we can all imagine this wouldn't have sat too well with someone as outspoken and opinionated as Anne, who no doubt would have fought the decision. It's thought that Percy, too, tried to win his father round when he came to London to confront his son about the scandal in June 1523. Yet his father was not for turning, and told Percy in no uncertain terms he was to break this apparent promise to marry Anne, avoid her company entirely or be disinherited.[71] This threat did the trick and Percy was quick to concede defeat, reluctantly following through with his commitment to marry Mary Talbot the following year.

What did Anne think of her dashing earl now? Like him, did she see the situation as hopeless, or did she think him spineless for backing down so quickly? We appear to get our answer in her defiance at accepting their fate, because the king decided it would be best if she was 'sent home again to her father' for a season to cool the rebellious romance down.[72]

It seems Anne was all riled up and ready to challenge the system, but was perhaps picking the wrong fight.

Considering his role as the English ambassador, Thomas Boleyn would have been as horrified at the unfolding situation as everyone else, and so was likely to have supported the king's decision for Anne to leave.[73] It certainly wasn't the kind of scandal the daughter of a high-profile royal diplomat should be involved in. But attempting to arrange her own marriage was the extent of it. Aside from an obvious lack of evidence to the contrary, it makes little sense that a smart and deeply religious woman who'd had a respectable upbringing like Anne's would have risked jeopardising a potential match to the son of an earl with anything as unholy as an illicit sexual affair.

So, if the hapless Wolsey was simply acting on the king's orders,[74] as was the nature of his role, why would Anne shoot the messenger to the extent she's been accused of doing? For isn't this meant to be the very point at which she began to harbour a deep resentment of the cardinal? It is, and it all comes back to that public dressing-down he gave Henry Percy.

Cavendish reports that Wolsey berated Percy for attempting to marry without consulting his father or the king, who would have 'matched you according to your estate and honour'. Ouch. Wolsey's public declaration that he deemed Anne too lowly to marry the son of an earl would have made for salacious gossip at court, and soon enough it got back to Anne, who was understandably mortified at the slur.[75] Cavendish reported she was 'greatly offended', apparently saying, 'If it ever lay within her power, she would work the cardinal as much displeasure.'[76]

This statement, I believe, could very well have been true. It sounds like the kind of childish threat Anne was known to have made in the heat of the moment when hurt and embarrassed. But would it be the grudge that Cavendish claims brought about Wolsey's downfall years later?[77] Oh no, for there were several more years and opportunities ahead for the cardinal to greatly offend the increasingly zealous reformer Anne Boleyn.

So Anne was sent home to Hever Castle 'for a season', where it was said she 'she smoked', so angry was she at being placed under what must have felt like house arrest.[78] She wouldn't have been alone during her time back home, as her old governess, Mrs Orchard, was still in attendance at the castle, as was Anne's grandmother Lady Margaret. In fact, Margaret lived at Hever until her death in 1539, and outlived almost the entire family, although she was said to have not been of sound mind with what we would today diagnose as dementia. So, it's likely that Anne would have helped to care for her, possibly alongside her mother, Elizabeth, who may have accompanied her during her stint back at Hever.

But as nice as this quality family time surely was, there's no doubt it still would have been a frustrating time for Anne, halting her religious mission before it had even begun.

Of course, the big question historians feel compelled to stop and ask here is: was religion really Anne Boleyn's driving force? Either that or they downright dismiss all notions of her having had any true religious intent, too sexual and power-hungry was she to have ever been a good woman.

Yes, it may have started as sixteenth-century propaganda so the king didn't come out of Anne Boleyn's murder looking like the bad guy, but there are a depressing number of contemporary historians who have bought into the lie that to be a powerful woman your intentions have to be bad, to achieve greatness you had to have slept your way to the top, as well as the old classic that Anne had too strong and fiery a personality for religion to have been her true motivation. It's apparently hard to swallow that someone so steely could be motivated by something as pure and delicate as religion. After all, religion is meant to be about piety, prayer, peace and love.

While it might be fair to argue that, for the elite few who ruled the Church, religion was less about salvation in the afterlife and more about gaining power here on earth, we can't deny that for the people, it was about having a deeper connection to God and the gospel.

And you're telling me someone who had quick-witted comebacks and putdowns for those who challenged her had religion and faith in her heart?

As though the two simply don't go together. But as history has taught us, indeed they do.

Thomas More tortured people for wanting to read the Bible in English. Henry VIII had people executed for refusing to accept him as the head of the Church of England. For centuries to come, Protestants and Catholics would regularly take it in turns to hack each other to death, all in the name of religion. These were forceful men willing to kill for their faith; not something any of us condone, but we do readily accept that men fight wars in the name of religion.

Yet we struggle to accept that Anne Boleyn could have been religiously motivated because, you know, *she had quite a harsh tongue and could be rather sharp with people!* I think if we were a bit more honest with ourselves, we might admit that it comes down to the fact that she was a woman.

While the men could hang, draw and quarter someone in the name of faith, we appear to expect our religious women to have been peace-keepers, spreading their good mission calmly and in a loving manner. Like Florence Nightingale or Mother Teresa. Why else do we struggle with allowing Anne Boleyn to have been angry, frustrated and fighting for her religious beliefs with the same unapologetic gusto as her husband? Yet the idea crops up time and time again with baffled biographers that because Anne would sometimes lash out with harsh insults, this subsequently cancelled out her lifelong faith.

Or is the issue more to do with her having been a cheeky flirt who was seen as potently sexual to men? Even Anne's most neutral biographer concludes that she 'radiated sex',[79] and this is something many historians have decided doesn't sit well with her being a religious woman.

Sixteenth-century historian de Carles spoke of her 'eyes always most attractive, which she knew well how to use with effect, sometimes, leaving them at rest, and at other, sending a message'.[80]

Can we have a collective eye roll, please?

Firstly, may I point out that the contemporary reports as to how alluring Anne was come from men, who appear to be blaming her for their being attracted to her. Sadly, it was Anne's misfortune, and that of all sixteenth-century women, that her character and indeed life were left solely in the hands of male record-keepers, to be interpreted and written from their viewpoint. So, it's not difficult to see how the misogynistic narrative of Anne Boleyn's story began. What's harder to accept, however, is how it's been upheld for so long in the modern world, not only by men but an alarming number of female writers. These are the historians who reason that because Anne had once been happy to play along with her friends in the game of courtly love, she was somehow the one courtier who wasn't deeply religious, whose world didn't revolve around an almost hourly devotion to God. That because she had a flirty manner, she couldn't have also been angered into rebellion by the misdemeanours of the Church.

Henry VIII was a notorious philanderer, regularly taking a mistress, yet we never question his Catholic beliefs because of it. In 1525, Martin Luther, priest and leader of the religious reformation, married a former nun, Katharina von Bora, to prove that vows of celibacy got you no closer to God than raising a family and enjoying a bit of hanky-panky. (You heard me, ladies and gentlemen, *hanky-panky*!)

Reformists like Anne were liberated by this new evangelical understanding that no amount of self-punishment and deprivation would advance your salvation before God. Meaning that, alongside her daily prayers, there was no harm in Anne Boleyn enjoying the flirty traditions of court life, so long as she had true faith in her heart and never took it any further than writing a silly poem and making eye contact with the opposite sex. It didn't have to result in affairs or dalliances; a flirt does not a slut make. Yet people really struggle with this one – as though good girls do not laugh and dance. There is to be no joy when you are a true woman of God, apparently.

Of course, there are a smattering of historians from #TeamAragon who claim Anne was only an evangelical to be fashionable. Now, knowing how closely she grew up with the religious reformists of the French court, it's not surprising to learn that she owned many controversial works by evangelicals such as fellow courtier Clément Marot, who, as we've seen, translated the Psalms into French. Ignoring the ban on English Bibles, Anne defiantly owned a copy of Tyndale's 1534 English translation of the New Testament and Jacques Lefèvre d'Étaples's French translation of the Bible, which caused just as much outrage to the authorities as its English counterpart, and was burned en masse. Anne also owned two other highly controversial works by Lefèvre, *The Pistellis and Gospelles* and *The Ecclesiaste* of 1531.[81] Rose Hickman, a friend of sixteenth-century historian John Foxe, also remembered that Anne had her father import manuscripts of the scriptures written in French, an incredibly risky move at a time when freedom of religious expression was essentially illegal.[82]

By the time Anne was arrested in 1536, among her seized possessions were forty progressive reformist books and manuscripts.[83] There were strict bans on owning most of these works, and individuals caught in possession of them could face arrest, imprisonment and punishment as a heretic. So, forgive me if I don't buy into the idea that Anne risked her career at court and any possibility of a prestigious marriage match simply to be seen as 'on trend' and a bit edgy. Lest we forget, her father was a high-profile royal diplomat and right-hand man to Cardinal Wolsey,[84] who was the all-powerful and devoutly Catholic adviser to the king of England. If Anne ever put that in jeopardy it was going to be for something she truly believed in. She was not playing games.

But perhaps the biggest clue that her true motivation was religion comes from Anne herself, in one of her few surviving written messages: the simple note of 'Le temps viendra' in her *Book of Hours*, which translates to 'The time will come.' This haunting handwritten note can be viewed to this day at the Boleyn family home of Hever Castle. But writers and historians alike, myself included for some time, have wondered exactly what Anne was alluding to. Was it her pursuit of power? Her quest to be queen? A prophecy for her daughter's future on the throne? As it turns out, it is none of the above.

I have discovered a note written by Jacques Lefèvre D'Étaples in his *Commentarii initiatorii in quatuor evangelia* in 1522, during Anne's first year at the Tudor court, which reads: *'Le temps viendra bientôt où Christ sera prêché purement et sans mélange de traditions humaines, ce qui ne se fait pas maintenant . . .* [85] which translates as: 'The time will soon come in which Christ will be preached purely, unsullied by human traditions, which is not being done now.'

His words 'Christ will be preached purely' relate to the evangelical quest to have a French translation of the Bible, a fight that Anne was personally to champion in her time. Then the line about 'unsullied by human traditions' is what Lefèvre sees as the priests' misinterpretation of the scripture and the man-made rules they fed their congregations while hiding behind the language barrier of the Latin text. The note as a whole is a direct reference to the religious reformation that was whipping everyone into rebellious angst.

So, with Anne collecting Lefèvre's work and here, it appears, cryptically quoting him in her *Book of Hours*, the connection is an obvious one and possibly the first indication that she was motivated by religion from the moment she set foot back on English soil.

Yet it appears to be only modern historians who question Anne's religious conviction, because sixteenth-century supporters and enemies alike saw her as an evangelical reformer who championed the work of religious activists.

Chapuys, the Spanish ambassador in England during Anne's ascent to the throne, regularly complained in letters home of her being 'the cause and nurse of the spread of Lutheranism in this country'.[86] It was also Chapuys who said Anne was 'more Lutheran than Luther himself',[87] quite the statement knowing, as we do, how passionate Luther was about reform. Not that she held quite the same extreme religious beliefs as Luther; but it was a telling thing for Chapuys to claim.

Nicholas Sander, the propagandist responsible for a steady stream of vitriol about Anne over the years, believed it was Marguerite d'Angoulême who corrupted her, and Anne in turn who 'corrupted' England.[88]

Jeez, no word of a thanks!

John Aylmer, who was later to become the bishop of London, wrote *An Harborowe for faithfull and Trewe Subjectes* in 1559, in which he confirms Anne's religious mission by explaining that, in his view, the Reformation was not started by men but by a certain woman: 'Was not queen Anne . . . the chief, first, and only cause of banishing the beast of Rome? Was there ever in England a greater feat wrought by any man than this by a woman?'

Not, he hastens to add, to take away from the work Henry VIII did, but 'yet the crop and root was the queen' and that Anne deserved her due praise, for she was the driving force of the Reformation, which he believed God had given her the wisdom and mindset to achieve.[89]

It appears John Foxe agreed with him, believing Anne was a martyr of the 'new religion' and 'zealous defender' of the gospel, who used her powerful position as queen to promote the evangelical cause.[90] So too did George Wyatt, who credits the Reformation and changing of religion to Anne, saying she 'bore a most great part in the great and remarkable conversion in the state of religion . . . which living she so courageously stood to support'.[91]

Then someone much closer to home, William Latymer, Anne's chaplain who went on to become one of her earliest biographers, confided that she dedicated her time to furthering the 'purity of the scriptures' and to the 'abolishing of the blind ignorance and abuses grown in this land' – clearly a reference to practices such as the sale of indulgences and fake holy relics.[92]

Even following Anne's death, Nicholas Shaxton wrote to Cromwell asking him to be as committed to spreading the 'honour of God and his Holy word than when the late queen was alive and often incited you thereto'.[93] Wyatt takes this one step further, controversially confirming that it was Anne's pushing for religious reform 'which has moved so many to write and speak falsely and foully of her'.[94]

On and on it goes, pages of eyewitness accounts from Anne's Tudor peers confirming the evangelical motivation behind every action in her life. Anyone who continues to overlook these statements is dismissing the very original sources on which our entire knowledge of Tudor history is built.

However, I suspect part of the reason modern historians have jumped to the conclusion that Anne's religious conviction wasn't as strong as the more gung-ho reformists was due to the fact that she championed 'moderate reform'. Indeed, there is a great deal of confusion over the meaning of this phrase, but let me clarify: when history speaks of moderate reformists, who were mostly Christian humanists, it didn't mean they were half-arsed about their religion. It simply meant that they were in support of reform in the main areas that needed change, as opposed to bull-in-a-china-shop, we're leaving, it's over, don't text me again!

Anne still fought hard for what she believed in and was deeply passionate, but the difference between her and, say, the Martin Luthers of the world, is that she wanted to see change rather than complete abolishment where reformers felt the Church was taking advantage of the congregation. But it's interesting to note that while many moderate reformers went on to become evangelical and eventually Protestant, many still remained Catholic.

You see, reformists didn't reject or deny Roman Catholic teachings; it's just that they felt the leaders of the Church didn't quite practise what they preached. And it appears this is where Anne sat in the theological debate. It explains why she didn't want the monasteries to be ripped apart in their entirety but *did* make the effort during her reign to visit them and help them reform their practices, as we will come to see.

But we have to remember that Anne Boleyn was a *first-generation evangelical*. It's called a 'new religion' for a reason. Anne was finding her feet, just like everyone else, figuring out where she stood with these new ideas versus the orthodox Catholic teachings. It was a time of religious growth and uncertainty, and hence we shouldn't chastise the Tudors for not knowing immediately where their beliefs lay.

So, historians who use the fact that Anne took holy communion and prayed before the sacrament while in prison as final proof she wasn't a true evangelical, really need to go take a theology lesson and hit us up when they're down with the basics.

By the time Anne was finally allowed back at court, the Butlers had given up on any hopes of a marriage between her and James.[95] So it's at this point that she found herself in London, for the first time unattached and ready to forge forward to find a marital alliance of worth. All scandal was in the past; nothing was going to ruin her mission this time.

Little did she know Henry VIII was about to bulldoze his way into her life.

CHAPTER 3

THE LOVE OF A KING AND SOCIOPATH

Historians have delighted in casting Henry VIII as the ultimate one-dimensional Tudor villain almost as much as they have Anne Boleyn, simplistically explaining away his actions as those of a narcissistic pampered prince. They've called him a tyrant, a murderer, an obsessive, paranoid, heartless egotist. And he clearly was. Don't worry, I'm not here to defend him and claim he too has been misrepresented all these years. But his behaviour *has* been misunderstood.

He harboured all these complexities and more. But what makes such traits manifest so cataclysmically in one person? What makes Henry's destructive patterns of behaviour, with all those seemingly irrational and evil decisions, slowly evolve his story from one of many brutal tales in history into a psychological evaluation?

The answer is mental illness.

The evidence I am about to present in these pages points unequivocally to Henry VIII being an undiagnosed sociopath.

If at this point your mind automatically veers towards Henry's infamous jousting accident of 1536, the year the king supposedly 'changed' from an easy-going, happy-go-lucky tyrant to a short-tempered one with a limp, then let me stop you right there. We are about to discover that Henry's issues were so much more deeply ingrained in his psychological make-up than history has ever considered before. So, while I definitely support the school of thought espoused by recent historians that the king's later accident did indeed affect him, the evidence we will dissect in this book proves that his head injury only served to exacerbate a clearly pre-existing, lifelong mental illness: one we can trace right back to its development in childhood and its grave effect on the people in his life, not months before Anne's death in 1536 but decades.

Which means Henry's entire relationship with Anne Boleyn suddenly goes from the world's most unconvincing love story to the chilling case study of a sociopath.

The key element of looking at the king's actions through the eyes of his mental illness is that it not only sheds brand-new light on his own life, but affects how we interpret Anne Boleyn's story in the most catastrophic way. It means she didn't have to have done anything drastic to cause his affections to wane; she didn't have to have been an impassioned wife on the warpath, throwing tantrums that caused him to tire of her – just *some* of the feeble explanations history has mustered so far.

It's human nature that when a break-up happens, we feel we have to lay the blame on someone in order for it to make sense, and the standard go-to with Henry and Anne seems to be: *what did she do to make him want to get rid of her so desperately?* Yes, it would appear society's favourite habit of blaming the woman was just as prevalent in the sixteenth century as it sadly still is today. But what if Anne didn't change or become tiresome? What if *he* was the one who suddenly switched? What if Henry's affections could do a 360 and turn to hatred without a justified cause and, more importantly, without a conscience?

The frustrating thing is that almost everyone has been quick to call Henry a psycho, dismissing it as a no-brainer while throwing around words such as mad and insane. But no one has ever stopped to apply the key traits of these mental illnesses to the king's notorious actions. Instead, for centuries, historians have continued to attempt to understand *rationally* how his relationship with Anne Boleyn unfolded the way it did, either brushing over the illogical sequence of events without striving for a more convincing explanation, or blaming other people, concocting theories based on the actions of those around him – namely Anne Boleyn – that *this* is what must have triggered him to . . . (insert irrational action here).

But the vital point to understand about sociopathy is that there *is* no rationale. If Henry genuinely had this debilitating mental disorder – which world-leading psychologists suggest in this chapter that he did – his actions can't be explained away logically or dissected as for a rational person. So, in order to fully understand Anne Boleyn's story, we must look at her entire relationship through the prism of Henry's mental illness.

But first, know this: to speak of mental illness is not an insult, and as a society we need to move beyond that stigmatised belief. It is simply an illness of the mind, in exactly the same way that a tumour might grow in the brain. But unlike a tumour it is harder to detect, easier to dismiss and it cannot be cut out. Those living with this condition are chained to their own destructive behaviour until the bitter end.

◆　◆　◆

The first thing you need to understand about a sociopath is that they have no conscience. As though someone flicked the switch on this part of their brain, giving them the emotional freedom to do whatever the hell they want, without that irritating voice of reason ruining all the fun. This means a sociopath is able to hurt those they supposedly love without a hint of guilt or a morsel of regret. It's almost incomprehensible to us that a person could never experience guilt, yet this we shall unfathomably witness, time and time again, in the story of Henry VIII and Anne Boleyn. It's not a case of the king's stubborn reluctance to experience true emotions; a sociopath's brain simply does not possess the capacity to process them. It is science, not logic. It's the kid who tortures animals without feeling bad. It's the person who doesn't lose sleep over getting a co-worker fired and taking their job. It's the king who can order the brutal death of the love of his life and get engaged to someone else the very next day. It's as liberating a prospect as it is a horrifying one.

So why sociopath and not psychopath?

Some psychologists say the distinction between the two is so minuscule they really should come under the same category, while others disagree, seeing them as worlds apart. But there are some key differences between the two that I believe place Henry VIII firmly in the sociopath category.

While they both display deceitful and manipulative behaviour, psychopaths are fearless, but sociopaths aren't. Now, while fear is an emotion, Dr Kevin Dutton PhD, a research psychologist at Oxford University, explains, 'There is a lot of cutting-edge, scientific evidence to show that sociopaths can actually experience fear *if* you draw their attention to something they should be frightened of.' So, whereas you and I might be scared of something that could cost us our lives in the pursuit of a goal, even if there is danger all around them a sociopath will not pay attention to it. But when grave danger is pointed out, this is where recent laboratory studies have found that sociopaths can experience that most debilitating of human emotions: true fear.[96]

This makes obvious sense as the majority of Henry's most shocking actions were most definitely driven by fear. The fear of God; fear of losing the throne – after all, it was only his father, Henry VII, who defeated King Richard III in battle and took the crown. So, it was an inbuilt family fear throughout the Tudors' reign that there would be an uprising and the throne would be taken back by a more rightful heir.

Henry also displayed an excessive fear of illness and death. You name it, Henry harboured an irrational fear of it. It's what made him so chilled and fun to be around.

Another difference is that psychopaths can't form attachments with others, whereas sociopaths can – even if they are pretty dysfunctional, as we'll see when we go on to dissect Henry's particular relationship with Anne Boleyn. Sociopaths see the object of their desire as just that: an 'object' they must win, not a person for whom they have developed deep emotions.

It will come as no surprise to anyone familiar with Henry's story that sociopaths are less emotionally stable than psychopaths. Where a psychopath can plan every last detail of a murder with a chilling sense of calm, sociopaths are highly impulsive and display erratic behaviour – like, say, ordering the murder of their wife within a matter of days after deciding they should break up. They lack patience. Act on compulsion. All sounding a little familiar?

Of course, one of the main differences between psychopaths and sociopaths is how the mental illness develops, and that's what they call *nature versus nurture*. Whereas psychopaths are born (nature), sociopathy can be due to childhood trauma such as abuse or neglect (nurture), or as previously mentioned, it can be the result of a brain injury.

But as we will discover, there is simply no getting away from the fact that Henry was at the mercy of his sociopathy during his entire relationship with Anne Boleyn; we see it in everything from his relentless, obsessive pursuit of her to the nonchalance with which he murdered her. Which means his mental illness could only have been the result of his disturbing youth.

Now, Henry's childhood is rarely delved into in great detail in the history books, as though this super-villain just materialised one day, morbidly obese, handing out death sentences from the throne. Yet Henry's mental illness was due to more than having grown up around a chorus of 'yes-men'. He experienced a deeply traumatic and isolated childhood, not to mention a dysfunctional relationship with his father, which was to have a profound effect upon his entire reign.

But this is where we have to agree that suffering is relative; while some may never know extreme poverty and the true horrors and abuses we hear of around the world, it doesn't mean that in their eyes, in their unique set of circumstances, life can't be *their version* of traumatic, and hence still have the same psychological impact. Mental illness does not discriminate. It can hit paupers and princes and be equally devastating. Of course, it's very easy to avoid giving too much significance to this part of the king's story, as there weren't too many well-balanced and functional childhoods in the sixteenth century. But the fact that there appears to have been an above average level of crazy in Tudor history should perhaps tell us it shouldn't be so lightly dismissed.

One of the king's biographers, John Matusiak, tells of how during these formative childhood years, from birth until the age of seven, those who surrounded Henry were passive figures, attending and providing at a distance rather than interacting and comforting as loving parental figures. Only weeks after his birth, Henry was taken away from his mother and father at Greenwich to live at Eltham Palace in Kent.[97] Here he was raised by his grandmother Lady Margaret Beaufort, who by all accounts was an incredibly intense woman. A devout Catholic, she took a vow of chastity at the age of sixty-one. She would wake at 5 a.m. every day to begin her prayers, and would wear a hair shirt. John Fisher described her as being continuously gripped with anxiety, in tears over past miseries and bemoaning what doom was to come.[98]

It was a belief of the time that around the age of seven, high-born boys should be 'taken from the company of all women', and Henry was henceforth taught exclusively by male tutors.[99] Until 1502, the main tutor was John Skelton, a man for whom biographers show a near-universal disdain due to his scathing sexist attacks on women, which once compelled an incensed little lady to send him the head of a dead man. Most worryingly, this occurred while he was living with the tender Prince Henry at Eltham.[100]

Throughout Henry's early childhood, his father's health deteriorated and the old king became increasingly bad-tempered, nasty and violent towards everyone he dealt with, including young Henry, who it's reported he attacked after his son apparently drove him into an almost trance-like pathological rage. The Spanish ambassador Fuensalida even told of how Henry's father once attacked him so violently it was 'as if to kill him'.[101]

So, not disturbing in the slightest that these should be the people who were raising the future king of England and Anne Boleyn's future husband. Not that Henry had always been the future king. In fact, for the first ten years of his life he grew up in the shadow of his older brother and original heir to the throne, Prince Arthur. But when Arthur died unexpectedly in 1502, their father became paranoid that ten-year-old Henry, who was now sole heir to the Tudor throne, would also die, exposing the kingdom to attack. So, he effectively locked his son away from all risk of physical harm and deadly diseases that had a nasty habit of snatching youngsters away all too soon. But as Matusiak rightly points out, animals raised in captivity aren't the most functional.

By the time Henry was thirteen, his father refused to let him take his place, like his brother before him, as prince of Wales at Ludlow Castle, instead keeping him locked within the safety of his own Palace of Westminster.[102] Again Fuensalida, who came to the Tudor court in 1508, described a disturbing scene: at seventeen, Henry was 'locked away as a woman' in a bedchamber just off from his father's that was only accessible via a private door.[103] Even though the young prince was said to have held his own miniature court, he never spoke in public, except to answer a question asked by his father,[104] and he was surrounded at all times by trusted attendants whose permission Henry needed to move anywhere within the palace walls.

While J. J. Scarisbrick, one of Henry VIII's most prominent biographers, backs up the reports that young Henry was raised in near isolation,[105] David Loades raises the obvious question as to how isolated he could really have been in the 'crowded environment' of the Tudor court. Indeed, Fuensalida was also to report Henry spending many a day jousting in the tiltyard at Richmond. Granted, he was watched closely by his father,[106] and Loades concedes that these were 'strictly private' activities in which Henry would probably joust or play tennis with only his instructor for company. It was said to be out of the question for the young prince ever to demonstrate his sporting skills to the rest of the court, and he went on to show his great upset at being excluded from the court's many summer activities.[107]

Alas, you see, the young Henry didn't need to be in solitary confinement every day of his childhood for the worrying lifestyle uncovered by historians to have had the damaging effect it clearly did on his psyche.

But what about the childhood friends we're told he was close to? We've already met the old rogue that was Charles Brandon. The king was also known to be close to a certain Henry Norris from a young age. So, can a sociopath have true friends?

No, not really. But 'friends' is a term we have labelled them with. Though Brandon came to be considered Henry's 'favourite' courtier,[108] accounts describe him more as a loyal apprentice who stayed close and obeyed his every demand. The fact that Brandon would turn to Henry's minister Wolsey for help in manipulating the king speaks more of him being a servant and court jester than a true friend.[109] Which would explain how, as with his treatment of Anne Boleyn, Henry was able, decades later, to banish Brandon from court and sentence Norris to death without so much as a second thought for his lifelong companions.

Back in 1503, Henry hardly had time to digest his brother's death and the enormity of his new future before he was hit with another, more devastating blow the following year when his mother, Elizabeth of York, died. Henry's mother was the daughter of Edward IV and the sister of the tragic princes who were presumed to have been murdered in the Tower of London by Richard III.[110] Although Henry spent much of his time away from his mother, this only served to elevate her to an untouchable, legendary status, and he was later to describe the death of 'my dearest mother' as 'hateful'.[111]

When you consider, then, that only six months later Henry's thirteen-year-old sister, Margaret Tudor, was shipped off to Scotland to marry the thirty-three-year-old King James IV, you get a real sense of every comfort being snatched away from him.

It's said that following Elizabeth's death the court lost all its fun, and by all accounts became a miserable place to live and work in. Henry's father refused to let him take part in official royal celebrations or festivities during the years leading up to his reign. You would have thought it might have been a good idea to prepare the future king, as he had done Arthur, but no. Henry never sat in on government proceedings, nor attended council meetings.[112] Matusiak confirms he was 'entirely untutored in the art of kingsmanship'.[113]

Then, when Henry was seventeen, his father died and he was thrust into the international spotlight, crowned king of England and handed all the power in the land.

Is there any wonder what happened next?

People have called Henry a narcissist, which is a mental disorder in itself but can also be one of the components of a sociopathic personality. Dr Kevin Dutton, author of *The Wisdom of Psychopaths*, explains that, just as a triathlon can feature various sporting events yet each one can stand in its own right, so too can narcissism be a symptom of sociopathy and also be a disorder on its own.

However, Dutton interestingly points out that sociopaths like to be the centre of attention because it gives them power which, in turn, enables them to pull the strings and manipulate other people. Something we can very much apply to Henry VIII and his life at court. So, for a sociopath, being the centre of attention is a means to an end, whereas for a person suffering from narcissistic disorder alone, being the centre of attention *is* the end goal. It fulfils a need for them to feel they are somebody, and Henry definitely wanted more than mere adulation. He wanted to get his own way.

Within weeks of his father's death, Henry married his late brother's widow, Katherine of Aragon, rescuing her from regal obscurity and placing her back on the throne that she had left her homeland of Spain for. And although Henry's grandmother, Margaret Beaufort, the woman who raised him from birth, died only days later on 29 June, her passing did not dampen the summer-long celebrations to mark his new role as king.[114] There were feasts, jousts, hunting and the odd beheading.

Ah yes, some of the first executions eighteen-year-old Henry ordered were those of Sir Richard Empson and Edmund Dudley, who'd helped his father amass the Tudors' vast fortune via an incredibly unpopular taxation and fine collection. As Henry's narcissism kicked in, and with it the desperation to gain public approval, on only the second day of his reign he concocted charges of treason and had the two men thrown in the Tower of London to await their execution.[115]

Just like that. Baby's First Murders ordered, seemingly without a flicker of guilt or remorse.[116] A sociopath was born, and long before his world was to collide with Anne Boleyn's.

Bizarrely, though, it has been argued that before his 1536 head injury, Henry was not the tyrant we have firm evidence of him being. This claim is based on reports by the king's tutors, ambassadors and contemporary chroniclers of his 'goodly personage', 'gentile friendliness', 'grace of nature' and 'how wisely he behaves', such that he has 'few equals in the world'.[117] But this fawning flattery was standard. We have to remember these people were speaking publicly about the king of England. What do we historians expect? His subjects to be giving a brutally honest critique of the monarch? Who on earth would risk their life to speak ill of Henry VIII?

Unfortunately, the erratic actions and behaviour we will come to witness from the king throughout this book clearly demonstrate that he suffered from a mental illness long before his horrifying decision to kill Anne Boleyn in 1536.

Alas, once you realise who Anne was dealing with I'm afraid it will change the way you view their 'romance' forever. However, now you understand the core components of Henry's psyche, we can begin to dissect the *real* reason that drove him to leave Katherine of Aragon. For it was not the simplistic quest for a son and heir, nor the passionate pursuit of his 'love' for Anne Boleyn. This is where the history books get it so wrong: not so much barking up the wrong tree as being in the wrong forest entirely.

Everyone has images of Henry VIII being this strong force of nature, and that was no accident. Everything about him was sending a signal to the world that he was a stronghold fortified tower of strength who was not to be messed with – from the power stance in his official portraits, with the unnaturally broad shoulders and those calf muscles, to the many public displays of macho bravado (jousting, wrestling, war; *my country's stronger than yours*). But this exterior was merely a carefully stage-managed cover for the worries and fears eating away at him on the inside. Henry was a tortured soul who feared everything, yet nothing ate away at him more than his fear of God's wrath.

It's no secret that he believed he was personally chosen by God to be the king of England; for this reason, he felt himself closer to the Almighty than everyone else. So he took it as a sign of the Lord's ardent displeasure when he failed to produce a son and heir to his hallowed throne with Katherine of Aragon. Although Henry was aware of the potential issues in marrying his brother's widow from the start, it wasn't until God made his anger known concerning the distinct lack of sons that he began to take it seriously. By the time a passage in the Book of Leviticus was brought to his attention, he knew he was in trouble. He obsessed over the scripture that stated in no uncertain terms: 'Thou shalt not uncover the nakedness of thy brother's wife; it is thy brother's nakedness. And if a man should take his brother's wife it is an unclean thing: they shall be childless.' Incidentally, this was deemed to apply only to male children because, lest we forget, Henry had a daughter by Katherine of Aragon, Princess Mary.

When it became clear that the queen was past childbearing age and they'd run out of chances for God to forgive them and bless their marriage with a son, the king was hell-bent on correcting his mistake and annulling the offending marriage to avoid the eternal damnation of his soul.

You see, the problem as Henry saw it wasn't that he *couldn't* have a son; his famous affair with Bessie Blount had given him an illegitimate son, whom he openly recognised as his own. The issue was that he couldn't have a son with Katherine.

And why not? *Because she was his brother's widow – I mean, keep up, old boy!*

Of course, there were many at the time who were sceptical about the king's argument, as most continue to be today. Particularly when there was additional scripture in Deuteronomy that seemingly con-tradicted Leviticus, stating, 'When brethren dwell together, and one of them dieth without children, the wife of the deceased shall not marry another; but his brother shall take her, and raise up seed for his brother.'[118]

But what we need to remember is that the text we are reading here is an English translation, and that Leviticus used the words *frater germa-nus*, which meant 'brother' in the true sense, whereas Deuteronomy used the word *cognatus*, meaning 'relative'.[119] It was this attention to detail that kept Henry VIII consumed with the fear that he had gone against God's word and needed to correct his sin. In fact, at the time of Henry's marrying Katherine, the Archbishop of Canterbury William

Warham had been explicitly against their union for the very same scriptural reasons.[120]

So, while it may have been repeatedly sold to us as *Henry VIII divorced Katherine and broke from Rome in order to marry Anne Boleyn* while citing Leviticus as the ultimate get-out-of-jail-free card, that doesn't actually appear to be the case. In fact, we have evidence that Henry was making secret enquiries about divorce long before he had the end goal of marrying Anne.

Wolsey's gentleman usher, George Cavendish, tells us his master went to France to meet Queen Claude's sister, Lady Renée, who was set to inherit the duchy of Brittany, as a possible new bride for the king.[121] At the same time, Wolsey was being instructed to find out about the possibility of an annulment. Then we have reports from the bishop of Lincoln, John Longland, who said in 1532 that he heard mutterings of the divorce 'nine or ten years ago', which dates the king's enquiries to as early as 1522 or 1523[122] – years before he was involved with Anne.

What this tells us is that something other than his lust for another woman was driving the king to divorce Katherine of Aragon.

Yet most still don't believe that Henry's fear of Leviticus was his genuine motivation.

Indeed, it's easy to interpret the king's pursuit of a male heir on a very superficial level, with many presuming his growing obsession to be no more than a legendary ego trying to correct his apparent 'failure as a man' to secure the crown and kingdom. While this may be a valid argument in the context of Henry's unique situation as king, and may very well have been how it all started, it becomes increasingly clear that when paired with his deteriorating mental health, the lack of a son soon took on a more ominous meaning for him.

The idea that Henry's quest for a male heir was driven by a fear of God's wrath rather than good old Tudor misogyny is further supported by the fact that it doesn't appear he was all too intimidated by the concept of a woman ruling England. This was first demonstrated when he left Katherine of Aragon to rule the kingdom in his absence in 1513, while he went away to war in France. He proclaimed her governor of the realm and captain-general of the forces,[123] during which time the English army defeated the Scots at Flodden.[124] But Katherine's victory clearly didn't emasculate the proud king to the extent some historians claim, because he later went on to decree in the 1535 Act of Succession that in the event of his own death, Anne Boleyn, *not his legitimate children*, would rule the country as sole queen regent. This was Henry VIII once again granting a woman equal rights, not just as a man but as a king. It doesn't get any bigger than that when trying to understand his stance on female rulers.

If Henry was opposed to the idea of a female heir for purely misogynistic reasons, he could have easily done some fancy footwork to ensure the crown went to another, albeit obscure relative, as many a monarch has done before and since. Case in point: there was serious talk at one time of him making his illegitimate son, Henry Fitzroy, his legal heir. He was the king of England; he could do what he wanted, as the Reformation proved. But vitally in this case he didn't, showing that he wanted that male heir born to confirm God had not forsaken him.

And so it was in the midst of this mental trauma, when he was at his most fraught and desperate, that the king's mind zeroed in on Anne Boleyn at court in 1526. What we perceive to have started out as a harmless light-hearted flirtation quickly spiralled into a devastating series of events that would change the course of not only Anne's life but British history.

But how do we know he didn't really love her?

Aside from the fact that he ordered a swordsman to decapitate her, I turned to neuroscientist Dr James Fallon for an explanation. Here, Fallon draws our attention to another disorder in Henry's sociopathic triathlon: borderline personality disorder.

People with this condition experience mood swings, and tend to view the world in extremes: a person will drastically become all good or all bad, with no reasonable middle ground. This causes their opinions of others to change quickly and without warning, meaning an individual who is seen as a friend one day can be considered an enemy or traitor the next.[125]

This is the Henry we recognise.

Dr Fallon's description of borderline personality disorder could almost be describing Henry's entire relationship with Anne Boleyn when he explains: 'Sufferers will idealise someone. They will become the most wonderful person they ever met. But inevitably, for any unpredictable reason, they will get disappointed, at which point they will devalue and then discard them.'[126]

It is this pattern of intense and unstable relationships, often swinging from extreme love (the idealisation phase) to extreme dislike (the devaluation/discard phase), that Henry VIII repeated time and time again with every single wife he took, but most importantly in his relationship with Anne Boleyn.[127]

And so, at last, 'idealise, devalue, discard' fills in the blanks and explains so many of the king's inexplicable actions within his relationship with Anne. In the 'idealise' phase, Anne became the target of Henry's game, in which he charmed, flattered and manipulated his way into winning her affections, single-mindedly pursuing her until she was his. But the thing you have to understand about sociopaths is that they are the world's most convincing method actors, who mimic the emotions they lack, meaning Henry might possibly have been the most charming person Anne Boleyn ever met. Over the years, he would have subconsciously absorbed how others acted in the pursuit of love. This means he wrote her the 'love letters', he sent her the gifts, he said all the right things in order to be the person he thought Anne wanted him to be.

However, the one thing she really needed him to be was single, so that's where his love-bombing essentially failed and he resorted to offering her marriage. But because Henry didn't have the emotional capacity to love Anne, he instead objectified her, meaning she was never the love of his life but an object of his desire, with emphasis on the word *object*.

'Idealise' does not refer to him idealising Anne as a human being, but as the glory of a prize to be won and owned. And idealise he certainly did. Henry held Anne up as the potential saviour of his kingdom and soul, deciding that she alone could provide him with God's good favour in the form of that all-hallowed male heir he had so far been denied.

So . . . no pressure, then.

But the problem with Henry idealising Anne as an object is that this apparent 'emotion' was only superficial, and could vanish as quickly as it came.

One thing history has struggled to understand in the whole Henry and Anne saga is the speed with which Henry not only lost interest in his new wife once they got married, but just how quickly his supposed love turned to loathing. This has been explained away in the past with quips that Henry discovered Anne to be too skilled in the bedroom to have been a virgin, and that she must have been corrupted in France.[128] But as we've already seen, that doesn't appear to ring true for the devout evangelical. More to the point, if those were Henry's true suspicions upon sleeping with Anne, why would he then go on to marry her one month later? As we will see when we discuss the dubious timing of their eventual marriage.

Easily dismissed, too, is the theory that after seven years together, Anne's fiery personality suddenly became just too much to deal with the moment they said, 'I do.'

Altogether pathetic suggestions that sound increasingly like excuses for why a man should want to kill his wife.

The problem here, I believe, is that we've been focusing on the wrong part of the relationship's timeline. We've been trying to figure out what went wrong later on – and, granted, plenty did; but in terms of their 'undying love' for one another, we need to realise it was never right to begin with. Only when we accept this do we realise how it could implode so spectacularly when it did, and at such breakneck speed.

And so it appears it was that same erratic, God-fearing angst that had driven Henry to divorce Katherine of Aragon that shocked him out of his blind obsession with Anne, bringing all his irrational fears of God's displeasure back to the surface and triggering the next devastating phase of 'devalue'.

One of the few emotional states a sociopath is capable of is contempt. As Anne became more human in the eyes of the king, failing to live up to the unobtainable ideals he held her to – namely, her ability to dictate the sex of their firstborn – so his valuation of her fell. In time, his obsession would turn to loathing, but the key thing we have to realise here is that Henry would blame *Anne* for his own disenchantment. It wasn't *his* fault his affection was waning. It wasn't *his* fault he no longer found her riveting. It wasn't *his* fault he wanted to kill her. It was Anne's.

Henry's sociopathy suddenly rendered him indifferent to his wife and partner of ten years; meaning that when someone said she was better off dead, he was able to turn away, move on and never look back with an unnerving ease we struggle to accept to this day.

We all know the harm that was about to befall Anne Boleyn in the final and fatal 'discard' phase; however, now we understand why the king had no little voice within telling him not to do it, for he had no conscience.

Disturbingly, you can chart Henry's pattern of 'idealise, devalue and discard' through all his marriages, apart from the two times natural death got in the way (his third wife, Jane Seymour's, and his own.)[129] But interestingly, this pattern was also repeated in some of the closest working relationships he had with the men who helped make him.

Yes, unfortunately for the courtiers and politicians of the Tudor court, Henry's relationship with Anne Boleyn is just one of many examples during the king's reign in which a diagnosis of sociopathy provides an explanation for his dreadful actions.

Alas, this is the Tudors' most baffling relationship explained through the chilling kaleidoscope of Henry VIII's mental illness. Now we are ready to dissect how things unfolded from Anne Boleyn's viewpoint – and, as you're about to see, it's not at all as you've been led to believe . . .

CHAPTER 4

THE YEAR THAT HISTORY ERASED

Ah yes, the year that ruins the entire theory that Anne Boleyn seduced the king and her father pimped her out to the crown to further his own career . . . No wonder this part of her story has been erased from history. But I think almost five centuries of censorship is enough, so let's go back to the core evidence and uncover exactly what happened in that missing year, the one that began in the summer of 1526.

With her suitor Henry Percy now safely married off, it was at last deemed acceptable for Anne to return to court; gone was the risk of the rebellious couple reigniting the flames of passion and putting a stop to Percy's wedding. Cavendish states that Anne was back before the Battle of Pavia, which took place in February 1525, and Wyatt reports that her parents were at court with her when she returned. However, we know her father, Thomas, left again by the early months of that same year, and it's been said that Anne was left under the supervision of her younger brother, George, who was returning from university. But George became a page to the king in 1514 around the age of eleven and had been a permanent fixture in court since then, with no evidence that he left to go to Cambridge at all.[130]

It is understood that Anne's sister, Mary, who had married William Carey by this point, gave birth to her two children between 1524 and 1526. Information on Mary is sketchy to say the least, and there are question marks over pretty much every event in her life. The only reason we know she had an affair with Henry VIII in the first place is due to detail in the dispensation he later sought to marry Anne that allowed for him having slept with a member of her family. Also, from the fact that he didn't deny sleeping with Mary when accused by Sir George Throckmorton. But the birth of Mary's children within this time frame tell us two things: that her relationship with the king was over by late 1525 – after all, nothing kills the saucy vibe like a heavily pregnant mistress; also, that it's likely she would have retired from court to give birth and recover around the time of Anne's return.

Mary's absence from court would certainly make sense for the events that were to follow, but it would also mean that Anne turned to George as her confidant at a time when she would have been paranoid that the entire court was gossiping about her return following the whole Henry Percy debacle.

Indeed, over time, George would prove to be the only one Anne could truly trust at court, no doubt bonding over their mutual love of evangelism, reform and a good old theology debate. Although Chapuys reported when he first met George he found him to be charming, courteous and with a refreshing frankness,[131] the Spanish ambassador would later go on to say that he hated being entertained by him, as the enthusiastic courtier had an exhausting habit of embroiling him in a religious debate every time they met.[132] Similarly, William Latymer was to say of Anne that whenever she sat down to eat with the king, she would be passionately debating scripture. By all accounts, George and Anne sound like kindred spirits, sharing the same work ethic, bolshie can-do attitude and, it has to be said, rather naughty sense of humour. Indeed, it was this humour that often pushed the boundaries of acceptable sixteenth-century banter and had a habit of erring on the dark side.

But one thing is clear from the many controversial conversations that have come to light between the two: George was someone with whom Anne felt safe enough to let her guard down and be herself – a true luxury in the duplicitous and backstabbing court of Henry VIII.

But, of course, it's at this infamous point in history that Anne set her sights on the king of England and pursued him like the skilled huntress she was. At least that's what we've always been told in the endless books, documentaries and dramas. If her sister could bed the king of England, then so could she, but with one vital difference: Anne was aiming higher than mere mistress; her goal was marriage. She wanted to be queen of England and so she charmed him, played him, tricked him, seduced him. She conspired with her pimp of a father and her wicked uncle, the duke of Norfolk, to snare the hapless king and tempt him away from his heirless marriage so she could replace his unwitting wife as queen.

Don't get me wrong, it makes for a great story, but let's just assess how logical it was for this to have been the Boleyn family's dastardly plan.

The first problem we come up against is the simple fact that commoners didn't marry into the royal family. The last known case of a commoner marrying a king was Elizabeth Woodville, who married King Edward IV in 1464. But this was two generations earlier. So much had changed politically since then: the Wars of the Roses, Richard III, the Tudor 'usurpers' who were now clinging on to the throne through sheer force and political manoeuvring. This meant that every royal marriage had to bring an international alliance to further secure their reign against threats of war and invasion.

Besides, hadn't Anne just been told she wasn't of high enough social ranking to marry the son of an earl? What on earth would make her return to court under the impression she could snare a king instead?

Of course, if we're going to get all pedantic, I should also point out that Elizabeth Woodville never required Edward IV to take the unprecedented step of divorcing his queen to take a new bride. And not just any old queen; Anne would need to replace Henry VIII's Spanish princess wife and in the process eradicate all the delicate international political ties she brought with her; and let's not forget that Katherine of Aragon's nephew was King Charles V of Spain, the Holy Roman Emperor and most powerful ruler in Europe. So it's laughable to conceive that Anne or her father would ever have thought that she, as an English commoner, could aim to replace the queen of England. Just look at the fight Henry and Anne *did* eventually go through to marry. Every step of the way, they were breaking new and controversial ground. When Henry eventually instructed Wolsey to write to 'all the bishops in this realm' to get their thoughts on how to potentially proceed with an annulment, Cavendish reports that this group of intellectuals and bishops considered it 'so obscure and doubtful' they simply could not see how he could do it.[133] This proves to us just how improbable a feat it would have been for any royal subject to believe themselves capable of achieving, meaning the idea of marriage could only have come from Henry himself.

Think about it: in order for Anne to have plotted to marry the king of England, or even just aimed higher than being a mistress, she would have had to believe that, first, Henry VIII had grounds to annul his marriage (divorce as a concept didn't exist in the sixteenth century, at least not before the Reformation); then believe he was willing to defy the pope's authority, risk excommunication, change the religion of the entire country and start a war with Spain to divorce their princess and marry a commoner. It's all so far-fetched, so ridiculous, so unrealistic that there is no way any member of the Boleyn family would have thought to conspire such a turn of events. There's ambition and then there's downright delusion.

Of course, we can't discuss any Boleyn schemes for the crown without talking about the shameless Tudor pimp that Anne's father supposedly was. Here, history would have you believe, was a man so desperate to launch his career that he placed his two daughters in Henry VIII's bed in order to get close to the king himself. The only thing that ruins this otherwise totally credible story is, once again, those pesky facts.

The first of these is that by 1526, when Anne came to the king's attention, Thomas Boleyn was forty-nine years old and had already enjoyed a twenty-year career as a highly respected royal courtier and diplomat. Historian Dr Lauren Mackay's PhD thesis confirms that Anne's father had 'an importance that pre-dated and was distinct from his daughter's'.[134]

Thomas's first royal appointment at court was as one of six coveted roles of 'esquires of the body' to Henry VIII's father. Upon the old king's death, both of Anne's parents were given the prestigious and symbolic honour of serving the new monarchs, Henry VIII and Katherine of Aragon, at the dinner the evening before their joint coronation in 1509. In that same year, Anne's father was made keeper of the foreign exchange, sheriff of Norfolk and Suffolk, becoming justice of the peace in both counties, with Anne's mother, Elizabeth, becoming baroness of the queen's chamber, where she was in charge of Katherine's wardrobe.[135]

Not only did Thomas go on to serve the king's adviser Wolsey, as his trusted ambassador and right-hand man,[136] becoming one of his top international negotiators, but over the years he was asked to perform a list of high-profile diplomatic and personal missions for the Crown, from welcoming Katherine of Aragon to England to escorting both the king's sisters to their respective weddings abroad. When Katherine of Aragon gave birth to Princess Mary in 1516, Thomas Boleyn was even one of the men appointed to hold the canopy over the princess at her christening.[137]

By 1521 Thomas had become 'part of a trustworthy and elite group of men' working directly for the king, and all before either of his daughters had been intimate with Henry.[138] So in 1522, as a reward for Thomas's unwavering loyalty and services to the Crown for the past thirteen years, he was nominated for the Most Noble Order of the Garter, which every historian since, bar his most recent biographer Mackay, has accredited to his daughter Mary beginning an affair with the king in the same year. An injustice that was to repeat itself in 1525, when the king made Thomas Viscount Rochford, an ennoblement that has been dismissed as nepotism by all who report it.[139]

But far from Thomas's career needing a boost from his daughters, there's a vital piece of evidence that ruins his ridiculous 'pimp' reputation: Thomas was away from court when both Mary and Anne became embroiled in their respective relationships with the monarch, rendering it impossible for him to have been behind any family prostitution plots. Of course, we can't rule out his having dispatched messengers back to England – but that would beg the obvious question as to whether a royal envoy of Thomas's standing would dare commit to paper or trust a messenger with instructions to trick and seduce the king of England.

Once we realise the Boleyns didn't set out to scheme their way to the throne, this changes things drastically – not only the way we interpret Anne's character, but her intentions for their entire marriage.

◆ ◆ ◆

In the year following Anne's return to court, she 'flourished in great estimation and favour', according to Cavendish, another unusually honest admission from a 'hostile source' who has nothing derogatory or scandalous to report about her character.[140] And indeed, by the end of 1525, it's safe to say her respectable decorum had captured the eye of the very man who had previously banished her from court: the king himself.

Quite what Anne would have made of Henry's sudden attention in those first few months is hard to imagine. She likely thought of it as nothing more than good-natured courtly love and so, no doubt, indulged the king in some light-hearted flirting. Playing along and having a bit of a jolly with His Majesty was all very well and innocent, but when he started to suggest they take it further in a sexual capacity, Anne would surely have panicked. Taking over from her sister as royal mistress would not have been the illustrious marriage alliance she had in mind.

But wait a second, wasn't the position of mistress to the king of England meant to be a pretty prestigious one, where he rewarded your, ahem, *services to the crown* by marrying you off to a gentleman of note? Indeed, although Mary Boleyn married the king's cousin two years before it's said she began her royal affair, so not something we can directly accredit to knowing the king intimately, Henry's other well-documented mistress, Bessie Blount, was married off to Gilbert Tailboys, 1st Baron Tailboys of Kyme, around the end of their affair.

Though it's not quite as good as marrying an earl, baroness is certainly not to be sniffed at, and in light of the controversy surrounding Anne's own social standing, it was a slightly more achievable goal. Perhaps if Anne had been as cold and ruthless as they make out, she might have considered this. However, being complicit in a marriage match was one thing; becoming a royal whore in order to achieve that marriage was quite another.

But by 1526, when Henry started to seriously pursue Anne, there would have been many more personal reasons as to why she would turn down the strapping, young and athletic king of England. Oh yes, Henry was quite the catch at this stage in life; there would be no beer belly and gout for another decade.

The first, slightly obvious and irksome reason would have been that he was her sister's ex, and perhaps the father of her two children. Yes, it's the timeless debate that stands no chance of ever being resolved; were Mary Boleyn's children the king's, or her husband William Carey's? With no firm dates for when her royal affair started or ended, the fact of the matter is simple: if Mary was sleeping with both Carey and the king within the same time frame, there is an equal chance that Anne's niece and nephew were Henry's. Particularly when we note the testimony of the vicar of Isleworth, John Hale, who said in 1535 that a Bridgettine of Syon Abbey once showed him 'young master Carey', saying he was the king's son.[141]

Maybe Anne Boleyn of the dastardly fictional novels might not have had a problem with pursuing her sister's ex, but the real-life young woman who was practically raised in a nunnery couldn't have failed to find it somewhat distasteful.

Biographer Wyatt then highlights another potential reason for Anne's refusal, one that no one ever addresses, and that is 'the love she bare to the queen whom she served'.[142] Of course, most people are so busy pitting the two women against each other, they completely overlook the fact that Anne may have initially held the belief that you don't have affairs with other women's husbands, let alone that of the queen of England whom you have been loyally serving for the past few years. Granted, Anne's resolve was clearly to weaken – and we are about to discover why – but it's perplexing that historians are so ready to assume that she would be happy to overlook the fact that Henry had a wife, when she had dismissed Wyatt for exactly the same reason not too long before.[143]

Of course, Anne also had to contend with the old killjoy of not believing in sex outside marriage. At this point in her life, she still held this act to be unlawful. And even if she were to put aside all morals and pride, logistically an affair with the king would have risked pregnancy; and unlike her sister, she had no husband to hide behind with that one.

Then there is the not-so-small matter of Henry being vehemently against everything Anne held near and dear to her heart: her passion and driving cause of evangelism. It was Martin Luther's controversial treatise of 1520, *The Babylonian Captivity of the Church*, which prompted the king to publicly condemn the 'blasphemous' work of the reformer, *not* his *Ninety-Five Theses*, as is widely reported. And what do you know? Henry managed to wrangle a fancy new title out of his efforts, too, with the pope naming him *Fidei Defensor* – Defender of the Faith.[144]

When the papal decree declaring the king's new title arrived in February 1522, there were huge celebrations at court. This was just about the time that Anne joined the royal household.[145] As a strong and passionate supporter of the new religion, she would have seen Henry's response to Luther as suppressive and ignorant.

So, you can start to understand why becoming mistress to the man who denounced everything she believed in didn't really appeal. However, I believe the real kicker for Anne was that she had just been told she wasn't good enough to marry the son of an earl, and now here was the king implying the only role she was worthy of was that of a royal whore. The humiliation had to be a slap in the face for the well-bred and hopeful young Anne. This is why it is vital we look at the psyche of the Tudors *alongside* the evidence in order to fully understand their decisions. Because only now, instead of seeing Anne in an emotionless pursuit of the king, can we begin to imagine the levels of insult and indignation she must have been experiencing, which sent her reeling back in shock and horror from Henry's progressively passionate advances.

Alas, there are only so many times you can politely refuse the king of England without offending or angering him. But when we start talking about how a woman can turn down the sexual advances of a man without upsetting him, we step into dangerous territory. Let me remind you that, in any given moment in history, when it comes to wooing a woman, not only has no *always* meant no, but if she's not really into it, if she is repeatedly turning down your advances and you persist, then you are wading into the murky waters of sexual harassment.

But he was the powerful king. He was in control of not just Anne's life at court, but the careers of her brother and father – so far, so Hollywood. Anne could hardly tell His Majesty to back off and jog on, as she had done with Wyatt, so she no doubt continued to play along in what was becoming an increasingly dangerous game of courtly love.

But then came that fateful day of the February 1526 Shrovetide joust. The day Henry made a public declaration of love for Anne by riding out into the field displaying the picture of 'a man's heart in a press with flames about it' accompanied by the motto, 'Declare, I dare not.'[146]

This would have served as a red flag, indicating just how serious Henry was getting – not only to Anne but to his wife, who it seems at this point also started to put the pressure on Anne.

According to Wyatt, the sole source of this now infamous Tudor story, Katherine is said to have entrapped Anne Boleyn in a game of cards, pointedly remarking, 'My lady Anne, you have good hap to stop at a king, but you are not like others: you will have all or none.'[147]

Of course, hindsight allows us, and Wyatt, to interpret this double entendre to mean that Katherine saw that Anne would not settle for being mistress, and would only accept being queen. But just like Anne herself, Katherine would have never imagined Anne could replace her as queen at this stage and 'have it all'. So, while I believe this passive-aggressive game may very well have taken place some time after the joust (not after Anne had accepted Henry, as it's often retold,[148] when both women were said to have avoided each other like the Tudor plague), I'm reluctant to put too much weight on these supposed words. As with all private conversations that were apparently recorded verbatim in these early biographies, unless it was a public address that could be corroborated by other witnesses, I'm always a little dubious.

But if, for the sake of argument, we are to take it that Katherine did indeed say this, a more realistic implication would be that she thought Anne was looking to take on the semi-official role as *maîtresse-en-titre*, similar to that of Francis I's mistress who took on official duties in place of the queen.[149] The fact that Henry would later go on to offer Anne that title certainly gives weight to this theory.

Of course, this notorious card game has also been retold as a way for Katherine to draw attention to the non-existent sixth finger on Anne's hand. But Wyatt also offers a more plausible, albeit less dramatic reason: that the queen hoped to keep Anne occupied, giving her less time to be preyed on by her husband.[150]

Either way, Anne couldn't have failed to feel the sudden heat of the queen's glare. Now her seemingly innocent flirtation was getting in the way of the royal marriage. She wouldn't have known which way to turn at this point without upsetting either the king or her mistress, the queen.

But as it turns out, Henry wasn't the only one pursuing Anne. It appears that after she returned to court, Wyatt renewed his attentions towards her. His grandson describes scenes of Wyatt being a pest, hovering around Anne while she remained aloof. It surely must have crossed her mind that he, too, hoped that now she realised marrying the son of an earl was above her station, she might reconsider a married man; this would certainly explain her reportedly bitter coolness towards an old friend.

On one occasion, Wyatt snatched a decorative jewel off Anne's dress and held it to his heart. She tried to get it back, but he refused, clearly hoping this would turn into some kind of flirtatious game. But exasperated by his childish antics, Anne simply walked off and left it with him.[151]

Then the king, who loved a bit of boisterous banter and had noticed how Wyatt fawned over Anne, decided to rub his nose in the fact that he himself was closer to her. During a game of bowls, Henry made an extravagant show of stating that the 'next game' was his, pointing with his finger on which he was wearing a ring he had taken from Anne (what was it about courtly love in the sixteenth century that turned men into jewel thieves?).

Recognising Anne's ring immediately, Wyatt supposedly responded by stating 'the game' was actually *his*, and showing the jewel he'd stolen from Anne hanging from a lace around his neck; at which point the banter stopped dead. Henry is said to have stormed off to Anne, demanding to know why she was playing two men at the same time.

She was quick to explain that the jewel was not a gift but in fact had been stolen. Henry apparently accepted this explanation, and the matter was done with.[152]

Why is this ridiculous story even relevant? Because it illustrates one important thing: Henry was willing to challenge any other man who pursued Anne. No, Anne didn't want Wyatt, but if Henry scared *him* off, did that mean other potential suitors were holding back for fear of getting into a love match with the king of England?

This, and the attention from the queen, would have undoubtedly been a huge wake-up call for Anne. She was wasting valuable time in which to find a proper match while she kept up this flirtation with the king. She didn't need to encourage it; she needed to stop it.[153]

So she made the extreme decision to remove herself from the Tudor court, and stayed away for almost a year.

Oh yes, that little nugget of information they conveniently forget to include in the majority of modern retellings of Anne's story.

But how do we know she really left court? What proof do we have?

Oh, you know, just the small matter of a handwritten letter to Anne by the king himself, in which he states: 'Since my parting from you, I have been told that the opinion in which I left you is totally changed, and that you would not come to court either with your mother, if you could, or in any other manner.'[154]

As I believe Anne's biggest concern would have been how to leave without making a fuss and offending the king, it makes sense that she would have waited for the royals to leave on summer progress in July 1526, then made her escape back home to join her father at Hever Castle, where he had recently relocated for work.[155] This explains Henry's statement 'since my parting from you', indicating he left court first on progress.

Fellow Boleyn historian Eric Ives has calculated that Henry wrote his first letter to Anne in the autumn, and now we know why: he had only just returned to court to find that she had gone.

No doubt the hapless task of relaying the bad news fell to Anne's poor brother, George, who had stayed on at court as a cupbearer after being moved from page in the privy chamber in Wolsey's January cutbacks. Over the coming year, George was to be used as a messenger, delivering letters from the king to Anne at Hever Castle. It's hard to know if George would have seen this as an ideal opportunity to become closer to Henry, or a severe waste of his talents and time. But with George's being by Anne's side during the most emotional moments of her life, as she received the king's dramatic letters and verbal messages, this surely would have bonded brother and sister more tightly than ever before.

A final indication that she left court after the king in July is that James Butler returned to Ireland shortly after, around 27 August,[156] suggesting he had no cause to stay if Anne had gone for good.

But hear this: if Anne had wanted Henry, she would have stayed at court and taken full advantage of being the object of his desires. Her leaving proves his attention was unwanted. Which begs this awful question: how far did she feel she had to go to placate the king before she went? I make a point of asking because the dispensation Henry sought to eventually marry Anne allowed for the fact that he could have already slept with her. Now most agree with Scarisbrick that this was an 'optimistic provision for the future',[157] meaning they could share a bed no matter how long the fight for an annulment continued. While I share his opinion, I do also believe it is possible that things could have gone too far, if only once, during this dangerous time at court. Could this be what prompted her to leave? Or was it merely a build-up of events?

Either way, the very nature of Anne's leaving rings alarm bells. There was no goodbye, no sultry farewell of 'Remember me' played up for dramatic effect. She left without saying a word, and stayed away for a year before giving in to his advances. She was clearly running away.

Yet so skilled was Anne at outmanoeuvring the unwanted sexual advances of men without causing upset or embarrassment that the king was completely unaware of her lack of interest. In his first letter, you can see his utter confusion at her leaving. As far as he was concerned, everything was going well. So engrossed in the chase was he that her polite refusals and unwillingness to take things further didn't even register with him.

After all, what woman would really mean *no* when the king of England was pursuing her? Upon returning to court in the autumn to be told that Anne had left and was not interested, Henry refused to take this seriously and proceeded to send her desperate 'love letters', begging her to be with him. These letters show that he was fully aware that Anne wasn't returning his affections.

And yet he continued.

He even started to get angry and frustrated that she wouldn't give in to his advances. It's at this stage that phase one of 'idealise, devalue, discard' kicked in, triggering Henry's sociopathic obsession.

And so to Henry VIII's love letters.

Firstly, can we stop calling them 'love letters'? The seventeen that survive span the course of almost three years, from approximately autumn 1526, when Anne had left court, to spring 1529.

Ah yes, that's another thing. They were all undated. (If you listen very closely, you can hear the frustrated screams of historians the world over.) Any order you ever see these letters placed in is down to that writer or historian's own conclusions, so it will come as no surprise to hear they have often been placed in an unusual order to fit a particular angle. Yet luckily for most of the letters, due to the topics Henry references throughout, we can get to the truth quite easily and place them within the right season or year.

On the basis of the tone and language, it's clear that a good chunk of them were written either before or after Anne accepted his advances

– the begging and pleading gives way to a more relaxed familiarity and, it has to be said, mundane updates of life at court.

But as far as being love letters, only three of them are frustrated odes to Anne in an attempt to predatorily hunt her down. Oh, I mean, 'romantically woo her'.

His pursuit was relentless and, yes, this came from a man who avoided writing at all costs, which certainly says something . . . but is that something love? Or the frenzied, obsessive, desperate letters of a sociopath who would move heaven and earth to win his prize? This may appear a rather cynical way to interpret a few letters. However, when we put them into context of everything we know about Henry's mental illness and Anne's persistent, if polite, refusal of his advances up until this point, not to mention his eventual murder of her, it quickly moves from cynical brush-off to logical explanation.

People have struggled – myself included – to understand how their relationship could have gone from these deeply passionate declarations to decapitation . . . but once you replace 'passionate love letters' with 'obsessive targeted hounding', the shocking change of emotions not too far down the line no longer seems so out of place.

But what of these letters? All of Henry's survive intact to this day in the Vatican, stolen from Anne, it was suspected but not proven, by Cardinal Campeggio, who came to London in 1528 from Rome to hear Henry's case for an annulment. (Officials searched Campeggio's bags when they later went missing, indicating they strongly suspected him.)

However, all and any of Anne's replies to Henry have been destroyed. Which begs the question: *why?*

If there was anything in her letters that portrayed her in a negative light, her enemies would have used them as evidence against her and her marriage to the king.

So why do you suppose they were destroyed?

Could it be because they didn't support the image her adversaries were trying to create of her? Even in the letter where Anne accepts the king's proposal of marriage, she asks for his forgiveness for offending him, presumably in the way she had ignored and distanced herself from him. We know this from Henry's reply, in which he mirrors her request, saying: 'If at any time before this I have in any way offended you, that you would give me the same absolution that you ask.'[158]

Yet, for those spinning the Great Legend of Anne Boleyn, when Henry's letters are read alone it conveniently allows them to make loaded assumptions about her replies – one even going so far as to describe them as 'the saucy words of Anne Boleyn'. How do we know they were saucy? We've never read her letters![159]

But you can see how it's easily done; for example, when Henry writes, 'The demonstrations of your affection are such, and the beautiful words of your letter are so cordially phrased,' this could be taken to mean Anne was the seductress, weaving her web and confessing her undying love. But the reality could just have easily been innocent, with Anne merely a loyal subject politely flattering the king of England. Yet, without her responses to defend her virtue, historians are conveniently allowed to spin this one-sided love story to suit themselves.

The letters' suspicious disappearance certainly rings more of censorship than of a heartbroken sociopath wanting to get rid of his lover's passionate words; especially when we read Henry's letters in their entirety, and it becomes abundantly clear that Anne was ignoring him for the most part – not responding, not encouraging and certainly not ruthlessly pursuing him with saucy words.

In what could logically only be the first letter from the king, Henry mentions that Anne has left court, having not seen her for a while, and complains that no news has been sent of her via a messenger. This is the note in which he writes, 'Since my parting from you, I have been told that the opinion in which I left you is totally changed, and that you would not come to court either with your mother, if you could, or in any other manner.'

Disturbingly, Henry goes on to state that old classic, that a woman *owes* it to a man to return his affections and that it is rude of her to turn him down: 'It seems a very poor return for the great love which I bear you to keep me at a distance both from the speech and the person of the woman that I esteem most in the world.'

He goes on, wanting confirmation that she left court specifically to get away from him, saying 'if I knew for certain that you voluntarily desired [to be away from me]'.[160]

Now this is dangerous territory for Anne. Leaving was supposed to ensure that she wouldn't have to confront awkward situations like this, or tell him directly she didn't want to be around him. But here he was, posing the dreaded question in writing. You can almost feel her squirming as she read it, wondering how on earth she could reply diplomatically. Which we can only presume she did, for this was not the moment he decapitated her.

In what appears to have been his next letter, Henry declares he has been in love with Anne for a year, with his famous phrase of being 'stricken with the dart of love'; this places the note around January or February 1527 (this being approximately one year after the joust): 'On turning over in my mind the contents of your last letters, I have put myself into great agony, not knowing how to interpret them, whether to my disadvantage, as you show in some places, or to my advantage, as I understand them in some others.'[161]

Henry's wording here is incredibly important. He admits Anne turns him down in her missing letter, making her feelings clear: 'to my disadvantage, *as you show*'. He is openly admitting that the only encouragement in her letter is his own interpretation of her words: '*as I understand them*'. Yet, even after admitting that she is plainly showing a lack of interest, Henry persists that it is 'absolutely necessary for me to obtain this answer'.

Mate, she's not saying yes – I think you've got your answer!

It is also in this letter that Henry offers to make Anne his one and only mistress – 'I promise you that not only the name shall be given you, but also that I will take you for my only mistress.'[162]

People see this as proof of the depth of his love for her, but all that jumps out at me is that up until now, while he's been declaring his undying love, stricken by the dart of love for a year, he's been sleeping with other mistresses.

Indeed, they were right – this is true love personified!

Henry's next letter could not be more important in highlighting not only Anne's refusal of him but her severe lack of encouragement, for he opens with the blunt statement that: 'It has not pleased you to remember the promise you made me when I was last with you – that is, to hear good news from you, and to have an answer to my last letter.'[163]

This is an obvious reference to his offer to make her his only mistress, yet numerous historians have placed this letter much later in their correspondence, sometime around his trial for divorce from Katherine. However, it makes zero sense for Anne to be ignoring Henry's letters at a time when she was back at Hever, keeping a low profile and hankering after every bit of news concerning her future as the queen of England. Especially when other letters from Henry around that time apologise for not giving her news fast enough, which shows us Anne's impatience for constant updates.

Frankly, there is no way she would fail to reply at any point after she had accepted the king. Once she had agreed to be his wife, things got serious. It was no longer a coy game of courtly love, or the avoiding of an unwanted suitor. Her reputation was now at stake – her cause, her chance of becoming queen. Which means Henry's scolding letter can only realistically be dated to *before* she accepted his advances – proof that far from encouraging him, Anne actually ignored some of his letters.

Then there's the line 'when I was last with you' – implying that even after removing herself from court, she could not escape the king, who possibly orchestrated a meeting in between letters. It's certainly not out of the question that he may have visited her at Hever, as we know he did various times in the course of their later fight to marry.[164]

Now, for the modern historians and writers who *have* acknowledged Anne's leaving court, it has been described time and time again as 'a masterstroke', her refusal a 'strategy',[165] a calculated tactic to whip the king into a sexual frenzy. But in the sixteenth century there's playing hard to get and then there's telling the guy you don't love him and moving away with no means of frequent communication to ensure you stay in his thoughts. If Anne seriously wanted Henry, she wouldn't have played such a risky game. How many factions at court were desperate to place a woman in the king's bed and have access to him at any given time? It was relentless. She wouldn't have left him alone with the buzzards circling.

And if Thomas Boleyn was meant to have been playing his poor daughter like a puppet, there's no way he would have allowed her to leave when it was clear she was in the unique position of having the king of England wrapped around her little finger.

Remember, it was Wolsey and the king who sent Anne away from court during the Henry Percy debacle in order to cool off their romance, which proves that leaving court was seen as something that would stop a romance, not encourage it. Oh yes. That old chestnut.

Still, Anne found a diplomatic way to respond to Henry's increasingly frustrated letters by telling him she was always his humble servant, because he was to reply in his third letter, 'Though it is not fitting for a gentleman to take his lady in the place of a servant, yet, complying with your desire, I willingly grant it you.'

Then everything changed in the most drastic way.

In a letter that can only be placed next in the sequence, Henry is suddenly ecstatic at Anne's 'too humble submission' and 'great humanity and favour, which I have always sought to seek'.

This was Henry VIII acknowledging Anne's acceptance of his offer of marriage – apparently accompanied by a gift from her: a trinket of a female figure on a ship crashing through stormy seas. Interpret that as you wish.

Hang on a second, though. He offered marriage to a commoner? She accepted the man she had been avoiding for months? Can we back up a little?

Yes, this is just one of the gaping holes history has left in the story of Anne Boleyn, allowing historians to fill in the blanks with scandal and drama. But how about we fill in the gaps with a few facts?

Anne clearly didn't accept Henry's proposal in person, instead sending a letter and a gift. However, we can only presume the king *made* his proposal in person, as we don't have evidence of it in any of his letters.

In early 1527, we only have one record of Anne being back at court, and that was on 5 May, when she returned briefly to attend a ball for the French ambassador in the chambers of Henry's daughter, Princess Mary. It is here that Henry was said to have led Anne out in a dance – though not in any official capacity as his mistress or bride-to-be, I hasten to add.

Anne's brief return to court came at a tense time, as it was that very same month that Henry first told Katherine that he had serious doubts about their marriage.[166]

It's a huge leap from this first, painful conversation between king and queen to proposing marriage to another woman, yet this is the timeline history has left us with, allowing us to draw our own conclusions as to what prompted such an unprecedented move. Was this the peak of Henry's all-consuming obsession with Anne, when he suddenly saw her in the flesh and was gripped by the desperation not to lose his prize? Was it the growing panic over his heirless relationship with Katherine and the impending wrath of God? Or could it have been an explosive combination of the two? Either way, the timeline suggests that it was during Anne's visit in May that Henry took the extraordinary step of offering her, an English commoner, his hand in marriage. The very fact that he was willing to overlook the opportunity to remarry into another international political alliance adds more weight to the analysis that his quest for a son was about God's wrath and *not* about securing the kingdom with an heir. If his motivation was the safety and future of the Tudor throne, then without a doubt he would have backed that up with a new political marriage.

The very fact that Anne gave her response via letter rather than an immediate response in person tells us all we need to know about her dumbfounded reaction to such a shocking proposal. She must have asked for time to consider and then left once more for Hever, perhaps reluctant to accept straight away, if only out of pure scepticism. What was she honestly meant to make of this offer? Were these just passionate words spoken in the heat of the moment? A lothario's ploy to get her into bed with outlandish promises he didn't intend to keep?

Whatever the truth, this was no simple case of 'Yes, I'll marry you, sweetheart,' as we've been repeatedly sold. There were a lot of very real, very dire consequences for Anne to weigh up before accepting this monumental position as the next queen of England.

As a royal envoy and ambassador, Anne's father would have been well aware of just how precarious a political situation it would create were the king to attempt to obtain an annulment from his imperial queen. If he failed it could end badly, not just for his daughter Anne but for the whole country; it could start a war between England and Spain. So in reality, it seems highly likely that her father would have felt some reluctance for her to wade into such a dangerous situation.

But what could have prompted this almighty turnaround on Anne's part?

Well, first, the obvious point is that this was at last a respectable prospect she could consider: queen of England. Not too shabby!

Not only that; after Anne left court in the late summer of 1526, the evangelical fight for reform began to pick up pace. In October, the bishop of London confiscated and burned six thousand copies of Tyndale's English Bible, which had been illegally smuggled into the country from Cologne in Germany. Yet the more the Church tried to oppress the people, the more they fought back, and within eight years twenty thousand English Bibles would be smuggled into England.

Anne would have also heard through her brother, who had his ear to the ground back at court, of an incident two months later, when London lawyer Simon Fish satirised the king's closest adviser Cardinal Wolsey in a controversial Christmas play at The Grey's Inn. When Wolsey got word of this, along with news of Fish selling contraband religious books, the lawyer was forced to escape the country and joined Tyndale hiding out in Antwerp.[167] Wolsey's extreme response, causing a man to flee for his life, would no doubt have angered Anne, who, as we will go on to see, was herself a huge supporter of these illegal religious manuscripts.

While away from court, she would have been further riled by news the following month of Bishop Warham burning Tyndale's English translation of what is now the New Testament in yet another public show of outrage in January 1527.[168] At a high risk to those who owned them, these controversial religious books continued to be smuggled into England by merchants and travellers, with a secret Lutheran group regularly meeting in Cambridge at the White Horse tavern. Anne could see that the reformists needed protection from someone in a position of power. Everywhere around her there were reports of people laying down their lives for their religious beliefs. So, is it any surprise that when the king proposed marriage in the midst of this growing unrest Anne realised just how much she could do for evangelical reform from the position of queen?[169]

Like Henry, Anne would have seen herself as 'chosen by God' when this most unique opportunity was placed in her lap. She had to take it.

But at what point did she accept? This, again, is another hotly debated issue.

Henry is said to have been consulting lawyers in April 1527, a month *before* Anne's appearance back at the royal court on 5 May, when it's likely he proposed. Then, weeks later, on 17 May, the king held his first formal, yet top secret, divorce meeting.[170] It's believed that, spurred on by the encouragement received in this meeting, Henry told a devastated Katherine he was pursuing an annulment of their marriage. Then he did something strange. In the following month of June, he brought his illegitimate son, Henry Fitzroy, out of obscurity and made him the duke of Richmond, some say lining him up as a potential legal heir.[171] Again, this proves the king had options for securing the Tudor throne other than producing a legitimate male heir, and was apparently considering them.

We must remember that at this point Anne may not have written to accept Henry's offer of marriage. In fact, Eric Ives believes that it was unlikely she would have agreed to marry the king until she had the security that he was officially and safely separated from his wife.

So, in June 1527 it appears Henry was making arrangements for a life without Katherine, but also potentially without Anne. This all starts to fall into place when we realise it was around this time that Wolsey was enquiring about a possible marriage for Henry to Lady Renée. So the mere fact that Henry pursued a divorce from Katherine before he potentially proposed to Anne in May reveals something pretty damning regarding the stories we've all been told: Henry was adamant he needed to end his marriage to Katherine, with or without Anne confirmed as a replacement. Meaning, Anne was not actually responsible for Henry abandoning his wife.

But by the end of August, when Henry asked his secretary, William Knight, to officially seek a dispensation for him to remarry, it was pretty obvious that Anne had accepted his proposal. For the woman in question had been previously contracted in marriage (logically to James Butler, not Henry Percy, as this is the only marriage we have official correspondence of Wolsey planning for Anne). This woman was also related to the king in the 'first degree of affinity . . . from . . . forbidden wedlock' (i.e., related to his former mistress Mary Boleyn).[172] But had the king not learned anything? Was this not the exact same situation that was compelling him to leave Katherine in the first place?

Not quite, because the scripture specifically referred to a man lying with his own brother's widow. There were no scriptural rules about bedding two sisters – only ancient, man-made canon laws, which Henry was now trying to sidestep.

So, by August 1527 we at last have firm evidence of Anne accepting the king's proposal and of Henry ploughing ahead to free himself to marry her. 'Twas game on!

◆ ◆ ◆

At this point I can almost hear the romantics wailing, '*Did Anne love Henry at all?*'

Well, let's be honest, feeling that you were brought together by God probably goes a long way to making you fall for a person. Indeed, notes they wrote to each other in Anne's *Book of Hours* firmly indicate she believed her union with the king to have been divinely orchestrated.[173] One of these notes is symbolically situated beneath an image of the Annunciation, when Archangel Gabriel is supposed to have told the Virgin Mary she was to conceive the Son of God. Here Anne wrote to Henry, 'By daily proof you shall me find to be unto you both loving and kind.'[174]

In the past, this note has been mistakenly placed in the early days of the couple's timeline as yet another example of Anne manipulating the king's emotions to lure him from his wife with promises of a son. To be fair, it's easy to see why this message has been dated before Henry's offer of marriage, as she appears to have written it in response to a note Henry himself penned in the same *Book of Hours*: 'If you remember my love in your prayers as strongly as I adore you, I shall hardly be forgotten, for I am yours. Henry R. forever.'[175]

The fact that he wrote it under the 'Man of Sorrows', a biblical image that is associated with rejection and grief, tells us he did so while Anne was indeed rejecting him. However, we have no proof that her note to Henry was an immediate or direct response to his. In fact, considering that Henry was only offering Anne the role of royal mistress at this point, it rules out her replying with any suggestions of providing him with yet another illegitimate son. As we've already discussed, he didn't need another one of those. So it was more plausible that Anne accepted Henry's 'Man of Sorrows' note without reply; this wouldn't be the first time she didn't respond to a message from him. It would then have been later, during their seven-year battle to marry, that she decided to write a note for him on the Annunciation page to serve as a poignant reminder not only of his pursuit of her, but inspiration to them both that they had God on their side.

But in terms of Anne's attraction to Henry, her refusal of an illicit affair up until this point did not necessarily mean that she didn't find him alluring or charming; indeed, as we have learned, a sociopath can be the most charming person you will ever meet. She simply couldn't allow herself to compromise her reputation and risk becoming a pregnant mistress.

There seems little doubt that Anne would have been physically attracted to Henry. At over six feet two inches, he was described as 'the handsomest prince ever seen', an 'Adonis of fresh colour' with 'an extremely fine calf to his leg'![176]

All right, steady on, there might be kids reading!

Upon accepting his proposal, Anne could finally drop her guard and for the first time allow herself to enjoy being the object of his pursuit. After all, he was saying all the right things – there's no way she would have been aware, at this point, of the demons he was battling; and now, she had no reason to resist his seduction.

Over the next seven years, it's clear that they bonded over their shared goal of fighting for the country's independence from Rome, and would often have felt that it was 'us against the world': something that clearly sparked a passion, with Anne no doubt in time developing a deep affection for him. I'm sure, like anyone, she told herself along the way that she could change all the little things she didn't care for, like his annoying habit of killing those who opposed his religious views.

But let's not fool ourselves. As much as they were similar in their love of a fiery debate and a fight against the pope, they constantly clashed over their religious beliefs and political views. So, it wouldn't have blossomed into seven years of passionate romance.

Everyone says Henry met his match in Anne, and they're not wrong there. I'm sure he never thought the day would come when he could have the same banter with a mistress or a wife that he had with the boys. Even so, Anne's eyes were wide open, and she was fully aware of Henry's womanising ways – something she was able to laugh off, even in the early days of their marriage. We see this when she insulted the French ambassador by dissolving into fits of laughter during their discussion at a December banquet in 1533. However, the cause of her hysterics, she explained, was not him, but seeing her new husband across the room; he had gone to fetch an important guest to meet her, but had got distracted along the way by a beautiful woman, completely forgetting the task in hand. Anne's light-hearted reaction not only highlights her personality but shows she entered this marriage for something other than love.[177]

But it is here that we risk judging Anne, blasting her as cold-heartedly ambitious for wanting to marry for anything less than true romance; yet we have to understand that while it was socially acceptable in the sixteenth century for men to rise to positions of power from lowly beginnings – take your pick, we've got butcher's son Wolsey, we've got blacksmith's son Cromwell – the only thing women were expected to do was 'marry up' in a smart match.

Now, the very fact that the king had to approve a good chunk of the marriages at court, given that they were considered domestic political matches, says a lot about this being standard practice. So, when arranged marriages were the social norm, why do we tear Anne Boleyn down for playing along? Why does she get branded as cold and calculating when all Tudors had been conditioned to see marriage as an alliance, from nobility to merchants?

Because, while this may have been the only acceptable form of career advancement for women, it certainly didn't stop the men from pursuing business-minded marriages, too.

Just look at Henry Percy, who ended up marrying for money and prestige rather than following his heart. Charles Brandon made it his life's mission to seek out multiple marriage matches that brought great financial gain, as he was forever looking to escape the omnipresent debt that came with trying to keep up with the king. Even Cromwell, who started life in Putney and was found begging on the streets of Florence as a young man,[178] married in what his biographer Diarmaid MacCulloch describes as a 'local alliance' with Elizabeth Wykes, who came from a successful family back home.[179]

It was all about what dowry did a marriage match pay? How did the union elevate the family to a higher social ranking? What title did it bring?

Of course, we see it as distasteful in this day and age, but in the 1500s both men and women who wanted to influence society and make a difference knew this was the way the world worked. Particularly the women who wanted a voice and were not content to just sit by and let the men rule. These were the women who saw marriage as a business partnership and did the best with the cards their sex had been dealt.

But perhaps the real issue the modern world has with Anne is that, far from being forced into an arranged marriage, she actively chose to pursue a political match for herself. In the case of Henry Percy, we saw her fighting *for* it rather than against it, and aren't girls meant to lead from the heart and not the head? Well, Anne Boleyn wanted to take control of her own life; she pulled the strings. She wanted to make a difference in the world, and to do that she needed to forge an alliance with someone in possession of a prestigious title. If you want to understand Anne Boleyn, this needs to be seriously considered. Her choices did not make her frosty and unfeeling. They made her a progressive thinker in an oppressive world.

But maybe that's just another female issue we have. After all, we're allowed to look back on the men in history, on whom the king bestowed a similar power to Anne, with approval and admiration.

Didn't he do well? Look how far he came from such humble beginnings, using his business sense, intelligence and diplomatic skills.

While Anne is seen as a social climber accused of having used what? Her sexuality. Underhand scheming. Oh, and witchcraft, apparently. Although, may I use this moment to put to rest the witchcraft rumours once and for all?

It appears we have Spanish ambassador Chapuys to thank for turning this particular court gossip into historical fact. He was to report in January 1536 that a source told him that another source told them that the king told a principal courtier (it's a tenuous link, but stay with me) 'that he had been seduced and forced into this second marriage by means of sortileges and charms'.[180]

However, in terms of reliable evidence and formal accusations, having personally viewed the original trial records of Anne Boleyn, nowhere in her devastating list of charges does it state witchcraft. This was merely another rumour picked up by the negative propaganda at the time, along with the claims that she had a few outstanding parking fines.

But modern historians need to stop this sexist, double-standard analysis that has them call the self-made men shrewd for using their wit, diligence and industriousness[181] while they imply the women are whores and sluts who used their bodies to play the men like sexual puppeteers. This warped interpretation of Anne's actions needs to be left in the past if we want to really understand who she was and why her life unfolded the way it did.

Alas, while Anne has been labelled 'calculating', Henry continues to be described as a romantic who loved women, with one of our most prominent male Tudor historians stating that 'Henry was usually a very good husband . . . he liked women – that's why he married so many of them!'[182] Also, that the key aim of a 2001 documentary *The Six Wives of Henry VIII* was for viewers to 'grasp the romance of history'.[183] Oh dear. But even our female historians have fallen foul of pleading the case for Henry's 'romanticism' in interviews.[184]

Now, I hate to be pedantic about this, but we cannot call a man who murdered two of his wives 'romantic'. Henry's not being intimidated by strong women and making them his equal, while commendable and progressive, doesn't cancel out or override his violence towards women. Yet he gets featured in publications such as *Love Letters: 2000 Years of Romance* with the obsessive letters of harassment above used as evidence of his chivalrous nature.

Indeed, in historical biographies and documentaries we see historians swooning over Henry's letters ('all this is the stuff of love'[185]) with none of them in the least bit disturbed or haunted by the fact that the man who wrote those seemingly loving words would end up murdering the recipient.

Almost all media depictions exclusively sell the viewer the notion that Henry and Anne's relationship imploded with passion; when a man loves a woman to that extent, how else is he to vent his heartbreak? As though decapitation was inevitable. In fact, one historian recently told television viewers that what happened to Anne was a terrible 'mishap', concluding that Henry, 'feeling betrayed and hurt, sentenced the queen that he loved to death'.[186]

It needs to go on record here and now that you don't sentence the women you love to death. Also, that the word 'romantic' is off limits when reporting the actions of domestic violence perpetrators. And yes, ordering the death of two of your wives does indeed come under the category of domestic violence, whether committed by a king or a commoner, last week or five centuries ago. If a man can kill a woman, whatever the extenuating circumstances it was never love.

Even though we are now starting to understand that Henry was subject to the blind will of his mental illness, and that his actions were not calculated attacks carried out by a rational mind, we still need to change the rhetoric we put out there. Knowing how their story ends, we owe it to the victim, in this case Anne Boleyn, to interpret the warning signs without putting a dreamy spin on it in favour of the murderer; not least in order to understand the truth, for if we realise it wasn't a love story then we will continue to look for the real reason events unfolded the way they did. And, as historians, is that not meant to be our very job?

◆   ◆   ◆

For those who still hold Henry's so-called 'love letters' as proof that it was indeed love between the two – or at least on hapless Henry's part, with Anne Boleyn just using him for her own cruel gain – then this one's for you.

A year after Anne accepted Henry's offer of marriage, in the summer of 1528, a deadly disease broke out in London, claiming the lives of courtiers and commoners alike. Ambassador Jean du Bellay confirms that Henry and Anne were back together when her maid contracted the deadly sweating sickness, stating on 18 June that 'One of the filles de chambres of Mademoiselle de Boulen was attacked on Tuesday by the sweating sickness. The king left in great haste and went a dozen miles off.'[187]

In the following purported love letter sent to Anne from the utterly devoted king, Henry warns her: 'I think, if you would retire from Surrey, as we did, you would escape all danger.'[188]

As we did? Meaning he left without taking her with him? The supposed love of his life? Oh yes. Not only did he leave Anne behind, but he took his wife Katherine away instead.[189] But Henry reassured Anne that no women in his party were known to have been taken ill, so she should be safe. She wasn't. Anne and her father soon fell ill and left for the confines of Hever Castle to battle the disease.[190] It is here that Henry sent the following heartfelt love letter that writers have since described as frantic with worry and grief. But given that we now know the circumstances, his words suddenly ring incredibly hollow: 'To hear of the sickness of my mistress, whom I esteem more than all the world, and whose health I desire as I do my own, so that I would gladly bear half your illness to make you well.'[191]

But he didn't bear her illness, did he? He didn't even risk it. He ran away and left her, refusing to visit for fear of getting ill himself, as the life of his beloved perilously hung in the balance.[192]

Ah, young love!

Look, I'm not intentionally trying to ruin all your Tudor fantasies here. I, too, was disappointed when I first realised that Henry and Anne's was not the love story I'd always been told it was. But if writers are going to continue holding it up as the pinnacle of romantic escapism, then we need to get truthful about how their story unfolded. Which means, first, we must realise that Anne's flirty demeanour wasn't to blame for his year-long harassment. Her repeatedly turning him down wasn't the ultimate example of *when a girl says no she really means yes*. Her accepting him for reasons less than love doesn't mean she was ruthless and deserved her downfall, that she had it coming or 'paid the price'.

We need to stop normalising this disturbing interpretation of powerful women just as much as we need to stop romanticising these narratives from history. Henry and Anne's story is one of the most dark and perverse that history can provide. So, if you want drama, look no further; but if it's romance you're after, this might be the wrong couple for us to focus on.

CHAPTER 5

LET THE FIGHT BEGIN

And so we arrive at the most historic, albeit apocalyptic, part of the story that everyone thinks they know so well: Henry and Anne's war with the pope and England's break from Rome.

How, during this time, Anne conspired to bring down the king's all-powerful adviser Thomas Wolsey owing to their long-running feud over Henry Percy (*wrong*), after he failed to secure the king his annulment (*wrong again*). How Anne's scheming to be queen killed the frail old cardinal as he was arrested and brought back to London (*nope*); how Henry tore a reluctant country from Catholicism for his own selfish gain (*erm, not quite*) and fought the pope for seven years to be with the woman he loved (*you're kidding, right?!*).

How about I give you a rundown of the full story? No more cherry-picking of the highlights to twist the truth to fit preconceived ideas. No more diluting history on the assumption that readers aren't interested in the bits that don't involve a sex scandal. We're a smart bunch; if we can handle the politics of the twenty-first century, I dare say we can keep up with the intricacies of international and domestic diplomacy of 1529. After all, they're not too dissimilar.

◆ ◆ ◆

It is often suggested that while Anne obviously had a vested interest in Henry divorcing Katherine of Aragon – her very reputation now hung perilously in the balance – all she did for the next seven years was lurk ominously in the shadows, whispering seductive words of encouragement in the king's ear. (That was in between the endless partying and plots to kill Katherine and her daughter, Mary, of course.) But what many readers may not realise is the extent of Anne's political involvement in the king's controversial annulment. Then again, perhaps you're not surprised at all, imagining the little schemer did everything she could to realise her dreams of being queen.

Either way, the particular strategy and approach she used gives us further evidence that she accepted the king's proposal solely for her religious cause.

It was Anne, as an impassioned evangelical, who dared to introduce the king to the heretical religious works of Bible translator Tyndale, prompting Henry VIII to have an epiphany: as king of England, he was answerable to no man on earth. No, not even the pope. Only God. Vitally, this meant that Henry's seven-year fight to marry Anne was not so much about love (that much I think we agree on by now) or even a sociopathic obsession to win his prize, but instead had quickly developed into him proving his God-given power as king over that of the pope. Who, it has to be said, was having none of this divorce malarkey, and told Henry his marriage to Katherine of Aragon could not be annulled.

So if Anne Boleyn is to be blamed for the break from Rome, then let's at least give the woman the credit she deserves; for she was not just an accidental catalyst for reform, a Helen of Troy whose face launched a thousand ships but left the real work to the men. No, Anne Boleyn was a key fighter for religious change, and it began with her marriage to the king.

The first evidence we have that she accepted Henry's proposal for religious purposes is a letter from Cardinal Wolsey's secretary, Stephen Gardiner, referencing private discussions with the king the previous year, 1528, about a potential alliance with the German Lutheran princes to help secure his annulment.[193]

Now, the princes were pretty much as their description suggests: German, royal and strongly in support of Martin Luther's fight for religious reform. This league of princes quickly began to serve as immense inspiration to many as the potential future for the English monarchy, not least to Anne Boleyn.[194] History has credited the king's future chief minister, Thomas Cromwell, with the entire German princes alliance, but Cromwell's biographer MacCulloch confirms that in 1528–29 he was working on other projects for his then master, Wolsey.[195]

In which case, who could possibly have been encouraging Henry to pursue a Lutheran alliance so early on?

Yes, gentleman at the back, it was *Anne Boleyn.*

G. W. Bernard argues that Henry alone was pulling the strings regarding this alliance, but ten bonus points to the reader who can tell me why anti-heretic Henry, self-professed Defender of the Faith, would be interested in an alliance with the decidedly *heretical* Lutheran leaders?

Yes, the young lady at the front is right, his evangelical fiancée, Anne Boleyn.

They even later sent Thomas Boleyn's godson, Thomas Theobald, to the German princes with the secret task of getting them to send Martin Luther's right-hand man Melanchthon to England.[196] Another move solely accredited to Cromwell; but why would political historians even consider Anne's involvement when she had been relegated to the subplot of scheming mistress? However, as we are about to find out, she became one of the most ferocious political figures of Tudor England. Her ability to argue the case to Henry VIII for a Lutheran alliance shows us firstly how seriously he took her advice, and also just how far her religious campaign had come in such a short space of time. Indeed, in July 1532, after Anne became patron to Cambridge scholar Thomas Cranmer, taking him into the heart of the Boleyn family, he was sent by the king to Nuremberg, where he had five days of meetings with the Lutheran princes.[197]

Now, not to diminish Anne's early political manoeuvres, but the reason Henry would have even considered such a shocking alliance was probably due to the fact that the pope – whom he so badly needed to approve his annulment to Katherine – had just been captured and held hostage by the most powerful ruler in Europe, Emperor Charles V, who, remember, was also king of Spain, and also happened to be Katherine of Aragon's nephew. Ah yes, that again.

So as dedicated as Henry was to Catholicism, and as much as he bowed in submission to the pope, he lived in fear of God far more; so he was willing to do anything to get out of his marriage. If that meant looking into some kind of agreement and alliance with this powerful league of German princes, then maybe it was worth it; and, perhaps more importantly, worth seeing how much power they had to counteract that of the all-conquering Charles V.

As Cromwell rose to power over the years and the negotiations rumbled on, in 1534 Nicholas Heath, who was Anne's closest faction member and Cranmer's leading assistant, was sent on a mission to Germany to renew efforts for an alliance;[198] Cromwell was told to draft a proposal to enter into a 'league or amity' with the Lutheran princes.[199] Notes from this assembly state it was 'set up through a few of the most distinguished people of the realm, though not endorsed by the king'.[200] Obviously, international negotiations such as these couldn't have taken place without the king's technical approval, but from this note it's clear Henry still wasn't totally sure about pursuing the alliance. But does that mean Cromwell was the main cheerleader? After all, history has told us he shared the same evangelical beliefs as Anne, and would take any opportunity to push for reform. But as various biographers of Cromwell have discovered, there is overwhelming evidence to the contrary in his early years serving the king. Not least are two rather shocking letters from Cromwell to Wolsey written in May 1530 (summarised by Thomas Master) in which he states he has 'discovered lately some who favour Luther's sect' and read 'pestiferous books' by Tyndale and Fish, which he feared would 'destroy the whole obedience and policy of this realm'.[201] It's in these letters that Cromwell also stated of William Tyndale, 'I [wish] he had never been born.'

Some modern historians on #TeamCromwell have tried to excuse these damaging statements as being either what the king would want him to say, or what Wolsey would want to hear. But the fact he said it in the first place shows Cromwell was not willing to publicly stand up and fight for his faith in the early years, if he truly harboured any deep evangelical faith at this stage at all.

As for all first-generation evangelicals, there could be a long process of understanding where your faith lay, so I'm certainly not about to reprimand Cromwell for taking his time to figure out what he believed. It only matters here in terms of understanding who was behind the German princes alliance from the start. So, for some slightly more telling evidence: in 1517, when Martin Luther was laying his life on the line by calling out the shocking abuse of indulgences, Cromwell was petitioning the pope for approval to sell a new indulgence himself back home to the people of Lincolnshire – which the pope granted him in a bull dated 24 February 1518.[202] A recent biographer speculates that it might have been the ease with which Cromwell found he could manipulate the pope that would later urge him to support the break from Rome. An interesting analysis to consider. Otherwise we're left with the distasteful story of the impoverished Putney lad who was willing to rip off his fellow common man to make a quick buck for himself.[203]

Further evidence presents itself around the time of the German alliance, when Cromwell was repeatedly asked to forward a copy of English reformer Robert Barnes's *A Supplication unto King Henry VIII*, in which the author appealed to the king to reform the Church. Yet, tellingly, Cromwell purposefully delayed in passing it on.[204] And so, we must logically conclude that it was Anne, not Cromwell, who was pushing for this Lutheran alliance in the early days. It was Anne who drew inspiration from the Lutheran princes and saw her marriage to the king as part of the process of reform, not just in the Church but within the monarchy itself – exactly as Marguerite d'Angoulême set out to do before her.

Alas, this will not be the last time history will credit Cromwell with Anne's good work, as you will discover soon enough.

◆ ◆ ◆

Even though a large portion of modern depictions of Anne's life barely even acknowledge her leaving court, the truth is that even after she accepted Henry's proposal, she spent most of 1527 and 1528 living at the family home of Hever Castle, with only the odd visit back to the royal court in London. However, in December 1528, it was considered diplomatically safe enough for Anne, as the king's controversial new fiancée, to finally be allowed to reside at court permanently.[205] But even the most rational historian has decided this was Anne's own plot to ensure she was on hand to coerce Henry to continue should he lose his nerve in pursuing the annulment,[206] devious conspirator that she was. It couldn't possibly have anything to do with her being isolated over in Kent and wanting to be in the midst of the action at court. Divorce proceedings were about to kick off, and frankly she needed to be advising and guiding everyone so they didn't mess it up – somewhat different, you must understand, to coercing and manipulating a man against his will. The truth of the matter was that now her relationship with the king was out in the open, if they failed to secure the annulment Anne would forever be seen as the very thing she had sought to avoid: a royal mistress. And not just any mistress, but one who had tried to dethrone the beloved queen. Her reputation would be permanently marred. There was no going back. Now she was in it, they had to succeed.

So, as the clock is ticking, and we draw closer to 1529 and the end of Wolsey's life, we find ourselves approaching the first of many accusations that Anne was responsible for the death of a dastardly foe at court.

I know we're repeatedly told that wicked Anne Boleyn had a penchant for conspiring the death of anyone who so much as looked at her the wrong way, but actual evidence to support these scandalous rumours is simply non-existent. As for masterminding Wolsey's epic downfall, it turns out her own efforts were not responsible for his fall from grace; it was instead a self-inflicted checkmate, resulting in a disaster of monumental proportions.

It's safe to say that Anne and Wolsey weren't the closest of allies. But far from being intent on wreaking revenge for how he dealt with the Henry Percy episode – a claim made by Wolsey's usher Cavendish, which has remained unchallenged over the centuries – Anne would have seen just how important Wolsey was for the annulment, and so would have put aside any personal grudges to form a united front; to the extent that on 3 March 1528, Anne complained that Wolsey was neglecting her, proving she wanted him to work with her, not disappear off the face of the earth, as most presume was her goal from the beginning.[207]

But try as she did to work with the man who had for so long been a close ally of both the king and her own father, worrying incidents started to occur that would make Anne resent the cardinal for far more legitimate reasons than having once mocked her status.

In what we shall label *Cataclysmic Clash #1* we can trace the rumblings of Wolsey and Anne's fresh feud to the autumn of 1528, when she appealed to him to help the 'Parson of Honey Lane'. Though the quaint title might suggest he was friends with a talking bear, the parson in question, Thomas Forman, was really quite the daredevil, selling extremely radical, not to mention dangerously illegal, books by Martin Luther to the students of Wolsey's very own Cardinal College (now

Christ Church, Oxford). Forman was subsequently arrested by Wolsey, who was horrified at the prospect of such progressive thinking infiltrating his orthodox college.

Behind the scenes, the bishop of London, Cuthbert Tunstall, who two years earlier had been responsible for burning Tyndale's English translation of the Bible, encouraged Wolsey to make an example of Forman. At this point, Anne intervened and tried to appeal for Forman's release, writing to Wolsey, 'I beseech your Grace with all my heart to remember the Parson of Honey Lane for my sake shortly.'[208]

However, Anne's simple yet loaded message was to be infuriatingly ignored, and Forman was to die mere months later, in October. With no official record of whether this was due to illness or at the hands of his captors, the suspicious timing leads us to presume the worst. In which case, we must realise how horrified Anne would have been, not only at the murder of an evangelical reformer, but her own lack of authority over the king's adviser to affect the very kind of life-or-death situations she rose to power to prevent. But things were only going to go from bad to worse with the cardinal.

Cataclysmic Clash #2 takes us back to the case of Simon Fish, another unfortunately named rebel who fled the country to escape Wolsey's wrath after daring to ridicule him in a play. After being forced to leave England, Fish wrote to Anne appealing for help, and to inform her and the king that he had found the answer to the issue of gaining an annulment from the pope.

While in exile, Fish had written *A Supplication for the Beggars*, a pamphlet that called out the immoral actions of the clergy, and, as he pointed out in his letter to Anne, how the pope made a mockery of England's laws. As it currently stood, if a man was excommunicated by the Church Henry could do nothing to challenge it, which essentially stripped him of any power.

This was a light-bulb moment for Anne, but did she dare propose the work of an exiled heretic to Henry? She discussed it with her brother, George, who urged her to take the risk and share it with the king. But she need not have worried, as Fish's words deeply resonated with an increasingly disillusioned Henry, who was forced to question more and more the matter of the pope's authority over his own. So, Henry quickly pardoned Fish and called him back to England to interview him;[209] they rode and talked together for hours, as a result of which the king promised Fish protection from those at court who were out to get him.

Unfortunately, Fish was later to run into trouble with Thomas More, who pointed out that this royal protection didn't extend to Fish's wife, and she was promptly arrested for refusing to allow Latin prayers to be heard in her house. More eventually released her to tend to her daughter when she fell victim to the plague, a disease that Fish himself was sadly to contract and subsequently die from within six months[210] – but not before making an almighty impact on British history by introducing the king to this life-changing text.

It's interesting to note that it has also been claimed by those eager to discredit Anne for any positive impact on British history, that it was Henry VIII's footmen who brought his attention to Fish's *A Supplication for the Beggars*. But in addition to sending a copy to Anne, Fish had distributed his pamphlet throughout London in the hope that one way or another it might reach the king. This would explain how Henry's footmen could have got hold of it, but does not explain why they would dare to be the ones who recommended heretical works to the king of England, particularly if his own fiancée was initially reluctant to do so. But even if both Anne and the footmen presented Henry with Fish's work, there is still no doubt that it could only have been Anne who had the power and gumption to push the king to pardon and speak to Fish directly.

Yet the very fact that Wolsey had men running from the country in fear of being killed for selling the religious works that Anne herself was fighting for would have added to her conviction that perhaps he wasn't a good man to be aligning herself with after all. If she was working towards a Lutheran alliance and introducing the king to the evangelical way, is there any surprise that Wolsey, with his persecution of heretics, had to go?[211]

However, if these incidents weren't enough to revolt Anne, other episodes were about to unfold that would trigger an intense loathing and contempt for the cardinal.

When Anne first returned to court in December 1528, she had received a message from her cousin Francis Bryan that Henry had a traitor among his advisers, and it didn't take long for her to form her suspicions as to who this might be.[212] Cardinal Campeggio had arrived from Rome two months earlier for Henry's divorce trial at the Legatine Court. But when by late January of the following year, 1529, the hearing had still failed to take place, Anne was seriously starting to suspect that Wolsey was trying to slow the divorce proceedings down – a suspicion that the imperial ambassador Iñigo de Mendoza confirms. So, it has been suggested that Anne formed a secret alliance with her brother, George, her uncle the duke of Norfolk and Charles Brandon, the duke of Suffolk, to investigate what he was up to.[213]

This secret investigation sounds like it was kept from the king initially, because by spring 1529 Wolsey had convinced Henry that the pope was a reasonable man who, under many layers of denial, actually wanted to help him out. So it would just be a case of persisting until they wore him down and broke his spirit until he saw no way out of the relentless bullying but to go against everything he believed and give in to the king's demands. A foolproof approach to the annulment, if ever there was one.

This was in spite of the fact that Francis Bryan had written to the king in March, explaining that he had been in Rome for three months before he was even granted an audience with the pope, whereupon the pontiff had made it clear he couldn't help with the annulment.[214] No wonder Anne suspected Wolsey was stalling a court case that he was in charge of setting up when they were getting news that this was to be the inevitable outcome.

In Wolsey's defence, he was probably somewhat clueless as to how to proceed without the pope's approval. Nevertheless, he continued to lead them down a dead end rather than save them time and hit the king with a few home truths about the pope's intentions.

So, at a time when Wolsey really needed to be reassuring Anne that he was working with her and not against her, he goes and instructs the dean of the chapel royal to get rid of all heretical books at court.[215] Yes, we can place *Cataclysmic Clash #3* to the time of a notorious story that Anne lent her cherished copy of Tyndale's *The Obedience of a Christian Man* to her gentlewoman Anne Gainsford. Gainsford's suitor and future husband, George Zouche, was then caught reading it by the dean, who passed the offending book to Wolsey. Anne refused to let her gentlewoman take the blame for being in possession of an illegal book and rushed to Henry before Wolsey snitched, proudly declaring it to be hers, saying, 'It shall be the dearest book that ever dean or cardinal took away.'[216]

But it was here that Anne saw an opportunity. She explained to Henry that, as with Fish's *A Supplication for the Beggars*, the book had some very interesting points that Henry would find of extreme interest with regard to the annulment. So, he got it back from Wolsey, and Anne proceeded to show him some of the most vital information that would eventually guide his breaking away from the clutches of Rome.

Tyndale's book reminded Henry that kings are accountable to God alone; that neither the pope nor any other authority on earth could rule a monarch. Henry liked the sound of this. It was metaphorical music to his ears as he declared, 'This is for me and all kings to read.'[217]

Ah, so this was it?

This was the moment Henry turned to the pope and said, 'Darling, it's over'?

Not quite. Henry going it alone and rising up against the pope's power was a radical step. A war. Basically a lot of work, and Henry realised it would be easier to simply have the pope give up and give him the go-ahead to wed. And so he waited.

The one thing you might be surprised to learn about psychopaths and sociopaths is that they will always choose the easy victims, and the pope was anything but. He came with a lot of headaches. The dangerous repercussions would have been repeatedly drawn to Henry's attention, so we can't rule out the possibility that he was scared of the consequences of a war with Rome and the dreaded sentence of excommunication.

Psychologist Dr Kevin Dutton says that although sociopaths are impulsive and won't usually delay short-term gratification in favour of long-term gain, if Henry was a very intelligent, high-functioning sociopath, it would make sense for him to hold out for the pope rather than take the extreme option of breaking from Rome at this early date.[218]

It is Wyatt who informs us that, sure enough, Wolsey did complain to the king about Anne's illegal book, in the hope it would make Henry realise she was a heretic and encourage him to give up all this annulment nonsense – which, incidentally, was starting to make them a lot of enemies in Europe. But Wolsey's approach didn't have the desired effect; it only served to annoy the king, and no doubt enrage Anne – not just because Wolsey was attempting to ruin her chance of becoming the queen of England, but because he was actively working to stamp out the freedom of religious expression that Anne was fighting so hard for.[219]

However, as an evangelical reformer set to replace England's Catholic queen, Anne had found herself becoming an increasingly controversial figure.[220] Indeed, Wyatt reports that in the midst of her and Henry's fight to marry, Anne received a death threat drawn in a book of old prophecies: a haunting image of her being beheaded. Wyatt doesn't date his story, but he has her discussing the death threat with 'Nan', indicating she was talking to her lady-in-waiting Anne Gainsford; so this would place the incident to when her intentions of marriage to the king were public, not before.

But who at court was behind the death threat? Frankly, it could have been any number of courtiers with access to Anne's chambers. But considering her suspicion of Wolsey at this time and his attempt to get rid of her, we can understand how this could only have served to heighten Anne's growing paranoia about the cardinal. Whether he was responsible or not, it's possible that in her eyes she saw this threat as *Cataclysmic Clash #4*.

It must be pointed out that although Wolsey's fall is often pinned on Henry and Anne, with the cardinal being the most powerful man at court and a mere butcher's son, there was no shortage of more qualified courtiers who had failed to gain as much favour with the king and were baying for his blood. Wolsey's gentleman usher Cavendish blames the lords of the council as working against him out of jealousy.[221] By this point, Anne was more than happy to get rid of him, but evidence does not point to her being the driving force behind the plot to bring him down, as is often presumed.

Anne's uncle the duke of Norfolk was Wolsey's main opponent over foreign policy. Lord Thomas Darcy's name also crops up regularly as a bitter rival who was equally eager to see him go.[222] This was mainly because he was against Wolsey's move to close a number of smaller monasteries to fund the launch of his own colleges (something we will touch on later), which Darcy saw as a gross misuse of Wolsey's powers.[223] Charles Brandon may have worked closely with Wolsey for many years, but when the king started to highlight his suspicions of his long-term adviser, Brandon was quick to turn against him to side with Henry. Similarly, we can only conclude that Wolsey's own right-hand man, Thomas Boleyn, turned against him out of family loyalty to support his daughter's growing suspicions.[224]

But before we feel compelled to fall back on earlier suspicions that of course Anne's father was conspiring to replace the most powerful man at court, and in the process manoeuvre his daughter on to the throne, let me stop you right there. Don't let Thomas's willingness to support his daughter at this stage convince you that he must, therefore, have always been by her side, plotting and conspiring. For evidence that Thomas Boleyn was once firmly against Anne's controversial marriage to the king has finally made its way, blinking, into the light, dazed and confused at having been hidden away from the public at large.

First, we have reports of a revelatory conversation between Anne and her father as her coronation loomed. With nerves frayed, Thomas suggested she shouldn't adjust her gowns to hide her growing pregnancy and instead be 'thankful to God for the state she was in'; to which Anne tersely replied that she was 'in a better plight than he would have wished her to be'.[225] Here we have Anne strongly implying that her father had not even supported her decision to accept the king's controversial offer of marriage, let alone been the mastermind behind it.[226]

But there exists yet more critical and conclusive evidence that disproves the worst lies we've been sold about Thomas. Straight from the quill of the opposition, we have a revealing letter from Chapuys stating that Thomas had 'hitherto, as the duke of Norfolk has frequently told me, tried to dissuade the king rather than otherwise from marriage'.[227]

Now this is quite the admission, and rings true as the concerned actions of an experienced ambassador and protective father who wanted to avoid placing his daughter, or for that matter the king of England, in a situation that would leave them open to attack.

Further proof is provided in the same report, where Chapuys confirms that the duke of Norfolk wanted it to be known that he 'had not been either the originator or promoter of this second marriage, but, on the contrary, had always been opposed to it'.[228] Not only that but Norfolk confided that had it not been for him and Thomas, Henry and Anne's marriage 'would have been secretly contracted a year ago'.[229] Chapuys then tells us of the extreme lengths Thomas Boleyn went to in order to protect his daughter from making a huge mistake by 'feigning an attack of frenzy'.[230]

Although Thomas may have tried his best to discourage both Henry and Anne in the early days, it's safe to say his better judgement was overlooked by all. It's clear from his eventual attempts to help the king's annulment that he felt he had no choice but to aid his headstrong daughter and the single-minded monarch in their quest as best he could, once he knew resistance was futile. But let this evidence be the final nail in the coffin of lies that tells us Thomas Boleyn was a pimp who schemed from the start to place his daughter on the throne.

Meanwhile in Rome, the pope was holding his ground.

As the years went on and Henry persisted, it's tempting to ask why the pontiff did not simply cave in to his demands. So why *was* he being so stubborn over the king's annulment? Many think it came down to the basic fact that Catholics didn't support divorce, while others believe that the pope wasn't buying what most still see as Henry's tactic of claiming his marriage went against scripture in the Bible.

However, it was a little bit trickier than that, as Henry had known full well that the scripture was an issue *before* entering into his marriage to Katherine. Even more damagingly, so had Rome, because it was the pope's predecessor who had signed a bull making it legal for Henry to marry his brother's widow in the first place.

So, Henry was effectively asking the pope to admit the Church was wrong and that it was all their fault, which, let's be honest, they were never going to do. The pope was also painfully aware by now that Henry intended to replace his Catholic queen with an evangelical reformist, something he would obstruct as much as he could.

As this impossible situation became increasingly clear back in England, Wolsey, who had been insisting to Henry that they simply needed to persist and the pope would change his mind, suddenly found himself having given years of bad advice.

Had they been wasting their time chasing the pope's consent? Yes, pretty much.

But instead of holding his hands up, Wolsey blamed the pope's deceit in stringing them along to cover up his own misjudgement.[231] But that excuse didn't quite wash with Anne; in fact, this would have proved her suspicions right, because she didn't just see it as Wolsey giving accidental bad advice. She saw this as Wolsey standing in the way of yet another marriage attempt. Don't forget, this was the second marriage match that Wolsey had potentially ruined for her; and now he was advising the king to pursue a route for the annulment that he knew would never succeed.

At this point, Anne could be forgiven for starting to think it was personal.

On 31 May 1529, the Legatine Court opened in Blackfriars, during one of the stints where Anne was packed off back to Hever to keep a low profile.[232] This was essentially Henry VIII and Katherine of Aragon's Tudor divorce trial. Cavendish described it as the 'strangest and newest sight . . . that a king and queen [should] appear in any court as common persons'.[233] It is here that both the king and queen made dramatic speeches that have been the focus of most 'six wives' biographies and dramatisations; though what is often carefully omitted from Henry and Anne's story is the shocking admission made by the supposedly love-struck king that Katherine had been a wonderful wife, and that if their union hadn't displeased God he would, as Cavendish confirms, have been happy to spend the rest of his life with her.[234]

Oh yes. He really said it. Let's just hope no one told Anne.

Yet for all the drama and controversy, the Legatine Court ended with something of an anticlimax for those involved. Cardinal Campeggio announced that he refused to make a judgement until he had relayed the proceedings to the pope back in Rome.[235] Though it's regularly inferred that this conclusion was frustrating for Anne and Henry simply because it was not the result they were fighting for, in fact it implied something much more catastrophic. Campeggio's decision was interpreted by all as a ploy to give Katherine enough time to appeal for the case to be heard in Rome, where Henry couldn't influence it.

They had been well and truly played. And, rightly or wrongly, Anne suspected that this had been Wolsey's plan all along.[236] In which case, I think we can officially label the failed Legatine Court as *Cataclysmic Clash #5*, and the straw that broke the camel's back.

The anti-Wolsey faction wasted no time in leaping into action. Although what followed in the summer of 1529 were two failed attempts to open the king's eyes to Wolsey's suspected deceit and possible secret dealings with Rome,[237] it took everyone by surprise when out of the blue on 9 October, Wolsey was informed he was to be charged with praemunire – the go-to charge whenever anyone followed the pope's laws over English laws; i.e., asserted papal jurisdiction in England.

But this didn't come from concocted evidence presented by Anne's faction or Wolsey's enemies at court. As much as we can see now why Anne was justified in wanting Wolsey gone, this arrest came from the king himself. What had Henry suddenly discovered? Actually, we're still not entirely sure, but the events that were about to explode give us a good indication.

This is another one of those times where many historians jump-cut ahead and mesh two huge events together. Call it artistic licence or distorting history to create a more succinct story, but it was *not* at this point, as we're often told, that the old man was summoned to London and died on the way due to the stress of being unable to give the king and his scheming mistress an annulment.

Instead, Wolsey was told to surrender the seal, that he was no longer cardinal and must immediately leave Hampton Court, which the king seized for himself.[238] But then, in what reads like a case study of *the sociopath at work*, far from being sent to the Tower of London as everyone expected, Wolsey was moved to Asher House, where the king subjected him to severe emotional whiplash over the coming weeks. One minute he was sending secret messages and gold rings, reassuring Wolsey he 'loved him as much as he ever did';[239] the next, the king's men were seizing his property and poaching his staff.[240]

But even though Wolsey had just been charged with a criminal offence, the bill presented in Parliament condemning him for treason failed to pass owing to the king's intervention.[241] It was at this point that Henry started lamenting that he missed his former adviser.

Ah! Isn't that a human emotion that flies in the face of this whole sociopathy theory?

No, and here's why: Wolsey was bloody good at his job. He had got the king out of all manner of international incidents over the past twenty years. As far as Henry was aware, Wolsey was still the only man who could sort this situation with the pope. *This* was the reason Henry was more reluctant to ditch his minister than any of his wives. Don't be fooled – it came down to business, not affection.

So by February of the following year, 1530, to the chilling fear of Wolsey's enemies and evangelical reformists alike, he had managed to wrangle his way back into royal favour. But Wolsey knew he was living on borrowed time. He knew full well he couldn't help with the king's annulment. He saw that Henry was surrounded by people who still didn't trust him and wouldn't rest until he was out for good – so that's when he is said to have made the decision to defect to the other side.[242]

In October 1530, Anne and the king were tipped off that preparations were underway for a scheme between Katherine of Aragon, Charles V and Rome, whereby a decree would be issued by the pope ordering Henry to return to his wife. And damningly, Wolsey was linked to the whole plot. His chaplain was intercepted carrying incriminating letters from Wolsey to Charles V, and his physician Agostini was found with letters from his master written in cypher.[243] Suddenly the conversation overheard by Cavendish, of the king producing a mysterious letter back in September the previous year and demanding of Wolsey, 'How can this be? Is this not your own hand?'[244] starts to make sense. Just how long had this secret correspondence been going on for?

Far from being thrilled at finally having her suspicions confirmed about Wolsey, from all reports Anne sounded distraught at the very real possibility that this marriage she had risked everything for might not happen thanks to the cardinal's secret plot. That she might now be cast aside, only to be remembered as the king's whore. More devastatingly, she would have lost out on the chance to fight for her religious cause from the only position of power that could incite real change in England. Some historians like to suggest that Anne's meltdown over the shocking revelations was 'calculated', and that she used emotional blackmail to provoke Henry into fighting back. However, we cannot deny that Anne's fear and upset at this point would have been entirely warranted and genuine.

We also can't presume she was the only one rocked by this betrayal. Indeed, Henry called Wolsey back to London immediately to answer to these new accusations.[245] But just in case anyone doubts whether Wolsey would have really been so reckless as to have begun secret negotiations with the opposition, we have evidence directly from the accused himself. Cavendish admits in his sixteenth-century biography that his master acknowledged he was being summoned to London for 'weighty matters yet depending . . . meaning the matter newly began between him and good Queen Katherine'[246] – a pretty conclusive admission by Wolsey's faithful servant.

So Wolsey's eventual downfall wasn't because he 'failed to secure the king a marriage annulment', as some historians have long suggested. Nor did Anne need to 'invent' a plot or 'conspire his ruin', for in the end he did it all himself. Alas, Wolsey never got his day in court to explain his secret communication with the other side, as he was to die dramatically on his way back to London. As for what killed him, various theories have been bandied about over the past five centuries, yet they all share one common denominator: Anne Boleyn.

Wolsey was at Cawood Castle in Yorkshire when Henry Percy was sent to arrest him for high treason and accompany him back to London on the king's request[247] (nice touch, sending Percy, which might back the claim that Anne was still harbouring at least *some* resentment for the way Wolsey dealt with that particular event). So they set off, stopping along the way – fatefully, it would turn out – in Sheffield Park with Percy's father-in-law, the earl of Shrewsbury.[248]

Over the centuries, historians have made out that Wolsey was a 'broken man',[249] who arrived sick and frail, his impending arrest at the hands of wicked Anne Boleyn having taken its toll on the ailing pensioner. But Cavendish, who was by his master's side the whole time, shoots that myth down with the revelation that on his travels Wolsey 'lacked no good cheer', with wine and entertainment aplenty.[250]

Even though he was wanted in London, Wolsey was clearly in no rush to face the music; he stayed at Sheffield Manor Lodge for eighteen days, where, according to Cavendish, they had 'a goodly and honourable entertainment'.[251]

But after two weeks, things took a terrible turn. Cavendish reports that Wolsey declared, 'I am suddenly taken about my stomach,'[252] and goes on to describe in shockingly candid detail Wolsey's 'new disease',[253] a testimony that ruins the other popular conspiracy theory – that Anne Boleyn poisoned him on his travels. For if this 'new disease' was the result of poisoning, who could possibly have done it? Wolsey had been in the safety of the Talbot household for over two weeks before falling ill – and there were absolutely no Boleyn supporters there willing to kill him. Even Percy himself surely couldn't have been disillusioned enough to still see his cancelled plans to marry Anne as being Wolsey's fault, instead of his own father's and the king's. And to be morbidly frank, no enemy would want to see Wolsey escape the humiliation of an interrogation and public beheading, and instead whimper away in a death by poisoning out in the countryside.

Speaking of which, back in London there was uneasiness at Wolsey's failure to turn up. The night he fell ill, William Kingston, the constable of the Tower of London, arrived to escort the former cardinal back to London, explaining 'report hath been made unto [the king], that ye should commit against his royal majesty, certain heinous crimes . . .'[254]

But before we go suspecting Kingston of poisoning Wolsey, let us point out that he fell ill before the constable arrived. In fact, unbeknown to them all, Wolsey was dying.[255]

So, if not the supposed perpetual schemer that was Anne Boleyn, what *did* kill him? A visit to Sheffield Manor Lodge, as it is now known, has uncovered the rather grim culprit, for Wolsey was lodged in a room directly above the toilet for a full two weeks before he fell ill.

Unlike most castles and palaces, where the faeces fell through a hole, down the side of the tower and into the moat, Sheffield Manor Lodge had to invent a whole new system for its ground-floor toilet. (Yes, we are actually talking faecal matter now – but an important matter nevertheless, so stay with me!) This new toilet system essentially consisted of leaving everything to stew on a bed of straw for two weeks, whereupon some hapless local kid climbed in and shovelled it out. Safe to say, this wasn't the kind of royal-standard sanitation Wolsey was used to; and with all that faecal matter inevitably contaminating everything he touched for two weeks, is there any wonder he caught what one of his biographers, John Matusiak, agrees must have been dysentery?

Cavendish reported that Wolsey 'took to the stool all night . . . unto the next day, he had above fifty stools.' Apparently 'the matter that he voided was wondrous black',[256] giving us all a delightful visual there. Thank you, Master Cavendish.

When the physician informed them that Wolsey had only four or five days left to live, Kingston hurriedly tried to get him back to London to speak with the king before he breathed his last. But it was no use. Wolsey died en route a few days later, on 29 November 1530.[257] He would never be held accountable for his actions, nor get to answer the accusations that sullied his final year. Perhaps if he had, there wouldn't have been room for Anne to be blamed for his downfall and death in the centuries to come.

CHAPTER 6

THE BOLEYN BRAVADO

It's the Anne Boleyn many readers should be familiar with who moved into Wolsey's former lodgings at York Place with the kind of heartless glee that only a Tudor super-villain could display. Confusingly, Anne is also sometimes depicted as still living with and serving the jilted queen, where she would spend her days taunting her former mistress with smarmy looks and catty remarks for no deserving reason, provoking many a haughty confrontation between the two rivals. All and anything to conjure up images of a reckless she-devil drunk on power. Never mind the evidence to the contrary. Never mind the illogicality of it all. This is the part readers and audiences live for, right? This is what they think we want to see?[258]

Actually, no.

At this point in our quest for the truth perhaps we should ask ourselves: why would Anne be smug as she took Katherine's place beside Henry? Katherine hadn't challenged or threatened her at this early stage, and so unless Anne had deep sadistic tendencies hidden under that evangelical activist exterior, she would have had no reason to want Katherine to suffer any more than she already had.

Though Anne finally lost the battle with her own conscience and gave in to Henry's pursuit, it did not have to mean that she was happy about hurting Katherine in the process. So, away from the vamped-up 'six wives' caricature, Anne the human being is more likely to have felt highly uncomfortable at the situation – embarrassed even, to have to pass her former queen in the courtyard. That's if they ever did.

On 25 December 1528, the French ambassador Jean du Bellay wrote: 'The whole court has retired to Greenwich, where open house is kept both by the King and Queen . . . Mademoiselle de Boulan is there also, having her establishment separate, as, I imagine, she does not like to meet with the Queen.'[259]

A year later, on 9 December 1529, Chapuys reported that the two highest-ranking noblewomen in the land – the king's sister Mary Tudor and Anne's aunt the duchess of Norfolk – were summoned to watch Anne appear at the king's side in place of the queen at a Christmas banquet.[260] However, it's rather telling that Anne refused to appear with him throughout the rest of the Christmas celebrations at Greenwich Palace.

Of course, this is described by most modern historians as a tactic to tempt Henry away to spend time with her alone at York Place, which is apparently what he ended up doing with most of his time by February of the following year. But why did this have to be a 'tactic'? Why not out of dignity, and uneasiness at being paraded around as the king's mistress while the queen was still very much part of the celebrations? For Katherine, indeed, spent Christmas with Henry that year,[261] and was still recognised as queen. She was even dining with him around the time that Cardinal Campeggio reported Henry as 'kissing [Anne] and treating her in public as though she were his wife'.

As a sociopath without a conscience, Henry lacked the emotional compass to know not to put on such an insensitive display. Yet I can't imagine Anne, with her conservatism and decorum, raised the way she was, being comfortable with such distasteful public scenes. No wonder she wanted to hide away in Wolsey's former lodgings at York Place – which was later remodelled as Whitehall Palace. Anne signed up for an honourable and legitimate marriage to the king, yet here she was being flaunted round in the dreaded role of 'mistress' that we've witnessed her adamantly avoiding.

◆ ◆ ◆

It was but a mere six months after Wolsey's death that Anne was hit with a devastating blow, and the first of many betrayals she was to suffer in her short lifetime. Charles Brandon, the duke of Suffolk, gentleman of the king's privy chamber and lifelong companion of her husband-to-be, secretly defected to the other side in May 1530.

Reports say Brandon felt increasingly sidelined in the king's affections by the new Boleyn faction. He also didn't like the way his previously high-profile princess wife Mary Tudor, whom he had controversially married back in 1515 before her return to England after being widowed by the king of France, had now been seemingly outranked by the up-and-coming Anne Boleyn.

Brandon was also yearning for the good old days, when the king preferred his company to that of any wife or mistress.

So, in a desperate bid to expose Anne and get Henry to abandon all this marriage nonsense, Brandon raked up a supposed love affair between Anne and Thomas Wyatt. Brandon was one of the men present at that infamous game of bowls years before, when the king had a bust-up with Wyatt over his flirtation with Anne. So Brandon knew there were old jealousies he could potentially play on; but as the king never seriously suspected Wyatt, Brandon's accusations had little effect. Not in 1530, at least. Six years later, Wyatt would blame Suffolk's spiteful little story as the main reason he ended up being arrested during the conspiracy to murder Anne Boleyn.

But Brandon's failure cut deep. Hurt that he had once again been ignored in favour of Anne, he disappeared from court, leading to speculation that he had been banished. But not before delivering his parting shot, urging the remaining councillors to reject an idea proposed in August or September 1530 for Henry and Anne to just go ahead with their marriage and hope the pope would accept it once it was done.[262]

Anne's supposed reaction to Brandon's slanderous attempt to ruin her name and relationship with the king has become the stuff of Tudor infamy: apparently, she hit back with lurid claims of Brandon having an affair with his son's fourteen-year-old fiancée. But that's a very diluted version of what really happened. The accusation I've discovered is far more disturbing than we have ever realised.

We know that Anne's opinion of Brandon was never very high to begin with, given his various indiscretions she had witnessed in her early years in France. But this accusation was no hot-headed retaliation for the events of 1530. In fact, it wasn't until over a year later, in July 1531, that Chapuys was to write in a letter that Anne 'wants to revenge herself on the duke of Suffolk, for having once brought a charge against her honour' and so 'accused him of meddling and copulating with his own daughter': '*Et pour se venger de ce que le due de sufforcq lauoit autres fois voulu charger de son honneur, luy a fait mectre sus quil mesloit et copuloit avec sa propre fille.*'[263]

People look for who this daughter figure could have been in 1531, with some concluding, as I say, that it was Brandon's son's fourteen-year-old fiancée, who Brandon did indeed go on to marry himself. But that can't be right, as Chapuys says it was Brandon's 'own daughter', which suddenly changes the accusation to one of incest.

Brandon's daughter would have been twenty-four when Anne made this accusation. However, there is nothing in Anne's claim to indicate she was alluding to a current affair, meaning it could very well have been an unsavoury suspicion she had been harbouring for a long time. I say this because there exists a little-known fact, rarely brought to light, that before Anne Boleyn left Margaret of Austria's court at the end of 1514, she had been educated alongside none other than Charles Brandon's daughter, who had been placed there at the time of his flirtation with Margaret. His daughter is believed to have been born in 1506 or 1507, and so was either seven or eight years old when she joined Anne in Mechelen;[264] we're always told the standard age to be educated abroad was thirteen, but in this case we have correspondence from Brandon recalling his daughter to England, proving she was indeed there.

So, did something come to light while the girls were growing up together? Did Brandon's daughter confide in Anne? Because there is some very important detail in the wording of Anne's accusations. She didn't accuse Brandon of an incestuous 'affair' or 'relationship'; she said he 'meddled/molested' and 'copulated with his own daughter'. This does not imply consent, but abuse, which is a very serious accusation to throw at someone out of the blue a year after an argument.

While everyone is quick to presume that this was Anne dishing out distasteful insults, perhaps we need to consider that there might have been something more to it? We will never know for sure, but the fact that Anne knew his daughter for some time as a child certainly sheds a whole new light on a disturbing and uneasy debate.

Regrettably, what Anne wasn't to realise at the time, and what we can't fully grasp ourselves without jumping ahead to the end of her life, is that this falling-out with Brandon was one day to be the final nail in her coffin.

◆ ◆ ◆

As it was to turn out, Brandon wasn't the only one who betrayed Anne at around that time. In 1531, just when the battle with the pope was about to get that much tougher and Anne needed the strength and unity of those around her, one by one key members of her inner circle, including her own family members, started to turn.

It feels almost inevitable under the circumstances. Not because she was such a cruel and insufferable person, as is often implied; no, the battle lines were drawn for a different reason. Everyone's loyalties and religious beliefs were being put to the test; were they for or against, not only the rise of this powerful and strong woman but the rise of evangelism?

As time went on, Anne began to represent so much more than just a new wife for the king. No longer the insignificant new girl at court, she was now a mature woman of thirty who had found her voice and knew what she wanted to achieve as queen. If you weren't completely aligned with her beliefs, jealousies could bubble to the surface without warning or provocation – causing people Anne had trusted and taken into her inner circle, like Brandon, to stab her in the back. Even her own aunt the duchess of Norfolk, hurt over an affair her husband was having with Bessie Holland, one of Anne's ladies, became extremely vocal in her disdain for the entire Boleyn family and her love for Queen Katherine. Needless to say, the duchess was asked to leave court once she had made her true feelings known.

So, how did Anne deal with these betrayals? By pretending it didn't hurt her, of course, and fighting back with what was soon to become her trademark: the famous Boleyn bravado.

Anne is always assumed to have been cold and ruthless because she held her nerve and stood up for herself at times when even the bravest among us might crumble. Yet let's not confuse the girl with her emotionally void fiancé. When the people she was closest to started to turn on her, it would have hit hard and hurt deeply. She would have felt increasingly isolated as those she trusted as close allies began to form factions against her – all for a position in life she never actively sought out.

But what's the number one rule when being bullied? Don't let them see it upsets you. So Anne toughened up. Dismissing Brandon's accusations in 1530, she adopted a cocky little motto inspired by the recently deceased Margaret of Austria: '*Ainsi sera, groigne qui groigne*', which roughly translates as, 'So it will be: those who grumble will grumble.'[265]

This is the sort of defiant, Tudor equivalent of 'Sticks and stones may break my bones, but stabbing me in the back and supporting my fiancé's ex-wife won't hurt me.'

◆ ◆ ◆

Now it may appear to some that with all the drama of Wolsey's demise, Anne had been distracted for several years by the sole obsession of bringing down this one insufferable enemy. However, all the incidents with Wolsey were unfolding at the exact same time as Anne was overseeing several almighty campaigns to free Henry from his first marriage. This, in reality, left her very little time to dedicate to giving the cardinal his comeuppance – a further indication that she was unlikely to have been the ringleader in his downfall and destruction.

You see, the first half of 1530 was taken up with researching how to escape the pope's authority. In October 1529, Edward Foxe and Boleyn faction newbie fresh from the opposition, Stephen Gardiner, arranged a meeting between the king and Thomas Cranmer. Cranmer was the Cambridge scholar who had previously declared over dinner with the two men that Henry and Anne were wasting their time with your bog-standard canon law. This was a theological issue that needed to be approached from a different angle: by consulting the scriptures.[266]

Was this not pretty much the same thing Anne had told Henry back when she showed him Tyndale's work in *The Obedience of a Christian Man*? Yes, it was – the only difference being that this time Henry was desperate and willing to try anything. So it was at this point that Henry sent Cranmer to live with Anne's brother, George, at Durham House while Cranmer worked with George and Thomas on consulting the theology faculties of the universities of Europe.[267]

This appointment was to kick-start a personal and professional bond between Cranmer and the Boleyns – most notably Anne, who would become his patron and ally, recalling him from a mission abroad on 1 October 1532 to elevate him from the role of chaplain to her father to that of archbishop of Canterbury.[268] Indeed, when Cranmer tried to thank the king, he was said to have replied that 'he ought to thank Anne Boleyn for this welcome promotion'.[269] From there, Cranmer's bond with Anne was only to strengthen. It would be he who eventually crowned her queen of England, later becoming godparent to her firstborn with the king.[270]

And to think this all came from that one unassuming conversation over dinner with Foxe and Gardiner.

So, in 1530, three attempts were made by the Boleyn faction to make this marriage happen.

Attempt number one in June was a presentation of the results of Cranmer's research at the universities, which, thank goodness, agreed with Henry's case for an annulment.[271] This was immediately followed by attempt number two, which was to be an open letter to the pope signed by the elite of England, further supporting the king. After toning down the initial anti-papal message, owing to a few objections from the more reserved members of the council, Thomas Wriothesley, Cromwell's future personal secretary, and William Brereton, the king's groom of the privy chamber, took the petition around the country. Here, it was backed and signed by an extensive list of high-profile abbots, bishops and senior royal officials who were all in favour of the annulment, proving wrong the widespread presumption that the majority were against Henry's subsequent marriage to Anne.

It was in light of this overwhelming response that the king floated Cranmer's idea of throwing caution to the wind and marrying without papal approval. This is what prompted Brandon's disapproval and all-round shock from the privy council, with advisers falling to their knees begging the king to reconsider.[272] That would be a no, then.

Weeks later came attempt number three: Henry was presented with the *Collectanea satis copiosa*,[273] which the Boleyn research team had been working on to argue that there was no basis to the idea that the pope was the supreme head of spiritual matters, and that, as king, Henry VIII was *already* the head of the Church of England.

The power and liberation of what he was being told gave Henry and his advisers more confidence that they were in the right, fighting as they were for independence.[274] But in private, the duke of Norfolk told Chapuys he thought this take too extreme.[275]

It's around this time that Robert Wakefield, a scholar whose patron was none other than Thomas Boleyn, provided vital confirmation to Henry that the passage in Leviticus referred to God's wrath specifically depriving him of sons, not just children in general.[276]

Yet by the following year, 1531, things still hadn't progressed.

Henry and Anne had just about had enough of the pope publicly humiliating him by repeatedly undermining his power as king. So, on 7 February, Henry demanded that he be recognised immediately as 'the sole protector and supreme head of the English church and clergy'. It was suggested they add 'so far as the law of Christ allows', which cleverly left it open to interpretation as to how much power Henry had.[277] Anne's reaction to his sudden and long overdue gumption was, apparently, as if she had 'gained paradise'.[278]

This was it!

Henry sent George Boleyn around the country with tracts to convince the people that their king was in fact already the supreme head of the Church, and it was the pope who was taking over where he had no right. A ballsy and courageous move by the monarch, it has to be said.

So, you can imagine Anne's confusion and mind-blowing frustration when the next two years were spent not acting on their new-found power but on blocking Katherine's attempt at a divorce hearing in Rome, which was exactly what they'd suspected she might try following the Legatine Court.

During this time, England also surprisingly continued to push for papal approval on the advice of their only ally in Europe, Francis I, who was desperate not to disrupt his own new-found peace with Charles V.[279]

In all likelihood, part of Henry would have been relieved to stall an official break from Rome, knowing just how much of a royal pain a reformation would be. But by the end of 1532 it was becoming increasingly clear that this waiting game was never going to pay off. If England wanted freedom, Henry had to take it.

So, what would have finally given the king the courage to do this? Ironically, it looks like it was the very people Henry called out as heretics. For if the reformist undercurrent hadn't been rumbling through England and Europe in the early 1500s, with overwhelming public support for whistle-blowers such as Martin Luther in Germany, Jacques Lefèvre d'Étaples in France, Huldrych Zwingli in Switzerland and William Tyndale in England, Henry VIII would never have dared to tear his country away from Europe's beating heart of Catholicism – not without fearing an almighty backlash and uprising from his people. If you thought the 1536 Catholic northern rebellion the Pilgrimage of Grace was bad, imagine if the whole country had joined in in unified horror?

So finally. Finally! This. Was. It . . . No, he really meant it this time!

Henry made Anne the lady marquess of Pembroke in September 1532 – an unprecedented move in itself, bestowing on a woman a male title and giving her land in her own right. But mainly, it was to ensure the king wasn't marrying a commoner.

Prior to sealing the deal, Henry and Anne embarked on an official diplomatic meeting in Calais with their biggest, and main, supporter in Europe, King Francis I. However, with Anne's former mistress Queen Claude having now sadly passed away, Francis had married Katherine of Aragon's niece Eleanor, who happened to be the sister of Henry's mortal enemy, Charles V. This meant they had to be as diplomatic as possible not to make this an official statement of France 'taking sides'.

Much has been made of the fact that no high-ranking women came to see Anne during the Calais trip, most notably Francis's sister, Marguerite d'Angoulême.[280] This has been taken as firm and final evidence that Anne had *not* served Marguerite in France, hence the two *never* having been close and Anne *not* being influenced by her, therefore *not really* a devout evangelical and *actually* a tarty little whore.

But as we've just seen, delicate European diplomacy is all the explanation we really need for Marguerite's absence and that of other French noblewomen. But far from this apparent snub meaning that Marguerite was against Anne, it was in fact while Anne's brother was on embassy in France that Marguerite expressed an understanding of his sister and the king's 'Great Matter'. Indeed, far from disapproving of their union, as many have been keen to imply, Marguerite was said to be excited by the idea of the English king's potential marriage to an evangelical reformist.[281] It was the duke of Norfolk who confirmed in 1533 that Marguerite supported Anne's cause, and would even encourage her brother, Francis I, to support Henry.[282] And why wouldn't she? With Anne's potential to take England forward in a reformist direction, it makes perfect sense for Marguerite to be *for*, not against, Anne.

Now, as we've seen, one of the more disturbing allegations that comes up time and again is how Anne allegedly used sex to get what she wanted with the king. Here she has been accused of repeatedly using her virginity as bait over the seven years until he made her queen (a girl would have to be pretty confident that her skills would live up to expectations after using them as a ploy for close to a decade). Some shockingly outdated schools of thought have in recent years labelled it 'sexual blackmail',[283] somehow implying that Henry was desperate for sex – and an illegitimate child – with Anne while she heartlessly held out for the big prize. Let's just pause for a moment to consider the senseless, not to mention appallingly sexist illogicality of this rhetoric – one that tells readers the only way a female could be favoured by Henry as highly as the men was for her to manipulate him with her sexuality. Never mind the fact that she outsmarted most of his members of the privy chamber; no, it was her body that impressed the king the most.

And of course, now Anne was meant to have used her body again to finally push Henry into action.

Yes, it is said something more monumental than a royal summit took place in Calais. Calculating the birth of Anne's daughter, the future Elizabeth I, it's been suggested that it was during the fateful trip to France, when storms delayed their return, that Henry and Anne slept together for the first time. But this was no consensual act of love. Anne was meant to have manipulated Henry in the belief that once she was pregnant he would have to marry her, launching us once more into wearily familiar scheming seductress territory.

They go on to argue that their theories prove true for, once the couple returned to England and the Christmas festivities were out of the way, Henry and Anne were married in a secret ceremony on 25 January 1533, her tactics having worked.

However, we run into a couple of problems with this theory straight away. Firstly, Elizabeth was born on 7 September, which means if the couple slept together in Calais in October that would have made it an epic eleven-month pregnancy. So, the dates don't add up there; in fact, by Anne's own calculations, she went into confinement on 26 August, which was traditionally one month before the due date – meaning she believed conception to have been sometime in late December, with Elizabeth then surprising them and arriving a couple of weeks early. Registered British midwife Judith E. Lewis backs up Anne's calculations by explaining that if Elizabeth was born at full term, bang on the forty-week mark, she would have been conceived on 20 December.[284]

But it is the wording of the very patent that made Anne marquess of Pembroke in September that disproves the whole 'sexual blackmail' theory. For the patent ensured that her new title would pass to *any* children born to her, not just legitimate ones. So, this was both Henry and Anne acknowledging that any premarital sex would not result in a shotgun wedding but simply an illegitimate child, as they still had no confirmation they would succeed in legitimately marrying.[285] Hence, this proves that Anne's finally sleeping with the king out of wedlock could not have been motivated by a scheme to get pregnant and push him into marrying her.

However, if they weren't married until 25 January and Anne believed she had conceived one month earlier, then that still leaves us with the sticky issue of sex out of wedlock. Indeed, it's the same wording of this patent that has led other historians to presume Henry and Anne were planning on consummating their relationship before saying 'I do.'

But why?

Is this not the same devoutly religious Anne Boleyn who saw these sorts of shenanigans as a firm '*Je crois pas*'? Where were her evangelical morals now?

Well, the couple's secret wedding was *so* secret that we have two dates for when it supposedly took place. The generally accepted date of 25 January was confirmed by Archbishop Cranmer, but the chronicler Edward Hall states the royal wedding occurred earlier, on 14 November 1532, saying: 'The king after his return, married purily the lady Anne Bulleyn, on Saint Erkenwaldes day, which marriage was kept so secret, that very few knew it, till she was great with child, at Easter.'[286]

This earlier date would certainly make more sense, given that their daughter was clearly conceived weeks later in December. It also doesn't have the couple waiting three months for no good reason after gaining approval and support from Francis I to go ahead and wed. But given that Cranmer was closer to the couple and hence more likely to know the real date, it could very well have been that Hall predated their wedding so it didn't appear Elizabeth was conceived out of wedlock. If so, what could justify Henry and Anne abandoning all caution and morals after seven years, rather than waiting a few more months to consummate the marriage on their wedding night?

I believe it probably came down to a rather hypocritical double standard; that by December they both saw their impending marriage as approved, not just by the king of France, but by God Almighty, and therefore it was a holy union exempt from the normal rules. Did they believe that, so long as the resulting baby wasn't born out of wedlock, there was no harm in sleeping together now, when they knew the marriage was a certainty? Possibly.

But I think it could just be a simple case of human beings falling short of the impossible moral standards they tried to uphold. Nothing more, nothing less. Either way, the king was fully aware that sex led to babies, so their sleeping together could only have been a mutual decision. To try and place a more calculating blame solely on Anne insults the intelligence of not just the king, but history readers the world over.

Alas, this was it. Officially together after an exhausting seven-year battle.

As Wyatt reports, 'And thus we see they lived and loved, tokens of increasing love perpetually increasing between them.'[287]

Quite. Until he decapitated her.

◆ ◆ ◆

Even though Henry and Anne were married in the early weeks of 1533, this news was to be kept secret from the public for the time being; only a select and reliable handful of people were trusted to know about it and, indeed, attend the ceremony. The elite congregation was made up of Anne's dependable brother, George, forever loyally by her side, her parents and omnipresent uncle the duke of Norfolk. Completing the wedding party were 'two intimate female friends' of Anne's who have managed to remain nameless throughout history.[288] Suspiciously absent was the Boleyn family's newest ally, Archbishop Cranmer, who admitted he only heard of the wedding two weeks later. This was probably an attempt by all to keep Cranmer, the appointed new judge of Henry's annulment, as unconnected to his new marriage as possible.[289]

Yet things couldn't stay secret for long, and when, by the summer, word of the wedding got out, Pope Clement retaliated by declaring Henry and Anne's marriage invalid, and hit the king with the sentence that drove fear into the hearts of all Catholics: he was to be excommunicated. But somewhat undermining the dramatic effect of his decision, he left the door open for Henry to put things right and reverse his actions by September. However, as the deadline came and went, the pope still hadn't confirmed his sentencing, proving he was just as reluctant as Henry to start an official war.[290] Finally, in March 1534, on the same day as the English government's legal approval of Henry's marriage to Anne, Pope Clement declared that he considered the king's first marriage to Katherine to be still valid; and Henry VIII was now officially excommunicated.

So, contrary to popular belief, in the end it was actually Rome that broke with England, not England that broke with Rome.[291]

But a vital shift had occurred. The king was no longer scared. Anne Boleyn and her reformist faction had sufficiently reassured him that not only were the people ready for religious reform but they passionately wanted it. So, it was in the belief that he would have unwavering public support in becoming the supreme head of the new Church of England that Henry finally made peace with the break from Rome.

Granted, he may have misjudged the situation somewhat, by presuming that the reformists would be happy with any religious regime so long as it wasn't Catholicism. He was soon to run into problems when everyone realised that Henry's Church was basically Catholicism with a new boss, and that it was still punishable to own a Bible written in English. Anne had been fighting for freedom of religious expression, so let's not make the mistake of thinking she was happy to be free from the Roman Catholics only to suppress the people with the king's new religious laws. This meant Anne's joy at achieving what she had set out to do by marrying Henry was decidedly short-lived.

It's hard to pinpoint at exactly what stage she would have come to the devastating realisation that her triumph in following the German Lutheran princes by establishing England's first evangelical monarchy had been shot down in flames. Almost immediately after the wedding, England was plunged into the murky waters of a confusing, non-papal-Catholic reformation. Nevertheless, Anne was still a beacon of hope, held up by reformists as their best chance for a religious reformation in England.

Which is why reports of overwhelming hostility at her coronation on 1 June 1533 sound suspiciously like Catholic propaganda by the Spanish tabloid of the day *Crónica del Rey Enrico Otavo de Ingalaterra*, a publication which Ives describes as featuring 'half-truth, rumour and nonsense'. There were certainly no local reports by eyewitnesses of negativity or booing; instead, as the Venetian ambassador reported, 'utmost tranquility and order'. [292]

But Anne didn't have time to wallow over the failure to lure Henry to evangelism. The girl from Norfolk had been crowned queen of England. She had work to do.

CHAPTER 7

THE WICKED QUEEN
(WHO ONLY DID GOOD)

Anne Boleyn is said to have wanted the crown for vanity and glory. For the chance to carry out spiteful acts unchallenged. For an empty life of pleasure and parties. For senseless power and selfish gain. So why, then, was every policy, project and plan of hers from the moment she gained said power based on charity, poverty and education?

She may have only reigned for three short years, but don't believe the lies they still try to sell you of a vacuous and cruel existence comprising only of pregnancy attempts and bullying. Anne spent her time on the throne fighting for what she believed in: championing the young and the poor, placing key evangelicals in high-profile religious roles around the country and becoming patron to a long list of reformists, even bringing them into the inner circles of the royal court to work directly with her. *This* was what she fought seven years for – as revealed by the overwhelming amount of evidence that gets buried deep beneath the tales of debauchery.

When I say Anne was a political figure, it's not a glib analogy for her playing the game in order to survive the Tudor court. She may not have been allowed a seat in Parliament due to her gender, but as you will discover here through to the final pages of her story, Anne was a politician in every other sense of the word. The core members of her team were like her own political party. Yes, there were members of the Boleyn faction who had their own agenda in supporting her rise to power – the duke of Norfolk, for one. But those who worked with her on a daily basis on the policies she pushed forward were as committed to reform as she was, and not just in religious spheres. Anne worked with a dedicated team around the country who would feed back news of where help was needed, so she could tend to these cases on her yearly summer progresses.

As we've seen, the general consensus is that Anne merely whispered seductively in Henry's ear at night, planting suggestions – Cavendish nicknamed her 'the night-crow' on this basis.[293] But evidence shows that she took her role as queen incredibly seriously. She worked for the people. In order to implement changes, she and her team would draw up plans and policies, drafts and documents and present them to the king, when she would have to argue her case for each cause she was fighting for.

It is important to remember, in the sixteenth century the monarchs of Europe had power equivalent to that of today's presidents and prime ministers. They still had to get approval from their councillors to back their policies, but their ability to instigate change was undeniable. And unlike any of Henry's wives before or after her, Anne was intent on using that power to its full effect.

During Anne's reign, the evil seductress was patron to a long list of underprivileged youths. Chaplain William Latymer said in his sixteenth-century biography of the frivolous flirt that 'she favoured good learning so much' that she paid large sums to cover their education at Cambridge University.[294] John Cheke wrote in 1535 how the morally corrupt schemer hugely increased her already generous donations to Cambridge, and that she would fund any impoverished student, just so long as one of her chaplains could vouch for them being a good, smart person with an inclination to learn.[295]

What a bitch.

So what other dastardly plots did she and her family conspire in during her reign?

Well, Foxe verifies Latymer and Cheke's claims that Anne was well known for supporting young students at Cambridge University, as were her brother and father. Among these students were Nicholas Heath, the future archbishop of York, Thomas Thirlby, future archbishop of Norwich, and William Paget, who would go on to become a lord.[296]

A lot of the students Anne championed had reformist connections, in line with her religious zeal for a future of change. Latymer reports Anne was patron to John Beckynsall, a scholar in Paris to whom she gave £40 a year to learn Greek. We might make the obvious connection that this could prompt further studies of the New Testament in its original Greek, or simply encourage more people to read and understand the scripture unhindered by translations; indeed, Beckynsall stayed in Paris beyond his studies, and went on to teach Greek to the next generation of students.[297]

In September 1535 another of Anne's chaplain's, Matthew Parker, petitioned for her to become patron to a certain William Bill, who was too poor to accept his recently offered fellowship at St John's College, Cambridge. So she funded his studies, and it's quite touching to learn that William went on to become almoner to her daughter, Elizabeth I, who also appointed him as dean of Westminster.[298]

Other scholars aided by Anne included William Barker, whom she put through his studies at Cambridge, which again led to favour with Elizabeth I.[299] In addition to these individual cases, Anne donated £80 a year directly to the universities of Oxford and Cambridge, and even persuaded the king to exempt both from a new clerical tax that stopped them from haemorrhaging cash and instead allowed them to plough it back into the education of their students.[300]

But not just satisfied with funding such established places of education, Anne also launched her own grammar school, making sure the teaching positions were well paid and that free education was provided for students who couldn't afford the tuition fees. On top of that, ten scholarships were set up, offering students a potential six years of further education at Cambridge.[301]

We also have evidence that Anne launched education initiatives within the area of reform she believed in most passionately: that of reading and understanding the scripture of the Bible. After placing chaplain Matthew Parker at the Stoke-by-Clare church near Sudbury, she appointed a lecturer to lead a Bible study group there four days a week. Here the congregation could begin to truly understand the undiluted word of God, which up until now they had heard only in Latin, a language reserved for those who could afford an education.

Bible study might be something modern-day Christians take for granted, but we have to understand how radical it was when Anne Boleyn first set this up in the 1500s.[302]

Not quite the depiction we see of her in the modern media today, is it?

Of course, you could argue that it was normal practice for royalty to fund individuals or educational institutions, and not even worthy of our attention when there are so many accusations of lewdness and depravity we could be focusing on. Yet the sheer extent of Anne's work in this area, and the level of involvement she clearly had, proves that it was not merely carried out in her name – it was personal. Every case we uncover has her fingerprints all over it as an opportunity for her to make a political impact, whether in relation to her religious cause or government policies. And as you're about to see, Anne's career in politics was just getting started.

Of course, it took a team of dedicated workers to help her achieve the mass humanitarianism we are about to uncover, and it was in the run-up to her taking the throne alongside Henry that a certain fellow named Thomas Cromwell made an appearance in Anne's life. The first evidence we have of her liaising with Cromwell was when she sent him a verbal message on 8 March 1529 at Hampton Court, his master Wolsey's residence.[303] It would be but a mere seven years later that he would plot her murder. How time flies when you're deceiving those who trust you.

By the time he came to know Anne, Thomas Cromwell had been an agent for Wolsey for fourteen years, jumping ship to the royal household during his master's fall from power. Yet he didn't move immediately into the direct service of the king, as is often presumed. Instead, he continued to oversee Wolsey's land and property, which had been seized by the Crown, until June 1530.[304] It's at this point that Anne took him in as part of the Boleyn research team working towards the annulment with the *Collectanea satis copiosa*.

But as an ally of Wolsey's for well over a decade, would she have ever entirely trusted Cromwell? You'd be inclined to think not, but quite a few key members of her faction defected from the other side. So did she ever really trust any of them? But whether she forged forward with blind trust or caution, we can't deny how closely the two were to work over the years before he went into the direct service of the king. That Cromwell organised Anne's coronation and the christening of her daughter, Elizabeth, indicates an impressive level of trust on Anne's part.[305]

But should we really be surprised? Even Cromwell's enemies conceded that his social skills, charm and hospitality were second to none.[306] Frankly, I would expect nothing less from the slick former lawyer who always knew the right thing to say, the right way to play every situation and could hold his nerve, as well as his tongue, when things got too heated.

Cromwell's biographer MacCulloch has recently debated whether he and Anne were as close as history has presumed. Here, a quote from Chapuys, who himself worked closely with Cromwell, is useful evidence to draw on: 'All I can say is that everyone here considers him Anne's right hand [man], as I myself told him some time ago.'[307]

And when we consider that Anne went on to appoint Cromwell as her high steward at £20 a year, it seems clear that they developed a close working relationship. Rather irritatingly, we have no confirmation of what year he was appointed, only evidence that he served in this role as late as 1535.[308]

But it was as early as 1532 that petitioners would often approach Anne through Cromwell, or simultaneously approach them both, proving it was common knowledge by this point that the two were working together and that he would pass any petitions on to her.[309] However, the difference between Cromwell and Anne was that, ever the businessman, he expected to be paid by his petitioners and, indeed, received money on the side for the help he gave.[310]

As we've seen, a large number of petitions sent to Anne were from students in need of financial support, but also a good portion were from reformists whose very lives were in danger owing to the cause for which they were fighting. This meant a large part of Anne's religious activism was about using her power as queen to help and protect fellow evangelicals who were soliciting the wrong kind of attention while out there campaigning for change.

One of our earliest recorded cases, at the end of 1530, shows Anne was too impatient to wait for the protection of the official title of queen before responding to an appeal from a Thomas Alwaye. Thomas wrote to Anne for aid after being arrested and imprisoned for owning an English Bible and other illegal religious books, later saying, 'I remembered how many deeds of pity your goodness had done within these few years . . . as well to strangers and aliens as to many of this land.'[311]

This was similar to the case of Thomas Patmore, who also petitioned Anne before she officially became queen. Patmore was an evangelical parson who was of the controversial reformist belief that priests should be allowed to marry, and so had been arrested for marrying his own priest to a housemaid. This, following earlier brushes with the law, when he was fined for distributing copies of Tyndale's New Testament, led him to being imprisoned for two years before he saw hope in Anne's impending reign. Patmore petitioned her in the few months before her wedding when she was marquess of Pembroke, allowing us to date this story to potentially as early as 1 September 1532. Anne is said to have taken the matter to the king and eventually Lord Chancellor Thomas Audley, Cromwell and Cranmer were appointed to investigate, at which point Thomas Patmore was released.[312]

This shows us that Anne most definitely did not shy away from controversial cases in those delicate early days, at a time we'd imagine she would be focused on gaining public approval or simply enjoying her newfound glory as queen-to-be.

As soon as she gained the power she has been accused of so mercilessly pursuing, she sought out those who were suffering at the hands of the Church; for example, she became patron to a traumatised Richard Tracy, who had been through the ordeal of having his father's dead body dug up and burned because his will made reference to his doubt that the Church, as opposed to God, could grant salvation to the dead. In 1534 Anne also helped the Antwerp merchant Richard Herman – who was cast out during Wolsey's reign for supporting an English Bible – gain reacceptance by his peers.[313]

Then, as well as reports that she helped childhood friend Clément Marot when he was wanted for translating the Psalms, we also have the curious case of the French humanist poet and religious reformer Nicolas Bourbon. Bourbon was jailed in 1533 for his provocative book *Nugae*, in which he thoroughly let rip on those who opposed the humanist new learnings. The interesting thing to note here is that Marguerite d'Angoulême became his patron in the 1520s, with Bourbon going on to tutor Marguerite's children in 1529. It's known that he was very close to Clément Marot, leading us to question if Anne also knew him personally from her final years in France. The fact that he would reach out to Anne for help in England over Marguerite in his homeland may tell us all we need to know here. Bourbon sent a letter to Anne via her cousin Dr Butts[314] and she convinced Henry VIII to intervene in his case.

Following Bourbon's successful release from prison, Anne offered him amnesty in England, paying all his expenses and introducing him to her trusted inner circle, where she also secured him a place in her cousin's household.[315] Tudor fans may recognise Dr Butts as being the king's physician, but something that is rarely highlighted is that he often worked with Anne, bringing her attention to people in need who she might be in a position to help.

Bourbon became eternally indebted to the entire Boleyn faction for taking him into their hearts and homes. Declaring his gratitude in a statement to the whole team, Bourbon thanked Butts, Latimer, Cranmer, Holbein and Cromwell, but none more so than Anne Boleyn herself, saying, 'Your pity lighted upon me from the ends of the earth, snatching me in my affliction, Anna, away from my troubles . . . How can I express my thanks, still less, Oh Queen, repay you?'[316]

When Bourbon released a new edition of *Nugae* in 1538 it was updated with stories of how Anne mediated for him in France and how generous she was to him in England.[317] Tellingly, Bourbon returned to France in the year of Anne's death, 1536.[318]

Yet, not just reserving such extreme acts of amnesty for those she was acquainted with, it's reported Anne went out of her way again in 1534 for a reformist scholar in Paris, Mr Sturmius, and appealed to the king to negotiate his release from prison. As it turned out, Sturmius continued to live in Paris until 1536 under the protection of Guillaume du Bellay, but it's clear from Latymer, who tells us the story, that Anne had extended an offer of further help that he thankfully didn't feel the need to take up.[319] Similarly, she helped a gentlewoman in France, Mrs Marye, to escape to safety in England 'for religion', as Latymer simply states. He doesn't give us the backstory, so we can only presume she was another outspoken reformist who caught the attention of the French authorities. Immediately after she arrived in England, Anne sent for her and apparently 'entertained her so lovingly and honourably as she confessed that her trouble had purchased her liberty, and that she gained more by her banishment than she could have hoped for at home.'[320]

Exactly how Anne convinced Henry to rescue the very heretics he was arresting and suppressing in England is uncertain. However, we should not underestimate the force of nature that Anne Boleyn must have been; nor should it be assumed that she used her sexual wiles to persuade him, as many would have us believe. The sheer number of people she got the king to save, not to mention the controversial causes she persuaded him to support, means that this approach would fast have become pretty exhausting. Cromwell and Wolsey had learned how to work effectively with the king over the years, implementing policies and encouraging him to pursue alliances that he wasn't totally behind; do we presume *they* turned on the seductive charm to get what they wanted? No, history has allowed them quick-witted intelligence. So how about we use our modern, rational minds to presume the same of Anne?

But what all these stories provide is *proof*, actual hard evidence of how Anne wanted to use her power as queen, and why she accepted Henry's marriage proposal in the first place. The reports you are reading are the result of that infamous 'ambition' we are repeatedly told she possessed. *Ambition*: the one word that features universally across all interpretations and analyses of Anne's character. Yet this is never a compliment on the part of modern biographers; it's never implied as a positive trait for a woman to have. Imagine you are playing historical bingo: blink and you would get a full house for the number of times they use the phrase 'ambition turned her head', almost as if she was a socially acceptable young lady until she had the brazen self-confidence to want to be more, once again backing up the rhetoric that to have ambitions of being a powerful woman your intentions have to be bad.

As though this apparent icy ambition automatically replaces other traits such as kindness, empathy and goodness.

Well, Anne Boleyn is just one example of the good that can be accomplished when an ambitious woman gains power.

Sadly, one life that Anne tried and failed to save was that of the most hunted of English reformers: the Bible translator William Tyndale. The authorities finally caught up with him in July 1535, imprisoning him for over a year. Thomas Boleyn's godson, Thomas Theobald, was sent to Antwerp to find out more about his arrest, and reported back to Cranmer in the hope that his patron Queen Anne could get the king to save him. Though she could not ultimately help, as she was arrested and killed herself mere months before Tyndale's execution,[321] Anne was to controversially show her solidarity with him shortly before she died. On 6 February 1536 she had Cranmer preach a sermon at Paul's Cross while the evangelical was still in prison, in which he reiterated Tyndale's sentiments in declaring the pope the Antichrist. As MacCulloch reminds us, Tyndale was the only major English writer at that time to have done this, so Cranmer's bold alliance with his condemned countryman is one that can't be missed – and one the archbishop of Canterbury would only have dared do with the absolute support of his evangelical patron, Queen Anne.[322]

Yet saving the lives of reformists was just one aspect of Anne's campaign. In July 1535, while on summer progress, she and Henry visited Sudeley Castle for five days. The king met with Cromwell at Winchcombe Abbey to plan the dissolution of the monasteries, and Anne spent her time investigating another major issue: the duping of the public with fake holy relics.

Hailes Abbey was brought to her attention due to the fact that it housed a notorious relic that was making huge amounts of cash, this being the 'blood of Christ'. Yes, the actual blood of Jesus Christ, supposedly taken from him while he was nailed to the cross and captured in a crystal container. Now, as modern-day readers, we must overlook the logistics, not to mention sacrilege of such an act, and remind ourselves that in the sixteenth century the existence of relics was an everyday fact of life. The people vehemently believed in their veracity. So the claim that this blood was said to have never congealed since the abbey received it in 1270 did not raise suspicions, but rather turned Hailes into one of the most famous pilgrimage sites in England. Thousands would pay every year to view and touch this 'holy relic' in the hope of being healed by its divine powers. Not only that, but visitors were told that they would only see it if their sins had been forgiven after confession, bringing us back to the whole contentious issue of whether priests could forgive your sins rather than God.

So, as an evangelical who was against such beliefs and determined to fight against all corrupt practices within the Church, Anne investigated. Latymer describes how she sent her chaplains to 'search and examine the truth of this abominable abuse,'[323] a quote that backs up her modest reform beliefs and proves she wasn't against the act of pilgrimage itself, just the deception and manipulation of the people. After all, shortly following her marriage to the king in early 1533, Anne was heard to have said to Norfolk that if she wasn't pregnant by Easter she would undertake a pilgrimage to pray to the Virgin Mary.[324]

And so, Anne's chaplains reported back that the relic was indeed a fake, the 'blood' actually being a resin made of honey and saffron (not duck's blood as was rumoured at the time). Horrified, Anne informed Henry, who clearly agreed this was unacceptable practice and had the offending relic removed.

However, Henry was forced to intervene again in 1538, as by this time the abbey had put the so-called 'blood' back on display, showing that 'abuse of pilgrimage' was one thing Henry was committed to stamping out, even after he had stamped out Anne herself.[325]

Since Anne's murder, this boundless stream of evidence of her good work has been censored and suppressed. When non-history-fanatics think of Anne Boleyn, do they recall her fighting for religious reform and freedom? No, they think six wives, six fingers and beheaded. Her truth has been suppressed for too long, and that's why this chapter needs to exist in its entirety. #WomenArentNumbers #SheIsMore #StopSuppressingHerTruthOrYoullHaveMeToDealWith

◆ ◆ ◆

Though Anne's religious work was clearly her driving force, it would be matched only by one other passion, and that was her extensive work in poverty relief. In the vital months leading up to her death, this cause would be exceptional for Anne in terms of the dramatic lengths she went to address it.[326]

But what would have prompted such dedication to poverty relief? After all, she didn't come from an underprivileged background herself. Was it perhaps the many carriage rides between the royal court in London and her family home of Hever Castle, during which she witnessed the real poverty of the people for herself? Or do we have the answer within the pages of one of her favourite reformist authors?

Jacques Lefèvre d'Étaples's popular book *The Ecclesiaste* encouraged those in positions of privilege, like Anne, to be generous to the poor. Lefèvre spoke of kings, princes and chancellors alike being those who should show a 'holy example of life', pointing out that it was in these walks of life that 'more injustice, more oppressions of poor widows and orphans' and 'more disorder in all manners' occurred.

These words obviously had an impact on Anne; her chaplain Latymer reports that in the months leading up to the yearly summer progress, Anne would request huge quantities of canvas, from which she and her ladies-in-waiting would make smocks and sheets for the poor. Foxe explains that Anne liked to have her ladies personally making clothes for the needy to show them what an exceptional position of privilege they were in, and to remember those less fortunate.[327] She would further request flannel material from which they would sew petticoats for men, women and children, which were then distributed to the parishes that Anne visited along the summer progress route. From there, it would be the priests' job to distribute them among the townsfolk who were most in need.[328]

Anne was apparently 'particularly receptive to female petitioners',[329] even helping her aunt Katherine Howard (no, not *that* Katherine Howard) in her attempt to divorce and escape her husband. Foxe tells us how Anne also gave generously to widows and families of very low income, and would donate £3 or £4 (approximately £1,300–£1,700 in today's money[330]) so that they could buy livestock to create an ongoing form of income and food supply.

On becoming queen, Anne was given multiple grants of lands, which provided her with income from the taxes of the people who lived there. This made her richer during her reign than any of Henry's other wives, before or after. It was this money that Anne gave away, sort of like a Tudor Robin Hood, taxing the rich to give to the poor. And notes show just how involved in the taxation process she became, proving she had a good head for business to support her charity work and political activism. She was no puppet merely acting out the standard duties expected of a queen.[331]

It was while on the summer progress of 1535 from Windsor to Bristol that Anne heard about a local evangelical couple who had lost their cattle and were being told it was God's punishment for turning against Catholicism. Anne invited them to visit her, whereupon she gave what sounds like an impromptu sermon, reassuring them that God was actually testing their strength. To help them get back on their feet, she gave the couple a lump sum of money, saying that if it wasn't enough to come back to her and she would see them right.[332]

But Anne's charity extended beyond her summer progress. It's reported she would send her sub-almoners to the towns around her permanent residences to make lists of the families most in need, and would then distribute money to them accordingly.[333] The duchess of

Richmond told Foxe that Anne would even carry a small purse with her every day to donate money to the people she passed on her travels.[334]

In addition to all this, Anne, of course, had her official royal alms to distribute – an allowance that all queens were given for charitable donation. This was the norm, and not exclusive to Anne; but it is interesting as a gauge to show just how far she went beyond the standard expectations of her role.

At the Royal Maundy service it was traditional for royalty to give alms to the poor, but it was said that Anne pushed to increase the usual amount; and, in fact, when she gave 'over and besides' the usual donation during one particular service, one woman told the almoner that she must have been given someone else's donation as it was far too much. He assured her it was the right amount, and when he relayed the story to Anne she said she wished she could have doubled it for the woman's honesty.[335] I suppose in the slippery Tudor court honesty was quite a rarity.

However, there has been great speculation over how much Anne's alms actually came to, with some saying Foxe hugely exaggerated her yearly donations.[336] But regardless, her almsgiving was just a drop in the ocean compared to the rest of her charitable work. It's certainly not something we need to exaggerate in order to prove her good intentions as queen. Even the Scottish theologian Alexander Alesius wrote of how he had heard great stories of Anne's charity to the poor, proving just how renowned she was for her generosity.[337] So much for being hated by all who knew of her.

So, you may understand the tinge of frustration felt when, alongside every acknowledgement of the overwhelming and undeniable good Anne did in her life, historians feel obliged to pick her true intentions to pieces.

Did she campaign for the people because she genuinely cared, or was it merely a ploy to outshine Katherine of Aragon's own charitable pursuits?

Similarly, did those who dedicated religious works to Anne do so because she shared the same faith, or because it was a queen's duty to be a patron and she actually cared not a jot for them?

Did she really support young reformists because she was passionate about education, or did she simply want to push for an evangelical future in order to break from Rome, gain royal supremacy and take over the world?!

She's not a comic-book super-villain!

Every good deed is pulled apart, with historians, novelists and screenwriters alike hunting for any potential ulterior motive Anne could possibly have had so they can keep selling you the notorious legend. It's perplexing and tiresome in equal measure. Particularly when modern biographies of Cromwell, Wolsey, Luther and Tyndale don't pick apart the motives for *their* good work in a similarly rabid way. I don't read accusations of Cromwell wanting to be the king's chief minister for the power and prestige. Instead, his biographies celebrate his rise from the doldrums of Putney, applaud the policies and laws he put in place and marvel at all the good he did for the country in spite of having Henry VIII to contend with. His murder plots are discussed, of course, but they are not the main focus, and they always come with an apologist slant.

Similarly, Wolsey is seen as a humble man of the church, the butcher's son turned cardinal who was committed to Catholicism and was browbeaten by the king, when all he wanted to do was run the country efficiently. But when his riches were exposed during his downfall – it took Cavendish three pages to list the inventory[338] – no one points out how excessive and vulgar it was. No, instead they focus on how Anne Boleyn went round to pick over the spoils herself, deflecting his greed on to her.[339]

So, is it then unreasonable to ask why it appears to be predominantly the women in history who are relentlessly accused of scheming their way to wealth and power purely for their own selfish gain? Are we being too sensitive when we question the standard rhetoric that they didn't *really* want to change the world? They just wanted jewels and gowns of cloth of gold to parade in at balls and feasts, where they could flirt and write silly little poems to boys in books and plot each other's demise (poisoning, of course).

Yes, there will always be exceptions to the rule, but as a progressive society this misogynistic trend is too prevalent to overlook. Readers need to be made aware of it because it's distorting how we understand and piece our history together. It basically comes down to bad writing, because only badly written characters are one-dimensional and intent solely on world domination. Which explains why Anne Boleyn makes a great fictional character, yet her story doesn't quite add up in the pages of the non-fiction history books.

So if you want to discover who Anne really was, it means considering that her good deeds could have been genuine. It certainly fits more realistically with the uncensored narrative of her story so far, wouldn't you agree?

I think the problem stems from the fact that many of the stories about Anne's activism come from 'martyrologist' John Foxe, whose *Acts and Monuments* (popularly known as *Foxe's Book of Martyrs*) was, as the title suggests, a round-up of the lives and work of evangelical/ Protestant activists. The reason Foxe's stories of Anne have been called into question over the centuries is because he features only a 'best of' compilation of her good deeds, hence presenting us with an unrealistic, saintly woman devoid of any human fault. But as Thomas S. Freeman points out, there were eight volumes of *Foxe's Book of Martyrs*, and with each one he added more and more evidence that Anne was in fact the opposite of the evil caricature that had been created following her death. Because of this, he has been accused of invention and embellishing the truth,[340] but his primary source for these stories was, among others, Anne Boleyn's own silkwoman Joan Wilkinson.

Joan was close enough to Anne that in 1536, when Latymer was sent to Europe to buy illegal religious books for his queen, the instructions were to pass them on to Joan, supposedly to appear as inconspicuous as possible. As it would turn out, on this occasion Latymer returned home to find Anne in prison.[341]

But here we have the statements of a woman who served within the very household that has been accused of running amok with revelry and depravity, as was described in the jolly biography *The Life of Jane Dormer*. Even though Dormer herself was not born until two years after Anne's death and the biography was written in 1645, reports that Anne spent her reign taking part in 'masks, dancing, plays and such corporal delights'[342] have been taken more seriously than eyewitness accounts of those in her household, like Wilkinson.

Jane Dormer married one of Princess Mary's closest advisers, so you can see why her biographer Henry Clifford might have had this vapid view of Anne's time as queen, as seen through the eyes of an enemy. But let us ask ourselves, why would Anne waste seven years fighting to be queen if she merely wanted to spend her days partying? She could have married any man of wealth to achieve such a lifestyle much more quickly and easily, not to mention without the ensuing international Catholic hate campaign and politically motivated murder.

Alas, from the varying accounts of life in the queen's chambers, it's clear that historians believe there could only have been one way in which Anne and her ladies spent their days. Either they were piously slaving away for the poor from the crack of dawn until they fell into their beds, only stopping along the way to pray in the solitude of the chapel;[343] or they spent their every waking hour dancing, flirting, plotting each other's downfall and having illicit sexual affairs, as though Anne's household was the Vegas of the Tudor court.[344]

May I interject as the voice of reason and propose that daily activities probably included a bit of both (minus the affairs and murder plots, of course). Why is it considered so improbable that Anne's household worked during the day – pausing regularly to pray, as a *Book of Hours* will attest was customary – then, like anyone, let their hair down in the evening with a dinner and dance?

Media depictions repeatedly have Anne wistfully spending her days doing nothing more than sitting on a throne, reading a book, surrounded by ladies doing needlework, like something from the pages of a Jane Austen novel. But the evidence of the sheer amount of work Anne got done during her few short years as queen prove her days would have been intense and full-on. Yes, she read many books, but the girl also had a lot of work to get through.

As a large part of her patronage to all those youths, and in addition to her refugee work and domestic charity, Anne would have had to read through daily appeals from petitioners. This would inevitably be followed by endless meetings with her advisers regarding who was the most in need, and how she wanted to proceed with each case. At the same time, she would be overseeing the year-round preparation for the summer progress 'charity drives', managing her ladies who were making the bedding and clothing ready for distribution around the country. Then, of course, she had to fit in Mass, which we know Henry VIII attended up to five times a day.

Yet 'work hard, play hard' was a phrase that could have been invented for Anne Boleyn. It has to be said, here was a queen who loved a good jolly, with contemporary reports telling us she was a talented singer and composer. Indeed, the Royal College of Music in London houses Anne's sixteenth-century music book, a compilation of the favourite pieces she liked to play during her many evenings of entertainment. She was a renowned patron of the arts, and this was reflected in her own joy and love of them that she shared with the ladies of her chamber.

But something we need to realise is that the royal court was built on feasts, tournaments, pageants and masques. What may seem to us like an endless stream of pointless parties was actually an integral part of court life and how you were expected to make your mark. The Tudors practically invented schmoozing; it was here, amid the dancing and revelry, that factions were forged, marriage alliances made and politics discussed, all over the innocence of a goblet of wine and a platter of sweetmeats. So, we must be aware of not misreading the traditions of the day.

A letter from Edward Baynton (Anne's vice-chamberlain) to George Boleyn on his trip to France in 1534 states:

> And as for pastime in the queen's chamber, [there] was never more. If any of you that be now departed have any ladies that ye thought favoured you and somewhat would mourn at parting of their servants, I can no whit perceive the same by their dancing and pastime they do use here, but that other takes place, as ever hath been the custume.[345]

Of course, it should come as no surprise that this letter has been jumped on over the centuries as proof that *all* Anne and her ladies ever did was spend their days frivolously partying. But it might appear to the more rational reader that his letter was just a bit of playful banter with the lads; Baynton teasing that Anne's ladies didn't miss the men and were having plenty of fun without them. He doesn't mention dancing with other men, and doesn't mention flirting. He doesn't even insinuate this is all the ladies ever did, simply that at that moment they were enjoying more free time than usual. (Something that, in itself, confirms the rest of their day was taken up with work.)

This does not make Anne and her women silly and vacuous. Nor does it undermine any of her political, religious and charitable work. It merely highlights how human the residents of the Tudor court were, unwinding after stressful days with dancing, singing and card games. Not that we can really blame them, when we hear the contrasting reports from those who directly served Anne, who confided that she was in fact an incredibly strict mistress during working hours.

Anne's chaplain William Latymer reports how she would 'rebuke' or 'sharply punish', even banish from court altogether, those ladies who did not uphold her high moral standards.[346] This sounds like the overly sensitive actions of a woman determined to prove just how seriously she took her prestigious new role. No doubt she was eager to replicate the renowned household of Queen Claude, in which she herself was raised.

Indeed, when Anne became queen and first appointed her chaplains, Latymer says she declared how they all must act, herself included, considering they were 'so high a personage; not found wantones, not pampered pleasures, not licentious liberties or trifling idleness, but virtuous demeanor, Godly conversation, sombre communication and integrity of life'.[347]

I suspect Anne was laying it on rather thick here. After all, she was addressing men of the church. But the general, overall sentiment of her words appears in alignment with the more realistic reports of life in Anne's household. Particularly when we hear she has been accused of adopting a rather holier-than-thou attitude – which is often highlighted as scathingly hypocritical, given what a renowned flirt they say she was back in her youth. (A holier-than-thou slut? Do you see how the negative propaganda often contradicts and catches itself out?) But not to dismiss the reports of this apparently condescending superiority, we must realise that by the time Anne held her own court and was responsible for a group of young ladies, she had done a lot of growing up. She was no longer the excitable new girl at court playing along with the games of courtly love. By the time she became queen of England, Anne's religious conviction had deepened greatly; so it's understandable that she might now advise her ladies to use their precious youth wisely, not waste it on the silly frivolities of courtly love; particularly knowing, as she now did, how it could come back to haunt you many years later.

To this end, she was known to have instructed even the minor members of her court to attend chapel daily and avoid 'infamous places' such as 'evil, lewd and ungodly brothels'. Latymer reveals she also lectured her chaplains, saying 'I assure you, you shall profit more in one day with good examples, than in a year with many lessons.'[348]

Yet for all the realities of Anne's strict household, it's reassuring to hear she still had the human touch, as illustrated in a story Latymer tells in his *Chronickille*. This is of a Mrs Jaskyne, a member of Anne's privy chamber whose husband fell ill at home in Essex while she was away on progress with the queen in Woodstock. Mrs Jaskyne wasn't allowed to go home to see him, so she pleaded her case to Latymer, who brought this to Anne's attention (we can only presume the person preventing her returning home was Edward Baynton, Anne's chamberlain).[349] As soon as she heard of this plight, not only did she grant the woman leave, but made sure she had provisions and more than enough money to cover her journey.[350] Stories like this seem to disprove that there was any distance and indifference between Anne and her staff. In fact, a report from the constable of the Tower while Anne was in prison tells us just how deeply she cared for the members of her household, as she was worried about who was making the accused men's beds for them, which cries more of maternal instinct than sexual prowess.[351]

But clearly these life lessons in honesty and integrity fell on deaf ears, as it was the members of Anne's very household who would, in just a few short years, conspire to frame her for adultery and treason.

CHAPTER 8

THEN IT ALL WENT WRONG

During her first year of marriage, in which Anne threw herself head first into her humanitarianism and many issues of reform, her personal life began disintegrating before her very eyes. But try as she might, she was ultimately powerless to stop it; for, unbeknown to her, Henry VIII was entering the 'devalue' phase of his sociopathic relationship with his coveted new queen.

And so it is with a mixture of weariness and trepidation that we approach the part of Anne's story that readers will be most familiar with. Indeed, the following tales of adultery and scheming are the only element of Anne's married life that most writers care to focus on – not wanting to sully their story of sex and scandal with anything as dull as helping the poor and rescuing refugees. But even then, the facts get distorted, mistold and muddied with apologist theories to excuse Henry's ensuing affairs (the old classics that she was 'too argumentative' or 'too skilled in the bedroom'). After all, when a man has an affair it's become standard modern practice to ask what the wife did to drive him to it.

Alas, as we've already discovered, Anne didn't have to do anything wrong herself for things to fall apart as spectacularly as they did. All she had to do was enter into a marriage with a sociopath.

It was around early February 1533 that Anne would have started to suspect she was pregnant for the first time. This welcome news was followed by her coronation on 1 June, by which point she would have been approximately five months pregnant.

It was in these later months of pregnancy, when it is said that she suffered terribly with sickness, that it's possible Henry took his first mistress. However, bizarrely, this is not an indication that their relationship was falling apart so soon. Of course, it signals the death knell of doom if you're of the belief that theirs was the most tragic love story of all time, and indeed it would be a sure-fire sign in any modern-day relationship. But a sixteenth-century royal marriage is not like any other, and Henry only seemed to take a lover during the later stages of pregnancies, when his wives were 'out of action'. I jest not when I say it was deemed bad for the health to abstain from sex, and yet frowned upon to have a little rumpy-pumpy when heavily pregnant. So what's a man to do? This was a medical issue. Honest, officer!

We have but one reference from Chapuys to indicate Henry may have cheated during Anne's first pregnancy, and that came the following year, when he wrote that Henry's new fling was a 'renewed' passion for a former flame, whom we will get to shortly.

But on 7 September 1533 the hallowed day at last arrived. Anne went into labour with the king's blessed child who had been anointed by God. This is what Henry had started an international war for. This is what he had left his wife and lifelong religion for. God was now to send his king the ultimate sign that he was once again in the comfort and safety of His good grace, having washed away the sin of marrying his brother's widow. There was peace and calm across the land.

Then Anne gave birth to a girl.

Knowing as we now do how much significance the people of the sixteenth century placed on religious signs from God, it cannot be emphasised enough just how devastating an impact this would have had on Henry's view of his relationship with Anne Boleyn. Can we even begin to conceive how this realisation registered within the destructive workings of a sociopathic mind? When the carrot that Anne had supposedly dangled before Henry for seven years turned out to be female, and not the male heir he had pinned his salvation on?

History will tell you that Anne had failed in the only job she had been hired to do. Damn women and their disobedient ovaries. Yes, she personally failed to control the forces of nature within her own body and produce a baby boy. The thing is that Anne didn't fail at all; Henry did. Five centuries of medical research later, and we now know that it is the sperm that determines the gender of a baby. The egg contains an X chromosome, but it is the sperm that has a chromosome that can be X, which results in a baby girl, or Y, resulting in a boy.[352] How's that for irony?

However, I would argue that in 1533 the problem wasn't that Henry saw this as *Anne's* failure. It was much more catastrophic than that. It was *God* who had once again denied him a son.

This was no mere disappointment at the lack of a male heir. The birth of a girl would have brought all Henry's irrational fears of God's wrath bubbling back to the surface, taunting him once again with the Holy Word of the scripture. Had his dispensation to marry Anne been just as risky as his first with Katherine? Had it not absolved his sin at all? Either way, the continued lack of a son clearly meant one thing; if the Lord was displeased with their union, so was Henry.

So, yes, *this* was what shocked the king out of his seven-year 'idealise' phase – only not for the exact reasons we have always presumed.

However, there are some historians who believe that Elizabeth's birth wasn't such a great disappointment for Henry VIII, because the king kept up a public show of nonchalance in the days and weeks that followed, pointing out that downgrading the celebrations was standard for the birth of a princess, which is indeed true.

But this was no ordinary birth. Henry had placed so much significance on the gender and how it represented his salvation that of course he had to project an outward appearance of confidence. Not only was this to keep those around him calm, but also to keep Charles V's imperial faction at bay and avoid them seeing this as the ultimate catastrophe for the new royal couple.

So in October 1533, the official line reported by Anne's ladies was that Henry loved Anne as much as ever.[353] Of course, it's also quite plausible that they could have convinced themselves this was God's plan all along: an older sister to support the future king. Yes, Henry needed that boy, but with the world watching this could not be the couple's ruin, and they knew it. If ever there was a time for the self-delusion that everything was juuuuust fine, that time was now.

Anne was young; she could conceive again. After all, in 1511, when Katherine of Aragon gave birth to a baby boy who sadly died only fifty-two days later, Henry didn't appear too worried, believing they still had time for God to bless their marriage with a son.[354]

Of course, the myth that just keeps building momentum is that this disappointment was simply too much, not for the mentally unstable father, but for the evil, cold-hearted mother.

Rumours still persist that Anne never bonded with or loved Elizabeth, solely because her child had failed to secure for her the role of mother to the future king; apparently, we need look no further than the fact that Elizabeth was sent away at only three months old and raised in a separate household. A great narrative for the terrible Boleyn legend, if it were not the case that, as we've seen with the childhood of Henry VIII and his siblings, this was a sad and somewhat bizarre royal tradition that was not in any way exclusive to Anne Boleyn. Yet only she is singled out as a bad mother for complying with the rules – an insinuation that is even more galling when we consider that Henry VIII is never called out for being an absent father.

It may appear that Anne shipped Elizabeth away and forgot about her, but that's only when historians purposefully refuse to mention the years' worth of correspondence and state papers that confirm Anne spent as much time as was allowed with her daughter, displaying a fierce and protective love for her baby.

Italian historian Gregorio Leti told how Anne fought against strict rules of handing her baby over to a wet nurse in the early months in order to breastfeed Elizabeth herself; a claim that, admittedly, has been called into question given Leti's lack of respect for the facts in his historical biographies.[355]

Um . . . is that the twenty-first-century pot calling the sixteenth-century kettle black?

Nevertheless, we have a multitude of other reports confirming that Anne doted on Elizabeth, and would proudly place a cushion underneath her canopy at court so her baby princess could take a regal place beside her throne.[356] Latymer confirms that Anne was anxious to personally oversee Elizabeth's education, confiding she 'vowed to almighty God that if it would please him to prolong her days to see the training up of her young and tender babe' that she would teach her all the languages of the scripture: Hebrew, Greek, Latin and, of course, her beloved French. Not exactly the intentions of an indifferent and neglectful mother, it has to be said.[357]

In terms of personal care, one of Anne's biographers confirms Anne was a 'fond, if distant mother' and visited as much as was permitted.[358] Indeed, her first visit was mere weeks after the three-month-old Elizabeth had been taken from her, indicating Anne struggled with this enforced separation early on. What's more, according to Chapuys, by March of the following year, 1534, after visiting Elizabeth at Hatfield Anne had demanded her baby be moved to the much closer palace of Eltham.[359] This was only five miles away from the royal residence in Greenwich, which would allow Anne to visit more frequently. We have to remember that Anne was a full-time working mother; now she was the queen of England, her schedule wasn't her own. Indeed, we have evidence of a visit only a few weeks after the move to Eltham on 18 April, where Sir William Kingston reported, 'Today the King and

Queen were at Eltham, and saw my lady Princess, as goodly a child as hath been seen, and her grace is much in the King's favour as goodly child should be.'[360]

Of course, the striking thing about this report is Kingston's need to point out that the king loved his daughter, indicating there had been gossip to the contrary over Henry's unease at the continued lack of a son.

We have further reports of Anne's visiting Elizabeth at Richmond Palace on 24 October, this time bringing her ladies and key members of the court to see their infant princess, including Anne's uncle Norfolk and Charles Brandon, indicating he had well and truly wheedled his way back into the fold by this point.[361]

Proving Anne was obviously struggling with the prolonged bouts of separation from her baby, she finally demanded Elizabeth be brought to live with her at court, where she stayed for five weeks in the early months of 1535.[362] This is something she repeated at Christmas, with Elizabeth living with her mother right through to the following year and subsequently throughout the final months of Anne's life. In fact, Elizabeth was still at court around the time of her mother's arrest in May,[363] a time when history recorded perhaps the biggest indicator of Anne's feelings towards her daughter: in her final days of freedom, she made desperate plans to ensure Elizabeth's safety and future care: a heartbreaking moment we will come to in time but one that cannot be overlooked now.

However, I fear we are focusing on the wrong people's reaction, as there were plenty of enemies at court who were positively gleeful that the new queen had given birth to what was considered a lowly girl. Elizabeth gave them hope that Anne's evangelical reign was not secure, and there was still a chance they could get her out – none more so than Henry's former wife, Katherine, and her daughter, Mary, who were still refusing to accept their newly demoted titles of Princess Dowager Katherine and Lady Mary.

But all was not lost for the king and his new queen; they were down but not out, and six months later, in April 1534, it became clear that Anne was pregnant again. Chapuys noted the king was confident that this time it would be a boy; but the poor little soul wasn't given a chance, as Anne miscarried around late July.

This would have been a particularly devastating blow to them both, as calculations suggest she lost her baby approximately one month before full term. With Henry's hopes of salvation for his seemingly unforgivable sins cruelly snatched away once again by the Almighty, things would have been at breaking point for him and Anne.

Locked away following her miscarriage, when a woman had to be 'churched' for the apparently unclean act of childbirth, Anne was helpless to stop her husband from falling into the arms of the mistress it's presumed he took during the later months of this pregnancy. But this was no innocent and forgettable fling. The mysterious Catholic woman in question remains to this day shrouded in secrecy. Known only as the Imperial Lady, due to her staunch support for the former queen, she was actively working with Anne's enemies to end her reign.

It was good old Spanish ambassador Chapuys who first reported in September 1534 that upon hearing the tragic news of Anne's miscarriage, which they had managed to keep secret until this point,[364] '[The king] has renewed and increased the love which he formerly bore to another very handsome young lady of this court.'[365]

Understandably, Anne was said to be horrified by the affair; but not merely at the thought of her husband wanting anyone but herself, as is the only way this affair has been reported throughout history. No, the true betrayal Anne would have felt is that Henry should find solace in someone so clearly against her and everything she stood for.

To make matters worse, this woman was said to have had the audacity to be openly hostile towards Anne. And so Anne attempted to get this Imperial Lady dismissed from her service – something that informs us she wasn't just a girl at court, but a girl whom Anne trusted within her very own household.

It was this attempt to control Henry that, according to Chapuys, prompted the king to send Anne the foreboding message that she 'ought to be satisfied with what he had done for her' and that 'she ought to consider where she came from', for apparently, if given the chance, the king would not go back and marry her again.[366]

However, Chapuys was not inclined to take this explosive threat too seriously, stating 'no great stress is to be laid on such words' due to what he describes as the king's ever-changing emotions and Anne's ability to manage them; a report that gives us a unique insight into the dynamics of their relationship.[367] However, the argument still rings true. It doesn't sound like a simple case of frayed nerves and overcharged emotions but, rather, very much in keeping with the 'devalue' stage of a sociopathic relationship.

◆ ◆ ◆

Things were to go from bad to worse for Anne when, the following month, she was dealt a political blow in that England's French allies were rumoured to be considering a marriage between Katherine's daughter, Mary, and the heir to the throne of France.

Henry was quick to intercede and propose that his new daughter Elizabeth, the only one he now deemed his legal heir, instead be the one to marry the duke of Angoulême.[368] But the damage had already been done for Anne. That her beloved French royal family would not consider her own daughter legitimate was too big an insult, and she made it known that she was not best pleased with Francis I.

The once unbreakable friendship between Anne and her childhood home of France continued to deteriorate so badly that by the following year, in July 1535, King Francis was bad-mouthing Anne to the pope's spokesman Rodolfo Pio, saying 'how little virtuously she has lived and lives now'.[369]

It's hate speech like this that has been taken out of context as further proof of Anne's moral corruption. Yet, when we discover not only the timing of these rumours but who they came from and the motivation behind them, it's pretty easy to see that they were just that: purposefully poisonous rumours and slanderous gossip.

But back in October 1534, personal relations between Henry and Anne also continued to deteriorate. Even though she had fully recovered from her miscarriage by this point, her husband showed no signs of giving up his controversial mistress. Anne felt forced to take extreme action to stop the situation slipping further out of control, and enlisted the help of her brother's wife, Jane Rochford.

The way in which Anne dealt with Henry's affair tells us a lot about her spirit. She didn't pine and beg him not to leave her; she approached it smartly and fought back with a plan. Admittedly, it was a crap plan. Together, Anne and her sister-in-law conspired somewhat unimaginatively for Jane to pick an argument with the Imperial Lady, so she would be banished from court.

Now, if Anne was the devious mastermind she was meant to have been, she surely would have come up with something slightly more foolproof than a quarrel between two ladies at court?

Unfortunately for her, Henry speedily cottoned on and, as Chapuys tells us on 13 October, had Jane banished from court instead of his mistress. Chapuys could barely conceal his excitement as he explained:

> The wife of Mr de Rochefort has lately been exiled from Court, owing to her having joined in a conspiracy to devise the means of sending away, through quarreling or otherwise, the young lady to whom the King is now attached. As the credit of this [Imperial Lady] is on the increase, and that of [Anne Boleyn] on the wane, she is visibly losing part of her pride and vainglory.

It was this victory over Anne's attempt to oust her that prompted the presumptuous Imperial Lady to send a message directly to Princess Mary, as Chapuys describes:

> . . . telling her to take good heart; that her tribulations will come to an end much sooner than she expected; and to be assured that, should the opportunity occur, she will show herself her true friend and devoted servant.[370]

This Imperial Lady was on a mission. And winning.

But what of the banished Jane Rochford? The anger she went on to display towards Anne tells us she never forgave her royal sister-in-law, not only for getting her into trouble with the king but for allowing her to suffer the embarrassment of being sent away.

However, it was during these months that Anne was in need of Henry's support in much more controversial cases than this. Alongside the personal trauma of miscarriages and plots to ruin her marriage, Anne was simultaneously fighting to rescue those in need of amnesty, campaigning for the youths' right to education and providing poverty relief for the people.

So, the fact that Anne felt scared to push her luck and challenge Henry over Jane's banishment suggests the Imperial Lady situation was becoming too volatile, and wasn't worth risking her relationship with the king over. This meant Anne had to diffuse the issue, not add fuel to the fire with more arguments. Yes, if ever there was a moment in history where it's safe to accuse Anne of seducing the king of England, that time would be now. She needed to go on a charm offensive if she wanted to lure her husband away from his dangerous mistress, who she could see was out to ruin her. I'm afraid that in the process, her sister-in-law, Jane, unwittingly became collateral damage.

People say that Anne was wracked with jealousy when Henry cheated because theirs was a marriage built on sweet, all-consuming love and desire; that Anne's reaction to Henry's mistress was more that of a broken-hearted wife than a distant queen, because unlike Katherine of Aragon before her, theirs was not a political match.

But I must point out that in the end, Henry and Anne's became the most political marriage of the sixteenth century. In eventually making Anne his wife, Henry was taking a stand against the pope. He was making a religious statement against Catholic dominance. He was aligning his country with France over the Holy Roman Empire. He was proving his power as king of England to all of Europe. And in Anne taking Henry as her husband, she was trying to give royal approval to the religious reformation, make England's stance on the abuses of the Church known and show exactly where their powerful monarchy stood on the controversial scriptural debate.

So, while it may have started out as an innocent sociopathic obsession, after a seven-year war with Europe and their own countrymen, Henry and Anne entered married life as a political match. Which means Anne's increasing anger at her husband cheating on her wasn't due to a broken heart, but the very real fear that he was slipping back into the arms of Catholicism and everything Katherine's imperial faction at court represented. It would have been the ultimate kick in the teeth as an evangelical.

Evidence that supports this are the reports that Anne worked with her cousin and avid supporter Margaret Shelton to have *her* replace the Imperial Lady as the king's mistress, which they successfully achieved by the following February of 1535.[371] Anne clearly trusted Margaret, as her mother had been governess to Elizabeth and Mary. But Anne's readiness to provide her husband with an alternative bedmate tells us loud and clear that she was less annoyed at the idea of him taking a mistress than of that mistress being an imperial and orthodox Catholic. He could cheat on her, but not on her faith. Indeed, it was in this same month, January 1535, that Chapuys reported Anne laughing off Henry's flirtation with another woman at a banquet.[372]

◆ ◆ ◆

It is while Henry was dealing with the aftermath of his excommunication and the unenviable task of forcing the more reluctant half of the country into denouncing their lifelong faith of Catholicism that we hear of a horrific event in the early months of 1535 that was to cast a dark shadow over this new reformation.

In April, Henry ordered the shocking executions of the Charterhouse monks who refused to accept him as the head of the Church of England and take the Oath of Succession. These were no mere beheadings; Henry made sure the monks suffered horrendously for disobeying their king. They were first dragged through the streets by horse, then forced to watch in turn as they were each hanged. Then, 'while still alive the hangman cut out their hearts and bowels and burned them'. It was only at this point, after they had succumbed to their torture, that they were beheaded and quartered.[373]

This barbaric and senseless cruelty, though an undeniable sign of the times, suddenly feels at extreme odds with the humanitarianism we've just witnessed from Anne. It's jarring to read the insinuation that she turned a blind eye, making no attempt to stop it.

But did she?

Henry and Anne were still on shaky ground following his affair with the Imperial Lady. If Anne didn't feel she was in a secure enough place to speak up for her sister-in-law mere months earlier, then she surely wasn't in a strong enough position to fight Henry on his decision to publicly torture and kill the monks now.

But she knew a man who was, who could act on her behalf – and often did.

Yes, it's curious to discover a desperate plea from Anne's man Thomas Cranmer in a rarely discussed letter to Cromwell shortly following the monks' condemnation. In this letter he begs Cromwell to spare the men's lives, reasoning that it would help the king win the whole country round if they were instead able to persuade the monks to change their minds by educating them with 'sincere doctrine'.[374]

Though Cranmer's appeal was to be largely ignored by Cromwell and the king, reports revealed that one young man, the vicar of Thistelworth, Robert Ferron, was pardoned. This was on account of his youth, it has since been presumed, and Cranmer's appeal.[375]

But could Anne have been behind this intervention?

Cranmer was one of her closest allies and most genuine member of the Boleyn faction, who vitally, like herself, had the ear of Cromwell and the king. In light of her extensive amnesty work that same year in saving religious men and women, it certainly makes sense that she might ask Cranmer to speak up where she thought she would not be heard. It's widely acknowledged that Anne's chaplains would often preach controversial messages on her behalf, so by that same reckoning it's valid to presume she would be in support of, or even the instigator behind, some of Cranmer's more contentious appeals. After all, this was the archbishop that Anne had appointed directly challenging the king's wish to execute the monks; would he have had the nerve to make such a bold request without secret encouragement from his patron, the queen? Given we know how strict Cranmer would be in the coming years over the punishment of heretics himself, his appeal here doesn't sound entirely like his own doing.

Perhaps the very fact that Cranmer's intervention has been brushed under the carpet and is rarely spoken of tells us all we need to know. What with his intimate connection to Anne Boleyn, there would be an obvious risk of her being linked to this act of mercy – and we can't have that, can we? While we will never reach a conclusive answer all these centuries later, it's certainly worth considering;[376] not least so we question the standard narrative that Anne forced the people to accept her as queen, whatever the cost to human life.

No doubt keen to surround herself with family members rather than traitorous young ladies out to seduce her husband, we hear news around this time of Anne accepting another loyal cousin into the service of her private household: a young girl Anne's relative Sir Francis Bryan could vouch for as trustworthy and not one to cause a fuss. This was a delightful country girl called Jane Seymour.[377] Anne definitely wasn't going to have any trouble with this one, and thank goodness, because by the summer of 1535 she was about to be rocked by yet another betrayal and would need all the support she could get.

Her brother's disgruntled wife, Jane Rochford, was back and out for revenge. Enlisting Anne's aunt Lady William Howard, Jane made a very public statement regarding her feelings towards her royal sister-in-law; she stormed the streets of Greenwich as part of a demonstration led by several London women in support of the very person who represented an orthodox Catholic monarchy: Princess Mary.

The demonstration caused enough of a riot for both Jane and Lady Howard to end up being arrested and thrown in the Tower of London. This was a huge scandal for the queen of England and so was understandably hushed up by the royal court, no doubt in a desperate attempt to keep up a united front at a time when they were struggling to get the country on board with the reformation that was already dividing the people.[378]

George Boleyn would have been as horrified by his wife's actions as his sister Anne. Not only was he part of the king's intimate inner circle of trusted friends and family, he also considered himself his sister's rock. He would have been enraged that someone so close to him could hurt his sibling and inevitably bring his own loyalty to the Crown into question. It's said that George and Jane never had the best relationship, so we can imagine this was only to drive a further wedge between them. In fact, George choosing loyalty to his sister and brother-in-law over his wife is the reason he would be dead in less than a year.

◆ ◆ ◆

While George was dealing with the embarrassment of his wife's arrest in London, Anne had more important issues to deal with, as this was the summer of the Reformation progress. All this 'love rivalry' and family infighting had served as too much of a distraction; Anne needed to renew her focus on why she had battled to be queen in the first place – to bring about reform.

Unfortunately, by this point she had lost one of her most powerful and skilled workers in Thomas Cromwell, who saw an opportunity to serve the king of England directly in his former master Wolsey's role. Yes, Cromwell had very wisely seen that wives could come and go, yet the king was here to stay, so he had to be on the right team. But exactly how did the self-educated courtier from Putney acquire the top job as adviser to the king of England?

During his time serving Cardinal Wolsey, long before Henry even considered breaking away from the Catholic authority of Rome, Cromwell was given the task of converting six monasteries into Cardinal College in Oxford. He went on to work on the dissolution of a further thirty monasteries, the money from which funded Wolsey's grammar school in Ipswich.[379] It was probably at this point that he realised just how much money could be raised from dissolving a monastery. Both Chapuys and Foxe separately state that Cromwell promised he could make the king 'the richest prince in Christendom'.[380]

So much for the great seductress Anne Boleyn – it appears Cromwell was actually the one who knew how to seduce Henry, with alluring promises of boundless streams of cash from the very people who were defying his authority as head of the Church of England. And so this is how their working relationship began.

But what's important to know about the early monasteries closed by Cromwell is that most of the tenants he threw out were poor men who were losing their homes and livelihoods.[381] So perhaps, having come to know Anne's values and plans for the country, Cromwell quietly realised that the new queen probably wouldn't get behind this scheme.

But he knew a monarch who would.

So, although Cromwell continued to serve Anne as high steward until as late as 1535, this shift in his priorities and loyalties was a catastrophic move that probably none of them grasped the enormity of at the time. In fact, we might wonder if Anne would have actively supported one of her own men moving into the direct service of the king, in the hope that he could influence him with her own political agenda. It's a bittersweet thought, knowing the events that were shortly to come.

As part of the same royal progress round the country that took Henry and Cromwell to Winchcombe Abbey to discuss the new nationwide dissolution of the monasteries, and Anne to Hailes Abbey to confront the priests over their fake 'blood of Christ' relic, Latymer also tells us that she paid a visit to the nuns of Syon.

In spite of, or perhaps pointedly because of the fact that Katherine of Aragon was their former patron, Anne stopped by the Syon nunnery to give them prayer books translated into English. This was no malicious act of spite, trying to get a rise out of the very people who opposed an English Bible; as Latymer explains, Anne wanted the nuns, like the rest of the country, to understand what they were actually praying for, in order to be 'stirred to more devotion'.[382]

Alas, they flatly refused to let her in, because she was a married woman – a confusing stance, considering their loyalty to Katherine of Aragon and refusal to acknowledge Anne's marriage to Henry. Perhaps it was a subtle attempt at sarcasm? But proving once again that she was a dab hand at persuasion, Anne finally managed to talk her way inside, whereupon she gave the nuns a lecture in theology – and a stack of English prayer books.[383]

Clearly there's nothing like a fight against the clergy to bring a couple together, as by the time Henry and Anne returned to court in the autumn of 1535, she was pregnant again. The happy news was out in the open at Christmas, and Henry was so overjoyed that God was giving him another chance of salvation that he decided he was not going to risk putting this baby in harm's way. That meant there would be strictly no more sex between him and Anne; and as his affair with Margaret Shelton was now over, Henry's attentions turned to Anne's other cousin – the new girl at court, Jane Seymour.

Jane had accompanied the couple on summer progress, where a royal visit to her family home of Wolf Hall would have given her a brief moment to shine and come to everyone's attention, including that of the king. So once back in London, Henry embarked on his favourite court pastime: the lusty pursuit of a virgin. However, unbeknown to Anne, she herself was starting the inevitable countdown to her death in a little over five months' time.

CHAPTER 9

ANNE BOLEYN: THE HUMAN BEING

In arguing the case against the censorship of evidence surrounding Anne Boleyn's life, it would be easy for me to risk giving an uneven character profile. While focusing on proving the truth behind the lies we may forget to acknowledge the human flaws that she inevitably possessed.

Well, not on my watch! Make no mistake, Anne Boleyn was no saint. Her excitability could often turn to cockiness. Her go-to trait was bravado when scared, overcompensating with arrogance when she found herself losing a fight. She would get angry when challenged and, good lord, we like an angry woman even less than a brazenly confident one.

If you have a problem, voice your opinion calmly, dear — don't shout and rant, it's not becoming of a fair maiden!

Yet although Anne's character and story have been staggeringly twisted and manipulated over the centuries, and subjected to sexist double standards that have us calling Cromwell's political work masterful while Anne's is labelled ruthless, I'm not here to dismiss all the bad. I'm not trying to explain away every negative report only to replace it with a happy, sunny, alternative version of events.

Instead, I am here to argue the case for *Anne Boleyn: the Human Being.*

This means she wasn't an infallible angel of virtuous perfection who should be worshipped at the altar of martyrdom; I'm not sure anyone on earth is worthy of such unbridled praise.

She was a complex multidimensional paradox – aren't we all? Yes, she had negative sides, and I'm not about to gloss over them to rehabilitate her image. That's not the purpose of this new analysis. In fact, in this chapter we are going to pick apart each and every flaw, every damning story we've heard, and every disappointing decision Anne Boleyn ever made, because a woman doesn't have to be perfect in order to be good.

It's the stories of Anne's short temper and sharp tongue that have had sceptics questioning how someone so angry at the world could also care about its people. But of the multiple reports of Anne cutting courtiers down to size, none have become as notorious as the story of her reaction in July 1532 to a priest who had been caught shaving gold clippings from coins to keep for himself. After the man was imprisoned by Henry VIII, Thomas Boleyn is said to have waded into the issue, asking Anne to spare him; at which point she rounded on her father, tearing into him for trying to save the man, declaring there were already too many priests in England.[384] The man was subsequently executed.

Now, this story leaves a bad taste for me. His was such a minor crime, and Anne had always been 'for the people', so how could she not step in and stop his death over such a petty theft?

Or have I just hit the nail on the head here?

Anne *was* for the people. Her whole fight was against the clergy who had been taking advantage of the people for their own financial gain, and here was yet another priest highlighting the corruption of the Church with an act of greed. In which case, should we really be surprised that his story riled Anne rather than tugged at her heartstrings? Of course, when her conscience kicked in, she hid behind the Boleyn bravado, throwing out her cocky retort about there being too many priests and stubbornly refusing to back down.

It's not a pretty trait, nor an endearing one. But this is what happens when you are presented with a human being rather than a fictional character. There are going to be ugly traits that come to light, stories that don't play out as we hoped they would. Human beings have this nasty habit of disappointing us, and I'm afraid Anne Boleyn is no different. Though we can perhaps start to understand why she reacted the way she did, there's still no doubt she should have helped, and it was searingly hypocritical of her not to.[385]

But what of those stories closer to home and Anne's treatment of her own sister, Mary Boleyn? In the summer of 1534, widowed six years earlier following William Carey's death from the sweating sickness, Mary caused a stir when she appeared at court, married . . . and pregnant.

Anne was stunned by Mary's blatant disregard for her position as sister to the queen of England. Not only had she broken with sixteenth-century royal protocol and married without the king's consent (even today's monarch must give consent up to the sixth in line to the throne), but Mary had married staggeringly beneath her status. Ives describes her new husband, William Stafford, as 'one of the hangers-on at court and second son of minor Midlands gentry', while elsewhere he is called 'a poor soldier with no prospects'.[386]

From Anne's reaction, it's clear she thought Mary's next marriage should have been an opportunity for a political or religious alliance. But here Anne shows what a blinkered outlook she had on life, for she failed to comprehend that not everyone was ready to lay down their life for the greater good. For Mary's part, she was no doubt sick of hearing about the bloody cause and simply wanted to be happy. But Anne couldn't understand such a notion; to be driven by personal desire rather than duty and morals was inconceivable. Which explains why she saw Mary's actions as irresponsible and careless.

So, Anne did what siblings do best and lashed out, thoroughly overreacting to the situation by banishing Mary from court, just as she herself had been banished years before.

But where some historians will purposefully mislead readers by concluding, 'Mary was obliged to stay away from court'[387] – after all, this was meant to be the climax of a long-running feud between the sisters, wasn't it? – you might be surprised to find that this is not how the story ended.

Not only did Anne, realising she'd been too harsh, bring Mary back to court soon after their argument, she also attended to her sister whilst in confinement during her final weeks of pregnancy.[388] This may sound like a surprising turnaround but not when we discover there is a lot more to the sisters' story than history cares to inform us; for example, when Mary's first husband died in 1528 leaving her in extreme financial difficulty, not only did Anne pay her a regular allowance but she personally took on Mary's son as her own ward[389] – something I imagine is rarely advertised for fear of ruining the infamy of their apparent feud. Anne also fell out with Wolsey while fighting to help Mary's sister-in-law, Eleanor Carey, gain the prestigious role of abbess of Wilton.[390] She even spent Christmas 1531 with Mary, and went on to take her sister as a personal companion on the fateful Calais trip shortly before her wedding.

Oh, bugger. We were meant to be highlighting Anne's shortcomings as a sister, and the truth just can't help but pop up and ruin that too. Perhaps, then, we should take a look at Anne's actions with her younger sibling, George, for it's when this excitable pair got together that we often hear of a jarring insensitivity in her personality.

Anne and George had what sounds like an incredibly close bond, heightened by the isolation the Tudor court could bring. But the two had fun. You wanted to be in their gang, yet it seems they rarely trusted others enough to let them in. Safe inside their little bubble, they appeared to be unaware of how their in-jokes and banter could make those on the outside feel. It was George's wife, Jane, who would go on to accuse the two of mocking everything from the king's clothing to his attempts at poetry.[391] While their teasing shows a certain degree of immaturity, it does still sound like the kind of playful family banter you might expect to find in any household, so perhaps not really worthy of our outrage. But what of the more serious accusations that Anne mocked Henry's virility, prompting George to question whether Elizabeth was indeed the king's child? Though quite the controversial subject to be mocking in the Tudor court, this appears to be the Boleyn black humour covering up a much deeper concern.

For Anne, her husband having problems in the bedroom was no laughing matter. Everything depended on them conceiving a son, all too aware was she of the very real and dire consequences of not producing an heir to the throne. So, it's highly doubtful that the siblings' conversation about Henry's performance in bed was one of malicious mockery, as it's all too often interpreted, but one of grave concern.

Not that this meant Anne turned to incest to remedy the problem, as she has been accused of, particularly as her brother had even less success at conceiving than Anne, with he and his wife never having children in all the years they were married.

Though these incidents hardly reveal endearing personality traits, I feel they are forgivable in the grand scheme of Anne's life. Who has not acted badly towards a family member, only to regret it later? Though, granted, failing to intervene in a man's execution may be somewhat less relatable for us.

But I'm fully aware these are not the reasons readers struggle to bond with Anne Boleyn. You don't know how many times I've heard people say things like, 'I *would* feel sorry for Anne but I simply can't after the way she treated Katherine and Mary!'

Not that I blame them, as some of the most popular 'six wives' biographies would have readers believe that Anne pursued the crown only to spend her reign tormenting Katherine and Mary purely for kicks. And while evidence thus far proves this is clearly not the case, we nevertheless have an abundance of nasty little stories to pick through when it comes to Katherine that are not all so easy to dismiss.

It's said that in 1534, Katherine was upset when she was told she could only hold her Maundy service as 'princess dowager' rather than queen. But Anne is credited with the extra touch of stopping the poor from approaching Katherine's home, believing her charity to be the only reason for Katherine's remaining popularity.

That Anne would stop anyone helping the poor when it was a cause that meant so much to her feels faintly ridiculous. But as I said, I'm not here to gloss over the accusations, so let's consider that Anne *did* advise Henry that he should put a stop to Katherine's charitable giving to hurt her popularity. It would have been a petty victory and a spiteful act that Anne had not fully thought through, losing sight of the fact that the only people she would really be hurting were those who needed help.[392]

It should probably be pointed out that a good number of the derogatory stories you are about to hear about Anne come from Chapuys, Katherine of Aragon's loyal Spanish ambassador and friend. As I've mentioned previously, the majority of his letters are extremely biased against Anne Boleyn, for obvious reasons, so we have to wade through the defamation and gossip to reach the probable truth behind little stories like Anne supposedly demanding Katherine's jewels so she could wear them herself.[393] As Anne's anger built with Katherine's refusal to take a dignified step back, were these the actions of a frustrated new wife caught up in her husband's bitter divorce battle? Or is it a case of Anne being blamed for Henry's own actions – a safe alternative to directly criticising the king?

But to be honest, these stories seem rather petty when in October 1534 came the more serious accusation that Princess Mary suspected Anne was working with members of her household to cause her 'bodily hurt'. Now this is something that needs clearing up.

It is Cromwell who admits in writing: 'True, it is that the King has occasionally shown displeasure at the Princess' and that 'some of the king's Privy Councillors who, imagining they were doing pleasure to [Anne], put forward certain measures and plans to the Princess's great disadvantage.'[394]

So not only is Cromwell solely blaming Henry here, he is also stating that no harm was ordered by Anne. It's also worth pointing out that at this particular time she was recovering from her devastating miscarriage at eight months, while also dealing with the attack on her marriage from the Imperial Lady. So I will leave it to the reader to decide if she would have simultaneously been scheming up ways to hurt her stepdaughter.

But stories like these cannot hold a candle to the most heartless and offensive tale of them all – that Anne wore yellow in celebration of Katherine's death. Somewhat more distasteful on Anne's part than jewels and alms, I'd say. So, is it true?

There was but one written account at the time, and that came from Chapuys. Well, nothing shocking there. He hated Anne and loved Katherine, taking any opportunity to highlight how evil Anne supposedly was towards her. In which case, you might be interested to hear that Chapuys did *not* say that Anne wore yellow, nor celebrated her death.

The king, yes, but not Anne.

Chapuys writes in his letter of 21 January 1536: 'You could not conceive the joy that the King and those who favour [Anne] have shown at the death of the good Queen . . . The King, on the Saturday he heard the news, exclaimed "God be praised that we are free from all suspicion of war."'[395]

This reaction certainly sounds more Henry than the unlikely and contradictory reports that he cried when he heard the news of her passing. (Unlikely for the simple fact that we know a sociopath does not have a conscience and therefore lacks the emotional capacity to experience such heartfelt grief.)

Chapuys continues:

> On the following day, Sunday, the King was clad all over in yellow, from top to toe, except the white feather he had in his bonnet, and the Little Bastard [three-year-old Elizabeth] was conducted to mass with trumpets and other great triumphs. After dinner the King entered the room in which the ladies danced, and there did several things like one transported with joy. At last he sent for his Little Bastard, and carrying her in his arms he showed her first to one and then to another. He has done the same on other days since, and has [jousted] at Greenwich.[396]

So, what do we make of the fact that Chapuys's extensive reports don't even mention Anne?

If she had been wearing yellow or celebrating or parading Elizabeth around, then Chapuys would have been lamenting her insensitivity as he always did. But nothing. Not one indication that Anne was even present at the celebrations.

Instead, Chapuys was alleged to have reported the unsavoury reactions of Anne's father and brother, 'the earl of Wiltshire and his son, who said it was a pity the Princess [Mary] did not keep company with [Katherine]'. Meaning they wished she had died too. However, as Chapuys's biographer recently revealed, this was a mistranslation in the *Letters and Papers, Foreign and Domestic, of the Reign of Henry VIII*; in Chapuys's original report he simply speculates that Thomas and George 'must have said to themselves, what a pity it was that the princess [Mary] had not kept her mother company'.[397]

But still no mention of Anne. Could that be because she behaved respectably? Or even refused to take part in these 'celebrations'?[398]

The only other sixteenth-century report that claims it was in fact Anne who wore yellow and not the king was written by the English chronicler and lawyer Edward Hall, who published his own account of what happened six years later in 1542. By this time Anne was long dead and the anti-Boleyn propaganda was in full swing, so it's easy to see why Chapuys's original eyewitness account got twisted so that Anne was the insensitive one wearing yellow and not the king.[399]

Towards the end of Chapuys's report we finally come to the only mention of Anne in this entire letter, which spans several days' worth of reports, explaining that she sent Mary a message via her governess 'that if she would lay aside her obstinacy and obey her father, [Anne] would be the best friend to her in the world and be like another mother, and would obtain for her anything she could ask, and that if she wished to come to court she would be exempted from [serving her]'.[400]

Perhaps not the most delicate olive branch Anne could have held out at such a sensitive time, if those were indeed her exact words; but the point is that this is all Chapuys has to say about Anne's initial response to Katherine of Aragon's death – and it is that of a caring parent, not an evil stepmother.

Eight days after writing this, Chapuys was desperately hunting for any hint that Anne reacted disrespectfully following Katherine's death, and indeed he finds it, writing that '[Anne] showed great joy at the news of the good Queen's death, and gave a good present to the messenger who brought her the intelligence'.

But you know it's flimsy evidence when even Chapuys is forced to admit that he heard this 'from various quarters, though I must say none sufficiently reliable'.[401]

Of course, the Spanish ambassador's doubts regarding Anne's reaction are never brought to readers' attention, in order to manipulate their opinions of the cold-hearted fairy-tale villain.

While the evidence here proves Anne did not react in the way we've been told, I have the niggling suspicion that some may remain adamant that *of course Anne celebrated if Henry did!* And given I was all set to explain Anne wearing yellow when I discovered she didn't, let's play devil's advocate for a moment and imagine these rumours were true: what would cause Anne to make such a poor choice in celebrating Katherine's death? Indeed, there would be no excusing this extreme lapse in judgement. Yet it would be quite easy to understand the psychology behind it. By the time Katherine died, she would have come to represent everything Anne was fighting against, while simultaneously being held up as the exemplar of everything she herself was not. And so Anne would have essentially dehumanised Katherine in her mind.

Dr Kevin Dutton explains:

> When we dehumanise others we deliver a shot of anaesthetic to our conscience to render cruel or hurtful behaviour painless. Anne would have had to subconsciously create a feeling of psychological distance to Katherine's death, and so reduced her to a status where she couldn't feel for her.[402]

Indeed, I would say this is why Princess Mary was said to have reacted with similar glee to Anne's own death later that year. They had all dehumanised each other to the point where they no longer saw their enemies as people but as vermin to be exterminated.

Which leads us neatly to the other rumour – that Anne was the one who killed Katherine. Any guesses as to how she was meant to have taken out her nemesis?

Yes, poisoning! Who saw that accusation coming?!

A post-mortem revealed that Katherine's heart was black, leading Chapuys to suspect foul play and, of course, Anne Boleyn. Yet, modern medical knowledge suggests this was more likely a sign that poor Katherine died of cancer.[403] Chapuys even admits in his letter that 'several of them confess, and even keep on saying that grief was the cause of [Katherine's] death, [and] to exclude suspicion of anything worse'.[404] He then immediately follows this up with the contrasting report that Anne had 'nevertheless, cried and lamented, herself on the occasion, fearing lest she herself might be brought to the same end as [Katherine]'. This in itself disproves his theory that Anne was responsible for Katherine's death, for if she were, she wouldn't be worried that she might be next. She was hardly going to poison herself now, was she?

Yes, it appears Chapuys gets lost in his own accusations at this point, but it must be said that he himself was severely grief-stricken at Katherine's death. He was trying to gather as much intelligence as possible, and all these contrasting reports are simply the various rumours that were swirling around court in the days following Katherine's passing. So, we can forgive him for not thinking straight, which might explain why he also failed to pick up on the fact that Anne seemed pretty surprised at the death of someone she was meant to have killed herself. Not only that, but the timing made no sense: why kill her now? Why not before Anne's marriage, when Katherine was a real obstacle? Why not shortly after, when the legitimacy of her marriage was in question? Besides, in the final months of her own life, as you will soon see, Anne had bigger things to focus on than her husband's banished ex-wife.

So, it appears that most stories of Anne Boleyn's cruelty towards Katherine have no real basis in fact, bar some possible ill-judged attempts at taking her jewellery and stopping her alms; however, it appears there is no escaping Anne's dealings with Henry's daughter Princess Mary. And herein lies Anne's real guilt and fault in character.

Mary was said to be as stubborn as Katherine when it came to accepting Anne, but this was no mere teenage rebellion from the royal seventeen-year-old. Mary would never accept Anne, not only out of loyalty to her ousted mother but for the plain and simple fact that she saw Anne as a heretic. Both she and her mother believed it was God's will for Katherine to be queen of England, Mary to be princess and Catholicism to reign supreme; meaning Mary's fight against her father and his new wife was motivated by her desperation to correct his sacrilegious mistake in depriving them of the throne.[405]

It also didn't help that from an early, impressionable age Mary was taught some pretty disturbing views by Spanish scholar Juan Luis Vives, such as that women were God's only imperfect creations, 'the devil's instrument and not Christ's'.[406] Charming! He advocated the whole 'women should be seen and not heard'; even then he wasn't such a great supporter of them being seen, saying they should be entirely covered when leaving the house. So it's not surprising that Mary was horrified beyond belief when evangelicals like Anne heralded new, liberated religious reform.

However, we have multiple accounts of Anne reaching out to her stepdaughter in order to make peace, all of which fly in the face of modern claims that Anne didn't approve of Henry visiting Mary and would apparently 'throw a tantrum' whenever he suggested it.[407] Even from a cynical point of view, to get Mary's approval for their marriage would help win over the Catholic faction at court and at large, so it made sense for Anne to treat Mary with honour and respect.

Admittedly, that didn't always go to plan.

The first recorded attempt at a reconciliation came nine months after Anne's coronation, in March 1534. When visiting Elizabeth at Eltham Palace, where she lived with Mary, it's reported by Chapuys that Anne 'urgently solicited [Mary] to visit her and honour her as queen, saying that it would be a means of reconciliation with the King' vowing Mary would be 'better treated than ever' if she did.[408]

Even though Mary came back with the reply that she knew no queen in England except her mother, Anne kept her cool and persisted, repeating the offer during the same visit. But when she continued to hit a brick wall, her restraint failed her and Anne's anger issues burst to the surface, apparently threatening to 'bring down the pride of this unbridled Spanish blood'.[409] Ah. And she started off so well.

Another well-documented yet undated attempt comes courtesy of *The Life of Jane Dormer*. Once again, while visiting Elizabeth at Eltham Palace, Anne heard Mass with Mary. However, unbeknown to Anne,

Mary was said to have acknowledged her with a curtsey as she left. When one of Anne's maids informed her of this, she immediately sent Mary a messenger, who explained:

> The queen salutes your grace with much affection and craves pardon . . . if she had seen [your curtsey] she would have answered you with the like; and she desires that this may be an entrance of friendly correspondence which [the queen] shall find to be completely embraced on her part.[410]

But Mary now responded by asking how the queen could have sent this message, as she was 'so far from this place', meaning, once again, that her mother was the only woman she recognised as queen; in other words, she threw Anne's olive branch back in her face.

With patience wearing thin – and Anne wasn't too good at keeping her temper under control at the best of times – the same source reports that Anne was 'maddened' by Mary's rude response. So it's becoming clear that here is a woman who would have benefited greatly from a course in anger management, her bouts of diplomatic restraint continuously wrestling with the overwhelming urge to fly off the handle.

Interestingly, Chapuys appears to report on one of her moments of attempted sensitivity when Mary fell ill later in September 1534, saying, 'The King sent his own physician to visit her, and permitted . . . her mother's . . . apothecary who has been her medical adviser for the last three years, should also be in attendance; which . . . has considerably helped to her recovery.'[411]

Considering that Anne is often accused of being behind the king's actions should we, by the same logic, presume she was behind this too? Or is it just the nasty and spiteful incidents that she was secretly responsible for? Perhaps in order to come to the most likely conclusion here we should ask ourselves if this sounds like the caring actions of a kind-hearted sociopath, or the maternal instinct of a stepmother keen to make amends after an argument?

Anne's final attempt at peace with Mary was, as we have just seen, following Katherine's death. As well intentioned as this may have been, the timing was probably not the best. Mary would have been overcome with grief, and now here was her wicked stepmother offering to take her mother's place. It's not surprising Mary lashed out and rejected her once again.

Did Anne take this raw emotion into account?

Of course she didn't. She just saw it as yet another unreasonable rebuff after she had gone out of her way to be kind. Which is why Anne fired off an angry and somewhat misjudged letter to Mary's governess Lady Shelton, telling her to stop pushing Mary closer to the king if Mary was so opposed to it, explaining that 'What I have done has been more for charity, for if I have a son, as I hope shortly, I know what will happen to her' and that 'considering the word of God, to do good to one's enemy, I wished to warn her beforehand' because she had 'daily wisdom' of the king's thoughts.[412]

We will see all too soon exactly what Anne's ominous warning of the king's actions related to. But for now, she ended her final letter with the usual go-to trait when hurt: that brash Boleyn bravado, saying she didn't *need* Mary and Mary couldn't hurt her anyway, so there![413]

On 29 January, Chapuys reports how Mary read Anne's letter and 'has been laughing ever since'.[414]

So it would appear that Anne dealt with Mary as immaturely as Mary dealt with Anne. Even though Anne evidently had moments of approaching her stepdaughter with delicacy and understanding, she was too quick to lash out in anger when her attempts to heal the situation were thrown back at her.

Of course, when added to the fact that Anne considered the young princess an 'enemy', you might be inclined to think she was viewing her stepdaughter in a somewhat overly dramatic light. But when put in the context of the times, we need to realise that Mary was always seen as more than a disobedient stepdaughter; she represented the potential threat of a Catholic uprising against Anne's 'heretical' evangelical mission. Though isolated, Mary was no powerless young girl. As the daughter of the former queen, most saw her as the rightful heir to the Tudor throne who had the might of the Holy Roman Empire behind her. Anne had to take Mary's threat of rebellion very seriously – a truth that often gets lost when the Tudor monarchs receive the soap opera treatment.

So if Mary was a genuine enemy, does that mean Anne was guilty of the other accusations – that she humiliated the girl and deliberately made her life a misery? Or would she have not risked antagonising her in such a spiteful way?

The king had already banned Mary from seeing her mother in an attempt to weaken their resolve to fight their demotion in the royal household. Some may assume Anne supported this decision, possibly in the belief that she had a better chance of winning Mary round without Katherine poisoning her ear with stories of her 'scheming stepmother'. There are, unsurprisingly, those who believe that Anne bullied the king into separating mother and daughter against his will – beleaguered and browbeaten husband that he was – in order to hurt and isolate them for not stepping aside quietly.

After all, when Anne's daughter, Elizabeth, replaced Mary as princess, we're told Mary was made to serve in her little sister's household as lady-in-waiting, conjuring up images of a Cinderella figure slaving away for her evil half-sister. (You know how history loves a good fairy tale.) But away from the fables, what truth is there in these reports?

It was in Chapuys's 1533 account of the latest court gossip where he wrote that 'I hear [Anne] has lately boasted that she will make of the Princess a maid of honour in her Royal household . . . or marry her to some varlet.'[415]

Can we pause a moment here and ask if we really believe Anne was planning to marry the king's daughter off to a member of the household staff? This was clearly a joke. And so too must be the quip about making her serve as a maid of honour. We've even just read a quote from 1536 where Anne specifically reassures Mary she would *not* serve in her household – perhaps indicating that she realised her silly remarks three years earlier had become the stuff of court legend and wanted to reassure her stepdaughter.

Yet Anne's wisecracks were jumped on with all the gravity of attempted murder, not just by Chapuys but by modern-day historians who have called them 'vulgar threats'.[416] But why let rationale get in the way of a salacious and dramatic plot point – even if it is meant to be a non-fiction biography. In actual fact, Mary was never made to serve Elizabeth, nor was she given any formal title of lady-in-waiting or maid of honour. Her main indignity was the loss of status. But far from her newborn half-sister ordering her to do chores, this merely meant things like Mary being asked to take her meals with the rest of the household – something she flatly refused to do, which consequently had a detrimental effect on her health.[417]

So, in light of this, and considering that royal protocol meant both Elizabeth and Mary were separated from their mothers, could it have been more that Anne thought it might be a comfort for the two sisters to grow up together with each other for company? Or perhaps, slightly more cynically, that she thought living with her baby sister might thaw Mary's iciness when it came to her new family set-up? Of course, the two girls lodging together at Eltham Palace could have simply been a convenience for when the king and queen came to visit and we're all just overthinking this! But that's probably far too boring an idea to contemplate. Let's discuss a death threat, pronto.

We've seen Anne throw around retorts to 'bring down the pride of this Spanish blood', along with many reports of her lashing out with other hot-headed empty threats, such as wishing 'all Spaniards at the bottom of the sea'.[418] While the king was away in France, Anne even once huffed that she wanted to have Mary killed while he was gone. *You know, quick, while he's not looking!*

However, when George tried to make light of his sister's controversial remarks by informing her that Henry wouldn't be best pleased, Anne retorted she didn't care if she would burn for it.[419] Now, does a rational mind take this seriously and believe that she was willing to die for the sake of murdering a stroppy teenager? Or are we to hazard a guess that this was Anne's dark and inappropriate sense of humour?

The fact of it was that if Charles V could storm Rome and kidnap the pope, or hold Francis I and his two young children hostage, he wouldn't think twice about launching an attack on England for the murder of his cousin Mary or aunt Katherine. This would appear to be all the proof we need that Anne's off-the-cuff remarks about wanting Mary dead were simply that damn Boleyn bravado once again.

Yet there is one statement Anne was meant to have said about Mary that feels more sinister than the empty death threats and bolshie retorts we have seen so far: 'She is my death and I am hers.' Considering this was reported a mere six months before Anne's execution, it may have been one of the few times she was deadly serious. Although we may question if she even said it at all, once we hear the source.

Charles V's representative Dr Ortiz said in a letter on 22 November 1535, '[Anne] has often said of [Mary] "She is my death and I am hers; so I will take care that she shall not laugh at me after my death."'[420]

However, I am tempted to believe the truth of this if only because while, no, neither Anne or her supporters tried to kill Mary . . . Mary's supporters *did* succeed in killing Anne, proving that for all Anne's 'big talk', her stepdaughter was indeed the dangerous one.

As we've touched on, when it comes to Henry's mistreatment of his ex-wife and child, such as sending Katherine to inhospitable castles to coerce her into submission, it has become standard practice to blame Anne as the brutish mastermind behind all his evil doings. As though the formidable force of nature that was King Henry VIII was a nervous child goaded and bullied daily by Anne Boleyn. A man who lived in fear of a good telling-off if he didn't carry out her senseless list of cruelties.

Here the melodrama of popular history threatens to become faintly ridiculous, so we need to bring it back to the bare facts – the most obvious being that Henry went on to carry out terrible acts of evil long after Anne had stopped supposedly whispering in his ear. This being due to the fact that the hapless and innocent king had decapitated her.

The best piece of evidence for this shortly followed Anne's death. In order for Mary to be welcomed back to the Tudor court, Henry demanded his daughter sign a document recognising him as the supreme head of the Church of England, and also accepting her own illegitimacy and the invalidity of her parents' marriage.

When Mary refused, Henry commenced plans for her to be tried for treason, which would have ended in the execution of his own daughter. Suddenly, those who helped in bringing down Anne Boleyn were targeted themselves, interrogated and imprisoned in the Tower.[421] Understanding the perilous position she and her supporters were in, Mary reluctantly signed the document, bullied into submission at last; at which point, Henry welcomed her back into the fold with open arms, as any loving, mentally unstable father would.

It is here he scolded the courtiers who were watching their tearful reunion, saying, 'Some of you were desirous that I should have put this jewel to death.'[422]

Upon hearing this admission, Mary is said to have fainted with shock. Evidence, if we really needed any more, that somewhat ruins the rhetoric that Henry 'was an affectionate man, happy to dote upon his children'.[423] Until they defied him – at which point he might murder them.

Yes. Such an affectionate and doting father.

Regardless of where you stand on this whole debate, it's interesting to note that Mary never came close to harm while Anne Boleyn was alive – it was only *after* Anne was dead and, some might argue, no longer there to protect her that she came perilously close to death. It's possible that due to this, Mary might have come to finally realise – granted, all too late – that her father's treatment of her and her mother wasn't so much Anne's doing after all.

◆ ◆ ◆

The stories and reports we've heard of Anne Boleyn up until now apparently cause confusion; the fun-loving flirt, the charitable activist, the frustrated new wife, the caring humanitarian, the abrasive boss, the religious warrior, the harsh sister, the loving mother.

Which one was she? Who was the real Anne Boleyn?

Allow me to let you in on a secret: she was all of them. Anne Boleyn can't be boxed into a neat little category of saint or sinner. It's these jarring contrasts and juxtapositions that reveal her to be a real and complex person as opposed to a flat fictional character. But because of these human flaws, perhaps one of the most disturbing conclusions to Anne's life and, ultimately death, is the belief that the new queen had it coming – a view that is common currency even today.

If only she hadn't been so ferocious. A little more 'grateful and gracious' – the exact words Chapuys expressed to Cromwell the day before her arrest.[424]

Well, excuse the crass analogy, but Anne Boleyn was no reality show contestant needing to be humble as well as talented in order to reach the semi-finals. She was a monumental queen in British history. We don't berate the pope for his lack of people skills when it comes to politics, and we rarely judge the likes of Charles V on his personality; the majority only note the historic impact his reign had on Europe. Yet with Anne Boleyn, we have to want to have been her best friend, or she was a bitch who deserved downfall and decapitation.

When she won victories, yes, she got overexcited and cocky; when she clashed with family, yes, she overreacted immensely. When frustrated and betrayed she would turn on that obnoxious bravado, fighting back harder for what she believed was right. She wasn't subtle; she was a bulldozer trying to achieve good. And the more she faced opposition, the louder, angrier and more abrasive she got.

Was this the right way to achieve things? Maybe not. Should she have learned better people skills from her father, the consummate diplomat? Most definitely. But for Anne, even he represented the stuffy ways of the past. She wanted to represent the future, and so her overeagerness to change the world sometimes rubbed people up the wrong way and did not always come across in the manner she intended. But we need to realise that, away from the vamped-up drama Anne Boleyn's story has now become, being human isn't a character fault worthy of euthanisation.

CHAPTER 10

THE COUNTDOWN TO ANNE'S ARREST

As all Tudor biographies reach 1536 the reader knows what's coming. In under five months Anne Boleyn will be dead. As the weeks tick by, we search for signs of what catastrophic events could possibly have led to the unprecedented murder of the queen of England. By now it seems painfully clear how Henry VIII could order the death of the woman he was meant to have been passionately in love with for the past decade; the sociopath without a conscience could plot her demise without flinching. The only thing is, he wasn't actually part of the conspiracy to frame her. The evidence we are about to discover proves the king didn't have any hand in Anne's takedown until the final days, when he called for her arrest and the death warrant had to be signed.

And so the countdown begins to Anne's execution on 19 May.

Following the previous summer's religious activism around the country, the fact that his wife was pregnant again gave the king hope that God was finally to bless him with a son and heir to his progressive new monarchy.

Yet, for Anne, as much as her pregnancy brought her reassurance and security, it also brought back deep-rooted fears as Henry sought his sexual kicks elsewhere while she was busy incubating the saviour of the kingdom. This meant the king suddenly fell prey to every Imperial Lady-wannabe at court, hoping to recreate her success at driving a wedge between the king and his evangelical wife. But Anne's cousin, the demure and unassuming Jane Seymour, was all too happy to step in and help keep him onside.

There was just one problem: Jane Seymour was not on Anne's side.

Jane was as devout a Catholic as she was fiercely loyal to Katherine and Mary, and suddenly it was déjà vu as Anne saw Henry fall for the charms of a young woman in her service who was out to ruin her. But this time the rules were about to change in favour of the imperial faction.

On 7 January 1536 the entire court, and indeed England and Europe, was rocked by the news that Katherine of Aragon had died. We've already seen how overjoyed Henry was at this, showing that he hadn't fully considered all the potential repercussions of his ex-wife no longer challenging the crown.

With Henry's former queen out of the picture, Princess Mary and her supporters suddenly saw themselves that much closer in their fight for Mary to outrank Anne's daughter, Elizabeth, as next in line to the throne. Think about it: while before, if Henry were to concede and place Mary back in the line of succession, it would mean him acknowledging his marriage to Katherine was valid. Something he would never do. But now, with Katherine gone, it was only a simple matter of relegitimising Mary in Parliament – which, incidentally, he did go on to do with both Mary and Elizabeth in his lifetime.

On top of that, all Mary's supporters who did not recognise the king's marriage to Anne believed that Katherine's death left Henry free to remarry. So the game had abruptly changed for the anti-Boleyn/anti-reformist faction at court. Anne would have been made all too aware of this by her diplomat father, who was fully in the loop with the delicate intricacies of international politics. So, does this explain Anne's absence from any celebrations of her enemy's death? Either way, it should serve as final proof against the theory that Anne poisoned Katherine, because her death placed Anne in a more perilous situation than ever before.

This much was made abundantly clear when, following Katherine's death, de Carles tells us Anne woke one day to a fire in her rooms. This story has been twisted since to insinuate that she had left a candle burning after 'entertaining a lover' through the night, but the timing points to it being something much more ominous. Was it a threat, a warning, or a real attempt on her life disguised as an accident? We'll never confirm the culprit's true intent, but I'm inclined to think it was the former: someone wanted Anne to know that she should be scared, and by all accounts it worked, with the queen clearly shaken that she and her unborn baby only narrowly escaped death.[425]

But things were about to get much worse. Mere weeks later, on 24 January 1536, Henry suffered his infamous and incredibly serious jousting accident.

Chapuys and Wriothesley both reported that even though the king 'fell so heavily that everyone thought it a miracle he was not hurt and killed'[426] and that Anne 'took a fright', they concluded that the king 'had no hurt'[427] and 'sustained no injury'. The fact that both failed to report the wound on Henry's leg that would turn ulcerous in time, causing him chronic pain for the rest of his life, suggests they were downplaying the accident in order to help the king appear strong, fit and well to outsiders. It was only Charles V's representative Dr Ortiz who reported a more worrying version of events when he wrote 'the French king said that the king of England had fallen from his horse, and been for two hours without speaking', meaning he was unconscious.[428]

External injuries are one thing, but as we have learned, severe trauma to the head is one of the causes of sociopathy; so there's no denying this accident had an irrevocable effect on the king's mental health. Not that he was a well-balanced individual in the years leading up to this moment. Just look at the wording Chapuys used in his letter regarding Henry's fall, comparing it to that of 'the other tyrant'[429] who escaped death. To be considered a tyrant in the sixteenth century meant your actions must have stood out as particularly psychotic, it being arguably one of the most brutal eras in British history. Meaning that this head injury only served to amplify every factor of Henry's pre-existing mental illness: the anger, the impulsiveness, the detachment from those he was supposed to have loved. Inevitably, this was to have a fateful and fatal impact on his reaction to Anne's downfall in the coming months.

But Henry wasn't the only one to be affected by his accident, for the shock was just one trauma too many for Anne. It's believed the stress of slowly losing her husband to another mistress, paired with her own brush with death days earlier, followed by her uncle Norfolk's scaremongering announcement of Henry's fall caused Anne to miscarry her baby on 29 January – in fact, the very same day as Katherine of Aragon's funeral. A sad coincidence that is repeatedly played up for dramatic effect, insinuating this was Anne's haunting comeuppance for celebrating the death of the former queen.

There could not have been a worse time for Anne to lose her safety net of the boy heir Henry needed – which in itself has been the subject of much debate.

Chapuys reported the foetus 'seemed to be a male child which she had not borne 3½ months'.[430] Had fate delivered its cruellest hand in aborting what could have been the much sought-after male heir? Was the foetus *really* a boy? With Wriothesley confirming a similar age, fifteen weeks, would it have even been possible to tell the sex of the child at such an early stage? Experts give mixed reports, some saying it is possible to tell at as early as twelve weeks, with others saying not before nineteen.

Midwife Judith E. Lewis confirms you can sometimes tell the gender of a baby at around fifteen weeks, but not always, and it is possible to get it wrong, concluding, 'The midwife examining Anne's baby could have seen certain developments and made an educated guess.'

While biographer Wyatt claims the king came to Anne 'bewailing and complaining unto her the loss of his boy',[431] we also have slightly contrasting reports that he declared 'I see God will not give me male children',[432] hinting that he saw the baby and believed it to be a girl, or not yet formed and perhaps mistaking it for a girl. Indeed, it was the baby's lack of form that prompted Catholic propagandist Nicholas Sander to start the tasteless rumour, while in exile during Elizabeth I's reign, that it was a 'shapeless mass of flesh' – an attempt to insinuate that Anne had miscarried a deformed child, proving it to be the demonic result of an unnatural incestuous affair.[433] But as this was the same man who started the rumour that Henry VIII was Anne Boleyn's father, I think we know how seriously to take him.

Anne was understandably distraught at the loss of her baby. Indeed, Wyatt reports that both she and Henry were in 'extreme grief', which would explain why Anne was said to have lashed out and blamed Henry for the miscarriage, an accusation the king apparently 'took hardly'. It is here Henry 'was then heard to say to her: he would "have no more boys by her". With clear emphasis upon the word "her".'[434]

Things were deteriorating fast.

With rumours swirling of a breakdown in the royal marriage, the anti-Boleyn faction suddenly saw Henry as ripe for the picking. If ever there was an opportunity to strike and take Anne out, this was it. It was at this point that Jane Seymour was advised to change tack. If she played the situation right, she could have more than her five minutes of glory in the king's bed.

But this much we know. After all, it's this Tudor catfight, which saw the two cousins scratching each other's eyes out, that has garnered so much attention from historians of the Mills & Boon generation. And if this was all that was unfolding in the early months of 1536, Anne would have survived it, as she had before.

But in spite of, or perhaps because of the fact that Anne saw herself increasingly cornered into a factional checkmate and felt her days on the throne numbered, she stepped up her political work. But this time it was to be a radical, all-or-nothing, national takeover in the name of the people.

◆　◆　◆

Now, anyone in the perilous situation Anne was in at this point might toe the line a little, waiting for a safer moment to continue their campaigns. But not our Anne.

Although, to the outside world in the spring of 1536, that's exactly what it appeared she was doing when Tristram Revel tried to present her with a controversial English version of Francis Lambertus's *Farrago rerum theologicarum* via her chaplain William Latymer.

This work has been called 'dangerously radical', yet Anne apparently said she 'would not trouble herself' with it.[435] Some historians have used this uncharacteristic response as final proof that she couldn't have been a true evangelical, and that therefore this was never the motivation behind her reign.

To put an end to that myth once and for all, allow me to point out several vital pieces of information. Firstly, Lambertus's book denied the sacrifice of Mass, something Anne Boleyn did not. So her reluctance to promote the book merely confirms, once again, that she was a *moderate reformer* who still believed in key practices of Catholicism.

As with all religious movements, there will always be radical offshoots (groups like the Anabaptists were notorious radicals at the time). Indeed, Revel had found himself under investigation in February of that year for his work, and so the evangelicals championing moderate reform had to be very careful as to whom they were seen to support, as they believed it was this kind of extremism that threatened to derail their own movement.[436]

Secondly, it must be pointed out that Revel first sent his controversial translation to Archbishop Cranmer and his brother, Edmund, the archdeacon of Canterbury, and to Hugh Latimer and William Latymer, all of whom declined to support the book before Anne said no herself.[437] But is these men's faith called into question on the basis of their refusals? Of course not. Only Anne's.

So don't be fooled by those who try to tell you she was playing it safe, too scared to stand up for her religious beliefs when things got serious; for as we are about to see, she was preparing to do quite the opposite. At this pivotal time Anne was picking her battles wisely, choosing to focus on her political campaigns that were already underway, and one of the biggest has been covered up for centuries.

Whether sixteenth-century politics is your jam or not – you'd be forgiven if it's the latter – you cannot fail to have come across the very basics of Anne's fall: that she and Cromwell fell out over the dissolution of the monasteries. Out of the millions of pounds being raised, Anne believed the religious houses bringing in less than £200 a year (approximately £88,000 in today's currency[438]) should be used for educational purposes and as refuges for the poor.

But if Cromwell plotting the murder of a queen over several thousand pounds of government money has never felt like a satisfactory explanation, and perhaps somewhat excessive, you would be right in your suspicions – for I have discovered the real reason for their almighty falling-out. Only two months before her death, Anne was involved in passing nationwide legislation to combat poverty. With her power increasing and now interfering with government acts, this provided Cromwell with a much more devastating reason to kill the king's wife, the woman who had helped raise him to the position he was now in.

Throughout history, the infamous Tudor Poor Law that was passed in 1536 has been accredited to Thomas Cromwell, but it actually originated from an abandoned draft by William Marshall, a pamphleteer and ardent reformer to whom Anne Boleyn was patron.[439] This draft was based on a report of a similar scheme run in the city of Ypres in Flanders, which Marshall translated and dedicated to Anne Boleyn back in 1534. In his dedication he explicitly asked her to petition the king to launch the scheme in England.[440]

Not only did Anne successfully pitch this to the king but Henry instructed his now top man, Cromwell, to oversee the scheme's proposal in Parliament and subsequent launch. And this is where we come to that vital discarded draft of the original Poor Law scheme, the contents of which were astonishingly ambitious and ahead of its time – in fact, very similar to the national laws in place in Britain today. The document has been identified as written in the autumn of 1535, and it is stated twice within its pages that it was intended for Henry VIII's Parliament, which was to open on 4 February 1536 – four months before Anne Boleyn's assassination.[441]

Coming as he did from an underprivileged working-class background, I have no doubt Cromwell approved of the core values of the proposal; not just helping the poor, but more usefully putting them to work. Yes, a key part of the initiative would provide those who were out of work with jobs on community projects, such as repairing harbours and the country's defences – something that is backed up by Cromwell's own notes of potential local projects that could be worked on.[442]

However, as it would cost the Crown heavily to put this national scheme into place it appears the downsides far outweighed the good for Cromwell. For, you see, a major part of this proposed law was a radical Tudor version of the National Health Service: where sick people would get free medical care in order to get them well enough to work again.[443] But fear not, Tudor England was no nanny state, and would be much tougher on those who failed to turn up for the work the government provided them with: skivers would be jailed and upon release 'burned on the ball of their right thumb'![444]

And yet this was not the most excessive part of the Poor Law.

The original draft proposed a council of eight people to oversee extensive nationwide work, starting on the first day of the impending parliamentary Easter Term in 1536 in order to launch the following year. Also, all local government officials around the country would have to swear an oath that they would enforce the act in their cities and towns.[445] This was monumental. This was Anne Boleyn looking to form a council to rival the powers of the king's privy council.[446] There is no mistaking that this would have been a major threat to Cromwell. But no doubt he calmed his nerves with the reassurance that the likelihood of such a revolutionary law getting the backing of Parliament was pretty slim.

That was until the king himself came to the House of Commons on 11 March 1536 to personally introduce it, and promised to contribute to the cost of running the scheme.[447] Ah. Suddenly Cromwell was faced with the king fighting in Parliament for a law his wife and her patronee were pushing. Not only was Anne Boleyn now effectively working as a politician and involved in laws passed in the Commons, but she had got the king to agree to use all this new money pouring in from the dissolution of the monasteries to fund it.

So, when people speak of Anne and Cromwell clashing over how to spend the money raised by the dissolution of the monasteries, in missing out this vital information it has made his plot to murder her seem a little over the top. But now, I believe the story is complete. Is this widespread, not to mention incredibly expensive-sounding, Poor Law what Anne Boleyn wanted to spend the new money on? It would appear so. And even more dangerously, the king agreed with her.

But the scheme never saw the light of day; Anne and Marshall's proposal never got off the ground, with the most ambitious version of their draft abandoned.

So, what happened? Did Cromwell sabotage it in some way? Is that why he was happy to be in charge of the scheme, to make sure he could control it? We question the motives behind all Anne's good work, so in the name of fairness and equality let's apply the same measure to Cromwell. If he opposed Anne's wish to use the smaller monastery money for charity – a theory widely accepted by historians, I hasten to add – why would he be so happy about backing a scheme that would heavily rely on funding from the Crown? And we're no longer talking £200 per monastery; this would be hundreds of thousands of pounds in Tudor currency, if not millions.

So, did Cromwell encourage Marshall and Anne to make this law as radical and extreme as possible, so that it would obviously be rejected by Parliament? Because that's exactly what happened. Following the king's appearance at the Commons on 11 March, opposition to this expensive bill was said to be so great it had to be withdrawn almost immediately.[448]

But wait. It just so happened that Cromwell had another version of the Poor Law up his sleeve and ready to propose. So Marshall and Anne's scheme was quickly replaced with a drastically diluted version that has since been deemed pretty ineffectual by historians the world over.

Funny, though, that Cromwell should be ready and waiting with another act that would appease the king and make it appear that he was helping yet he really wasn't.

The Poor Law that was passed in 1536 simply stated that local officials should find work for the unemployed. The rest of the act focused on banning begging, setting up basic and optional donation boxes in parishes, and that churchwardens should collect alms every Sunday and national holiday. Oh, and older children refusing to work were to be whipped.

But most importantly this version was *minus* the proposed income tax. (If they were going to tax the people then it should fund wars, not go straight back to the people themselves, right?) Lo and behold, this new bill was also minus the funding from the Crown. Oh, and minus the rival council.

Fun fact: between 1532 and 1540, when Cromwell was at the height of his power at court, he saw a staggering 333 acts that he proposed passed in Parliament. This astounding figure proves one thing: if he wanted to get a law passed, he did.[449] Even sixteenth-century political expert G. R. Elton is perplexed by the mission's failure to launch, stating that 'the failure . . . is surprising, especially because the government of the 1530s did not usually fail when administrative reforms were called for.'

The thing is, we know the Poor Law wasn't Cromwell's brainchild, having first come from Marshall via Anne, with Cromwell merely assigned to oversee the scheme by the king. But if we needed any further proof that it was not 'Cromwell's Poor Law', as it's repeatedly called, then look no further than the abandoned document on which it was all based. For it has no official writer. After centuries of trying to identify the author of this incredible draft, historians have concluded that it could only have been Anne's client William Marshall. Not only that, but after comparing handwriting and syntax styles, it's been determined that it definitely could not have been written by Cromwell himself, nor the king, nor any of their official draftsmen. The language of the draft clearly indicates it was not written by a government official, and even the style of its parchment – folded in half like a book – indicates the writer was a private individual and was not used to drafting official documents.[450]

With his experience of translating the similar Ypres scheme, I'm not here to challenge William Marshall as the author of the document; I do believe it was him. But I am here to pose the obvious question in light of our new analysis of Anne Boleyn's work, and that is – did she also work directly on the draft? Even Foxe references her involvement in a scheme to provide work for the poor around the country.[451] It would be bizarre that Anne was passionate enough about Marshall's appeal to get the king and Cromwell involved, only for her then to leave her protégé to it, never taking any interest in the scheme again. Particularly when we have just learned how committed she was to providing poverty relief from within her own household.

Who do you think got the king to personally lobby for it in Parliament? Is this not exactly the sort of thing Anne had done many times before, having Henry intervene in international cases of amnesty?[452]

All the evidence leads us to conclude that Anne Boleyn was the driving force behind this radical new law – a law that history has accredited to Cromwell ever since. Not surprising, really. When removing all trace of Anne after her death, were they honestly going to credit the dead adulteress with a powerful and positive government law?

Sadly, the fate of the scheme was almost as pathetic as what remained of it. When it came to its second renewal in 1539, the Poor Law didn't get passed and was finally laid to rest once and for all.[453]

Well, who saw that coming? I really thought Cromwell was going to push for it this time.

Historians have been mystified, baffled even, as to why Cromwell couldn't get his own measly little law passed again a mere three years after his initial supposed victory.

Hmmm, I wonder why? He never wanted it to pass in the first place.

But Anne and Marshall's work was not entirely in vain, and interestingly enough the closest Tudor England was ever to get to their original scheme was a law implemented by none other than Anne's own daughter, Elizabeth I. Was she finishing what her mother tried to start? G. R. Elton indirectly alludes to this when he points out that parts of the Elizabethan Poor Law are replicated word for word from Marshall and Anne's 1535 abandoned draft document.[454] Did Elizabeth know full well that she was implementing her mother's last mission before she was murdered? For closure and comfort, we might like to think so.

Anne Boleyn's mission may have failed in March 1536, but for Cromwell this had clearly got way too close for comfort. Something had to be done about the queen.

In trying to piece together what went wrong, Anne must have quickly come to realise that far from working *with* her on the scheme, Cromwell had been working against her all along. Her suspicions were seemingly confirmed when on 2 April Cromwell opposed her call to use the smaller monasteries for charity and education, the very themes of the failed Poor Law. William Latymer tells us how Anne wanted to convert the smaller abbeys and priories into places of study and continual relief for the poor.[455] The monasteries had always been a refuge for the sick and destitute, from children who had been orphaned to widows who couldn't support their families; not only did they give these people vital support but they kept them off the streets and from turning to crime in order to survive. So, Anne saw the monasteries as vital to the people and the safety of the country. But it would seem Cromwell did not.

The important thing about the Reformation's dissolution act is that it had a clause whereby the king could save any monasteries he wished. So, with Anne calling for him to do just that, and Henry's eagerness to support her poverty schemes only the month before, this must have been a scary prospect for Cromwell.[456] He knew the Crown needed all the money it could get for his plans to modernise the country's defences. Hey, wars weren't cheap!

However, undoubtedly still reeling from Cromwell's last political betrayal, Anne was not about to let him get his way with this one, and so she directed her full vengeance and fury his way. In fact, she hit just about everyone with a few home truths – her husband included.

In a daring act of defiance, Anne commanded her almoner John Skippe to preach a controversial sermon to the royal congregation on Passion Sunday that read like a war cry against their dodgy dealings. This infamous sermon has now gone down in history owing to the mass controversy it created. Skippe chose John, Chapter 8, Verse 46,[457] and accused them all of following the king blindly for personal gain. At which point he used King Solomon as a barbed example of how he became 'un-noble' in his 'carnal appetite' for taking many wives and mistresses – a nice little dig at Henry's increasingly serious affair with Jane Seymour.[458]

Yet how do we know Skippe was preaching this message at Anne's command? Because, as Ives has correctly pointed out, no cleric in Anne's household would have dared say such things without her explicit approval.[459]

Skippe ploughed on to the main event: Anne's scathing attack on Cromwell. This time he gave the rather accurate example of Ahasuerus of Persia and his evil councillor Haman, who set out to destroy the Persian Queen Esther.[460] As Latymer tells us, Skippe spoke of the 'good woman (which this gentle king Ahasuerus loved very well and put his trust in because he knew that she was ever his friend) and she gave unto the king contrary counsel.'[461] He finished his sermon with a daring and direct warning to the king that he needed to be wary of his counsellors 'for the malice that they bare towards many men'.

Now, because the story used in Skippe's analogy ends with the evil councillor being killed, it has been concluded by many that Cromwell saw this as a direct threat, and that his subsequent destruction of Anne was merely a pre-emptive strike in self-defence.

But as we've seen, with the timing of the Poor Law and dissolution of smaller monasteries, Cromwell had already struck her twice. This sermon was Anne fighting back, and not a perfectly understandable reason as to why that downtrodden man we've seen in *Wolf Hall* might be compelled to kill a woman.

Anne wanted to show Cromwell she was not scared of him, and with Skippe preaching this message so publicly in front of king and court, this was her drawing the battle lines. She was ready to fight – and not sneakily behind closed doors; the extent of Cromwell's political duplicity meant the time had passed for subtle point-scoring. This sermon was a serious statement that she knew would have real implications. But at the same time, she might have also hoped the dramatic scriptural guilt trip would urge the councillors to rethink advising the king purely for personal gain. It was a bold and daring move that showed her true nerve.

Safe to say the sermon went down like a lead balloon, with Skippe accused of treason, malice and inciting anarchy.

But Anne Boleyn did not stop.

Almost as if she knew she was running out of time, she refused to be frightened into submission. So, she instructed her chaplain Hugh Latimer to preach a new sermon with the same message, discouraging the total destruction of all religious houses and imploring the king to put them to better use. And she went on and on. Over and over. Urging all other preachers to ensure their sermons included 'continual and earnest petitions' of the same nature.[462]

Then something amazing happened. A delegation of the country's abbots and priors came to Anne to ask for her protection. Yes, the Catholic clergy wanted to work with Anne Boleyn – the woman who has been sold to us as the ultimate morally corrupt she-devil of the sixteenth century. Yet the Church in 1536 was starting to wake up to the fact that Anne wasn't the dastardly party in England's version of the Reformation – but all that came a little too late.[463]

Anne was willing to try and help them, but that doesn't mean she was about to let them off the hook that easily; and so, she thoroughly ripped into the priests and all the corruption they had imposed on the people thus far.

Latymer doesn't give many details as to how this came about, who exactly Anne was speaking to and where, but my goodness, it has all the drama and pay-off of a Shakespearian play.[464] They say Anne had a sharp tongue, but I couldn't help but cheer her on as I read her rant to the Catholic priests that day. Now, bearing in mind that I am providing a modern translation of what is essentially Latymer's recollection of her words, nevertheless you get the gist of why Anne had been campaigning for reform all these years:

> I am convinced that the godly persons who first erected your foundations wanted their priests to be focused on God's glory and to help the learned. I know they would have wanted you to be pure and diligent professors of God's word and not enjoying that charity for yourselves. But it's been clear for the world to see just how negligent you have been in performing your role. As for me, I am deeply disappointed to see how stubbornly you have departed from God's true religion, forsaken your sovereign and most cowardly given in to the bishop of Rome, whose detestable sleights and frivolous ceremonies you have taken to be the pillar of your fantastical religion. Like hypocrites, you have fed your false superstitions to the unwitting congregation who know no better. You do not listen to the preachers of God's word and sit either idle or keeping yourselves busy in your cloisters, completely devoid of knowledge. Neither will you give any charity or fund students in universities in the hopes of them giving back to the congregation and indeed the country. So, know this, that in my opinion the dissolution of your houses is a deserved plague from Almighty God who abhors your lewdness and blind ignorance, and until you cleanse and purify your corrupt life and senseless doctrine, God will not cease to send his plagues upon you until your downfall and ruin.[465]

And with that Anne stormed out, leaving the men, as Latymer describes, 'betwixte fear and heaviness half dismayed'.

Needless to say, her dramatic speech had a positive effect – or, at least, scared them into action – and the men ended up 'most liberally offering to her grace large [payments] and exhibitions to be distributed yearly to preachers and scholars by the only assignment of her majesty'.[466]

◆ ◆ ◆

Towards the end of her life, as the situation became increasingly perilous, Anne saw her chaplains as her crew, her family, as allies she could rely on. People that she could genuinely trust were all working towards the same shared goal. And so, it's only right that in her lifetime she repaid their loyalty and work with promotions for all; as we've seen very early on, Cranmer became archbishop of Canterbury, then later Shaxton was given the see of Sarum and Foxe the bishopric of Hereford.[467] But it was Hugh Latimer's appointment as bishop of Worcester that was a particularly symbolic victory for the evangelicals, as only two years earlier it was the very same clergy of Worcester who had been trying to condemn him for heresy.[468] And though Skippe was not to take over the bishopric of Hereford until three years after Anne's death, it was he who visited her regularly while she was imprisoned in the Tower, showing just how close she considered him to be.[469]

In an emotional statement William Latymer said, 'Before it pleased God to call her out of this transitory life she expressed thoroughly the wonderful affection she bare the preachers and vigilant pastors of God's flock.'[470]

This was a carefully loaded pronouncement. Latymer's talk of the 'vigilant pastors' subtly implied that the officials who should have been looking out for the people's best interests weren't doing their job, and so it fell to reformist campaigners like Anne and her chaplains to put the pressure on the authorities to clean up their act.

As we've seen, the Reformation made fighters and rebels out of the straightest, most law-abiding citizens – those who at first tried to play nice by being polite and compliant. But in angering their opponents, they were each forced to choose: were they going to back down in submission or rise up and fight?

We witnessed this change in Martin Luther, and to varying degrees in Anne Boleyn and even Henry VIII.

None of them set out to be as radical as they became, but as each experienced what they saw as an injustice, they grew stronger, their voices getting louder and more threatening every time they were challenged. The idea of things continuing as they were was so unthinkable that they realised they had to act and take on a rebellious role they never sought to play.

So, if you're wondering what on earth came over Anne Boleyn in those final months of her life, what gave her the strength and courage to journey on when she was obviously playing with fire, it comes down to the natural instinct of fight or flight. This is also known as acute stress response, a theory first founded in the 1920s by the physiologist Walter Cannon in relation to an animal's reaction to threat, which has since been discovered to apply equally to humans. The body releases hormones to aid either running away from danger or staying to fight. And in this instance, Anne stayed to fight. It is this adrenaline rush that powered her on in the face of growing opposition.

It is also this exact same instinct that caused Cromwell to realise he had picked a fight with the woman who had helped get rid of Wolsey, the very man he had replaced. Cromwell knew he could not go the same way as his former master. But by April 1536, the essential difference between Anne and Cromwell's plans for each other was that Anne simply wanted to overpower her oppressor. Cromwell, on the other hand, decided he must kill her.

CHAPTER 11

The Part Where They Blame It All On Another Woman in History

Over the years history has been keen to focus on Anne's rivalry with the king's next wife, Jane Seymour, with tales of fist fights, bitching and abandonment dominating the majority of media portrayals. Biographers and producers delight in homing in on this element of Anne's story, packaging it in the contrived style of a corset-busting period drama. As a consequence, readers and viewers can be forgiven for thinking Jane Seymour was the overriding factor in Anne being cast aside by her husband and partner of ten years. But as you may now be coming to realise, real life can't be neatly condensed into a three-act storyline. Well, I guess it can if they leave out the political wars, humanitarian efforts and international conflicts – effectively, every *real* reason for Anne's demise – but in doing so they dilute and dumb down history and do a great disservice to the reader, not to mention the truth.

Of course, that's not to say that Jane Seymour wasn't an important element in Anne's takedown; indeed, she was a potent ingredient in the melting pot of disaster that was starting to bubble away in this most grim of metaphorical Tudor kitchens.

While Anne was fighting her final political campaigns of 1536, she was simultaneously subjected to a tumultuous emotional attack on her so-called private life. As soon as Anne miscarried her baby at the end of January, Jane Seymour was suddenly advised to hold back from becoming Henry's mistress in a sexual capacity. They had a better plan for her: to inspire the king to do away with his increasingly problematic wife and take Jane as his new bride.

Where a commoner marrying the monarch had once been a ridiculously unrealistic prospect, Anne's own achievement had now left her exposed to attack from any woman who was up to the challenge. And Jane Seymour certainly was.

However, this doesn't mean she waited in the wings until the king was single and ready to be snapped up. In fact, we have only recently started to realise just how much of a shocking crossover took place in the months leading up to Anne's arrest, to the point that as soon as Henry heard confirmation of Anne's death he went straight to Jane, and the following day they were betrothed. Ten days later they were married.[471] The timing was seen as so distasteful that it was kept from the public until the king made Parliament 'demand' that he remarry urgently as a matter of national safety to secure the kingdom with an heir.[472] Only then did Henry pretend that he had stumbled upon Jane Seymour and gradually introduced her to the country.

At the time of Anne's takedown, from her arrest to the trial and, of course, her execution, Henry made sure Jane's name was kept out of the news and away from any hint of scandal, making it one of the biggest cover-ups of the 1500s. History has been complicit in promoting the royal propaganda, painting Jane as the simple, submissive wife, who somehow floated into the king's life in an unassuming cloud of moonbeams and innocent virtue.

Of course, it makes sense. Writers needed 'Wife Number Three' to be different from the hardened schemer that was Anne Boleyn, so this character description worked for them. Jane was the delicate good girl who never spoke out of turn. Placid. Obedient. Boring.

Guess what? Oh no, she wasn't.

But don't worry, we aren't about to pit yet another woman against Anne, even if that's what Tudor courtiers and historians alike have revelled in doing since 1535. But we still can't escape the unsettling fact that everything we have previously believed to be true of Anne Boleyn – that she calculatingly pursued and played the king to secure the crown – is ironically what Jane Seymour did. And this was no malicious rumour created to suppress yet another powerful woman's true story; we have written evidence of Jane's actions from within her camp at the time of their taking place. However, in spite of such seemingly heartless deeds, you may find it hard to dislike Jane due to a strange sense of awe and respect that builds the more you discover about her.

'Henry VIII's third queen' may have been repeatedly dismissed as a dim-witted and passive pawn, innocently placed in the king's path. Writers simultaneously credit her with demolishing the royal marriage while being too simple to know what she was doing. (Hey, she can't be seen to be as quick-witted as 'Wife Number Two'.) They ingeniously skirt round this issue by making Jane a mere puppet for the power-hungry men at court. But how much of that is actually true?

Jane's rise came at a time when she'd pretty much given up on life, because life had given up on her. She'd resigned herself to spinsterhood back home at Wolf Hall, with no marriage prospects and no hope of a career. Then she was given a lifeline: a chance of success back at court. You can almost feel the sense of having nothing to lose, and, my goodness, she went for it. Jane had played nice in the past and life had seemingly forgotten about her. Which is where we begin to understand why she was no hapless pawn in the court game of getting Anne Boleyn out; as Chapuys's evidence will reveal, Jane calculated every move with an amazing, albeit despicable, team around her, in order to have the ultimate shot at life.

On the surface, she appeared to be your average country girl. Unlike that of her cousin Anne Boleyn, Jane's education had nothing particularly radical about it; her recent biographer concludes she was probably taught by the family chaplain. It's recorded that it could have been between 1527 and 1529 that Jane followed her older brother, Edward, to court.[473] She would have been aged between nineteen and twenty-one, and this was the first time she had left her small village for court life in London. Jane would have grown up hearing all about her brother's glamorous life serving the king's sister, Mary Tudor, in France alongside their cousins Anne and Mary Boleyn,[474] and was no doubt yearning to experience that life for herself.

It was Sir Francis Bryan, a distant cousin of the Seymours, who secured Jane her first role at court, in the household of Katherine of Aragon.[475] But she was joining at a dramatic time in court history: the early stages of Katherine's scandalous annulment from Henry VIII.

Jane was to witness all the sad events as they unfolded, including the emotional trauma Katherine endured as a result of her husband's appalling treatment of her. It was probably the strong personal empathy Jane felt for Katherine that caused her to quickly become devoted to the queen and her daughter, Princess Mary. Chapuys later noted that Jane bore 'great love and reverence to the Princess'.[476]

So, when you understand where Jane's loyalties lay and the impact this would have had on how she viewed her cousin Anne Boleyn, you start to see why Jane may not have felt any guilt whatsoever in stealing Henry from Anne all those years later – if a husband can ever really be stolen.

Oi, give him back, for the poor man cannot speak for himself!

Of course, having seen the disturbing effects of Henry's mistreatment of Katherine for herself, Jane couldn't have had a very high opinion of him as husband material, which makes her designs on him in 1536 somewhat chilling

But back in 1533, it turns out that the breakdown of the king's marriage was to have a direct and detrimental effect on Jane's life. When Henry finally succeeded in his quest for an annulment, Katherine was no longer entitled to a royal household. This meant her staff was hugely reduced to only ten ladies, and unfortunately Jane didn't make the cut; she was forced to leave the glamorous Tudor court for village life at Wolf Hall once again.[477] (This is now feeling surprisingly similar to Anne's episode back at Hever Castle following the Henry Percy debacle.)

The return home would have been a devastating blow for Jane, signalling the end of her career in London with no future prospects. And who was the person she held responsible for her misery? On whom could she focus her anger and resentment? Anne Boleyn, of course.

In Jane's eyes, it was because of Anne that she went on to live a frustratingly dreary country life for two long years, from 1533 to 1535.[478] During this time, as a committed Catholic Jane would have watched the events of Anne's reign helplessly from the sidelines as the new religious regime of the Church of England took over.

However, Jane's prayers were finally answered in early 1535, when the perpetual knight in shining armour that was Sir Francis Bryan managed to secure her a new position back at court.[479] But this time it was in the household of her cousin and queen: Anne Boleyn.

And so, we find ourselves at the root of Jane's underlying contempt for Anne – how and why she could deliberately set out to ruin the cousin who had taken her in and given her a lifeline. Anne never saw the betrayal coming.

Contrary to popular belief, Jane didn't initially set out to replace Anne as queen, due to the simple fact that Anne's most recent pregnancy secured her position on the throne. But once she miscarried the baby everything changed – not just for Anne but for Jane, too. From that moment on, right up to her secret betrothal to the king, Jane was meticulously coached on how to act by those around her. At this point they believed that if Jane played it right she could replace Anne, not just in the royal bed but as the queen of England. She could be the saviour of the land, bringing England back to Catholicism and reinstating Henry's daughter Mary as next in line to the throne.

In forcing Jane Seymour into the constraints of her caricature within the 'six wives' gimmick, history has been keen to tell us she wasn't a political queen. But pursuing the crown and becoming queen in the first place was the most radically political thing Jane did.

For a girl who had been relegated to the sidelines her whole life, now that she was at the centre of the action it appears there was no way she was going to be anyone's submissive pawn. Contemporary reports of those who supported Jane's rise tell us she was fully complicit in her new faction's plan, with her dramatically making a show of returning the king's gifts and letters unopened.[480]

This has been interpreted by historians centuries later as Jane's attempt to recreate Anne's supposed success in further piquing Henry's interest by refusing to give in to him. Of course, as we now know, that wasn't quite how Anne 'played' it. It was Chapuys who reported that the king's friends were coaching Jane[481] on how to deal with Henry's complex personality (disorder), until he had before him an easy, uncomplicated, alternative bride at a time when Anne was causing him all kinds of religious and parliamentary controversies.

Chapuys wrote that Jane 'has been well taught by those intimate with the King, who hate [Anne Boleyn], that [Jane] must by *no means* comply with the King's wishes except [for accepting his hand in] marriage'. Vitally, Chapuys confirms these were instructions that Jane was 'firm' in following.[482]

He also detailed at this time that Jane was 'advised to tell the King boldly how his marriage is detested by the people and none consider it lawful'.[483] A rather underhand attempt to manipulate Henry against Anne, considering the lack of truth in this statement; for every Catholic who was against their marriage, there would have been an evangelical reformist in extreme support of it.

But Jane may very well have consoled herself with the idea that she was *only doing to Anne what she had done to Katherine*. But Jane didn't know the half of it. Lest we forget, Henry had decided his relationship with Katherine was over when Anne finally gave in to his sociopathic charms. Jane, on the other hand, was purposefully setting out to split up Henry and Anne while they were both very much committed to the marriage – even if only on a political level.

But how do we know we aren't making the same sexist presumptions about Jane Seymour that history has been guilty of in relation to Anne Boleyn?

Well, firstly, the accounts of Jane conspiring to seduce the king come from the people within the court and were recorded directly at the time, whereas Anne's supposed seduction and apparent sexual blackmail of the king were an analysis made by historians years and, mostly, centuries after the event.

Even Wolsey's gentleman usher Cavendish, an ardent enemy of Anne's, details only Henry's pursuit of her in his sixteenth-century biography of the cardinal, without even a hint of a targeted allurement from Anne.[484] This would have been all too obvious an opportunity for Cavendish to paint the king as the victim and Anne as the vixen if that were the general consensus at the time; but, rather tellingly, he does not.

Secondly, these reports of a calculated seduction by Jane weren't spiteful gossip coming from just anyone at court in an attempt to blacken her name. They came from Spanish ambassador Chapuys, to whom Jane wasn't considered an enemy. In fact, by his own admission, Chapuys was in support of Jane replacing Anne, stating, 'Certainly, it appears to me that if [Jane's plan] succeed[s], it will be a great thing both for the security of [Princess Mary] and to remedy the heresies here, of which [Anne Boleyn] is the cause and principal nurse.'[485]

So, you see, he had no reason to lie in order to paint Jane in a bad light, which makes his reports of her actions simply that; reports, not a malicious and sexist attack similar to those made on Anne over the centuries.

◆　◆　◆

In those final months it's evident Anne could see everything was falling apart, what with her being stabbed in the back politically by those she once worked with and trusted – and then, with the worst possible timing, Henry embarking on an affair with a member of the opposition.

Now was not the time for Anne to show those scheming against her that their plan was working. They *wanted* Anne to act out so that Henry would run to the peaceful and loving arms of Jane Seymour. Anne needed to remain unfazed and calm, putting on an unshakable, united front with the king. But at this crucial time, she did the complete opposite.

Running on raw emotions from her miscarriage, in the midst of the Poor Law catastrophe and riled up by her sermon war cry, Anne reacted to Henry's affair with Jane with a fury that became notorious.[486] When she caught her cousin sitting on her husband's knee,[487] she reportedly went ballistic at the audacity of the two adulterers. And later, when she spotted Jane wearing a necklace from Henry, Anne was said to have lost her cool entirely, viciously ripping it from her neck. Though these stories originally come from *The Life of Jane Dormer*, which doesn't feature a particularly positive account of Anne, this does ring true as a natural reaction to her cousin's duplicity and husband's infidelity, especially in the wake of an onslaught of personal trauma and political drama.[488] In which case, you may feel inclined to take a brief moment here to scream futilely, willing Anne not to rise to the bait. Alas, we must sit by and watch as her every emotion-fuelled reaction played perfectly into her enemy's hands. A cold-hearted schemer would have approached the situation with steely detachment, but once again may I remind you we are dealing with Anne Boleyn the human being.

She was publicly attacking the king with her chaplains, challenging his plans for the dissolution of the monasteries and yet was angry, surprised almost, when this resulted in Henry taunting her by taking another woman. Considering the warped dynamic of their relationship and knowing the way her husband worked, did Anne really expect any other outcome? So why react so damagingly to the discovery of this inevitable mistress?

Well – aside from what Jane represented religiously, and away from Henry and Anne's now being a political match – on a personal level, whether it was rational or not, every one of his affairs would have hurt Anne's pride. Henry was the one person who validated her entire existence by this point, and every time he chose another woman over her it was seen as a smug win for her enemies, who were so eager for the king to divorce her.

There was only so long Anne could hide behind the bravado of her relentless political attacks and 'fight or flight' instincts before the facade crumbled and the emotions she was so desperate to keep hidden spilled out, exposing her vulnerability. Emotions she may well have known made her appear weak and fragile to the opposition; as, indeed, they did.

Jane's success at getting close to Henry and under Anne's skin gave the Catholic anti-Boleyn faction that much more ammunition. They were determined to end her reign once and for all. And, rather devastatingly, they were succeeding.

◆　◆　◆

Even though Jane focused all her attention on replacing Anne, she surely couldn't have been aware that it would result in the unprecedented death of a queen. While there's no doubt, from the sheer numbers of those involved in the lies we are about to uncover, that she must have known her faction was framing Anne, could she ever have imagined the queen's punishment would be death? Did she merely expect Anne to be divorced like Katherine before her, or sent to a nunnery as Anne herself would go on to speculate?

I only ask as I try to pinpoint the exact moment Jane would have realised she'd had a hand in Anne Boleyn's murder. More worryingly, at what moment did she notice Henry's chillingly nonchalant attitude towards it? Exactly when did she become aware of the sociopathic capabilities of the man who was about to become her husband?

For a time, Jane may have revelled in giving the reformist Anne her comeuppance for the misery she had imposed on her Catholic country. But now Anne was to be executed to make way for Jane. Put to death at the hands of the man she herself was about to marry, a man she had also witnessed humiliate and discard his first wife. At this point Jane must have been terrified at what she'd got herself into. But she had come too far now; there was no going back. She was trapped in the nightmare she had helped create.

So, unsurprisingly, Jane blocked it all out, focusing instead on the monumentality of her upcoming wedding that would make her the next queen of England, and on the Henry she personally knew: the caring, loving and affectionate gentleman he was with her.

Because, let's be honest, what was the alternative? Face up to the fact that her husband-to-be was about to murder his wife?

CHAPTER 12

WHO KILLED ANNE BOLEYN?

By the end of April 1536, Anne knew she was living on borrowed time.

She had declared war on the most powerful people in the country and started to suspect that her risky strategy of fighting fire with fire had only served to ignite the powder keg on which she was precariously balanced. We know this gut-wrenching moment of realisation hit Anne in that last week of April because on the 26th she called her chaplain Matthew Parker for an emergency private meeting. Twenty-three years later Parker would reveal in a letter that Anne had heartbreakingly asked him to watch over Elizabeth, stating, 'not forgetting what words [Elizabeth's] mother said to me of her, not six days before her apprehension'. He further admitted in 1572, 'Yea, if I had not been so much bound to the mother, I would not so soon have granted to serve the daughter in this place.'[489] This referred to his later appointment as Elizabeth I's archbishop of Canterbury.

The fact that Anne felt desperate enough to put care into place for her daughter's spiritual well-being meant she had serious concerns she would not be there to see her grow up. Whether she imagined this would be due to her death, or a separation similar to that experienced by Katherine and Mary, we can't know for sure. But it proves Anne was aware in those final weeks of just how dirty Cromwell was willing to play, and how dangerous a man he was to challenge.

After all, she had been up against the anti-reformist faction at court for ten years now, but this was the first time that Master Cromwell was working against her. Anne must have been aware of what he was capable of for her to suddenly feel this afraid. As her paranoia built day by day, she knew something was coming; she just didn't know what or when.

Ironically, Cromwell was also working from a place of fear in Anne's final month. He wasn't plotting to kill her because she was evil or cruel, but because he was scared of her. He had come to the realisation that not only was she actively pushing for political policies that were in direct opposition to his own but she also had the power and intention to overrule his authority. You see, at this point in his career, Cromwell was not yet at the height of his political reign. That all-conquering dominance history knows him for would only come with the removal of this powerful queen and the key members of her faction. In fact, Ives calls him 'second division' in comparison to the personal favour and private influence enjoyed by men like Henry Norris and George Boleyn.[490] You can almost see it coming.

It's clear Cromwell felt restrained by his lack of control when only months before, the king warned him he was exceeding his authority. Of course, when we learn that Cromwell took over Thomas Boleyn's prestigious role of Lord Privy Seal following the murder of two of his children and the Boleyn family's fall from grace, we can see how his plans for dominance fell seamlessly into place.[491]

So how does a man with limited power get the queen of England sentenced to death?

◆　◆　◆

Despite Henry and Anne's catastrophic falling-out over her miscarriage and the Jane Seymour affair, and despite Anne following this up by publicly challenging her husband's questionable work on the dissolution act, surprisingly Henry wasn't the one who wanted Anne dead and gone in those early months of 1536.

No, Henry realised Anne was much more useful to him as a political bargaining tool. We know this because the king was still pushing for Europe to recognise his marriage to her as late as one month before her arrest. Not, you might note, the actions of a man preparing to dispose of his wife.

So, in March 1536, just around the time of the ill-fated Poor Law, a real war was rumbling once more in the on-again/off-again romance between Emperor Charles V and Francis I of France. What were they fighting over this time? Italy. Well, Milan to be precise, and both rulers wanted England on their side; so this meant, quite unbelievably, that Charles V was open to an alliance with Henry VIII.[492]

As in the Holy Roman Emperor. As in Katherine's nephew. As in *are you serious?* After everything that had happened? But remember, Charles's aunt was now gone, and family loyalty is important and all, but, you know: war!

However, a reconciliation with the Holy Roman Empire came with a clause. In order to bury the hatchet, not only did Charles V want military support, he also wanted his cousin Princess Mary back in the line of succession to the English throne. In turn, he was offering imperial support for Henry's marriage to Anne.[493]

Really!? A seven-year battle, then all to be forgiven over a potential war? Yes, apparently, because Henry was evidently open to a reconciliation. Sure, Charles had helped ruin his life but, guys, war!? We know this because Henry offered his daughter Elizabeth for an imperial marriage in late 1535, when negotiations had recently begun. However, his offer didn't get much of a response, which probably set a few alarm bells ringing for Henry.[494]

Of course, it can't have escaped Cromwell's notice that if it was Elizabeth who was the bastard child and not Mary, it would help immensely with this imperial alliance they were now pursuing.

Nevertheless, he kept negotiations going with Spanish ambassador Eustace Chapuys, the two having had so many discussions that the latter noted in June 1535:

> Cromwell said lately to me that were the Lady [Anne Boleyn] to know on what familiar terms he and I are, she would surely try to cause us both some trouble, and that only three days ago they spoke angrily together, the Lady telling him, among other things, that she would like to see his head off his shoulders. 'But,' added Cromwell, 'I have so much confidence in my master, that I fancy she cannot do me any harm.'

Even Chapuys was sceptical of this apparent threat from Anne, as he voices in the very next line of his letter – a statement that is conveniently omitted from historical biographies at large: 'I cannot tell whether this is an invention of Cromwell, in order to raise the value of what he has to offer.' This is when he concludes, 'All I can say is that everyone here considers him Anne's right hand [man], as I myself told him some time ago.'[495]

Considering that at this stage Anne had no reason to suspect foul play by Cromwell – and there being no evidence to suggest a falling-out in early 1535 to cause her to wish Cromwell dead – I feel we cannot take this as evidence that his subsequent plotting of her murder, a full year later, was an elaborate act of self-defence in retaliation for this mysterious argument. So, rationally, we may have to agree with Chapuys, that this was just a tactic from Cromwell to win over the Spanish; although it's very interesting to note that by April the following year, Chapuys was repeating this suspiciously false statement as fact in his letters to Charles V, conveniently forgetting his own earlier scepticism in order to paint Anne as the evil monster, saying, '[Cromwell] had previously told me [Anne] would like to see his head cut off. This I could not forget for the love I bore him.'[496]

Well, Cromwell's words certainly appeared to have done the trick. On 19 April 1536, exactly one month before Anne's execution, the king met with Chapuys at Greenwich to discuss this long-awaited potential reconciliation with Charles V. George Boleyn greeted Chapuys and invited him to meet Anne and kiss her hand. Not such an unreasonable request, if this new alliance meant complete acceptance of Henry's marriage to Anne. However, Chapuys declined.[497]

Ah. More alarm bells.

Chapuys was then taken to Mass and positioned by a doorway so that Anne would pass him as she entered. It's at this point the story gets twisted due to a mistranslation in the *Letters and Papers of Henry VIII*,[498] meaning that for centuries historians have told us Anne stopped and curtseyed to Chapuys[499] – a bizarre notion in the first place that a queen would curtsey to an ambassador – but the idea Anne was imagined to have had was that owing to courtly etiquette, and all eyes being on Chapuys, he would be forced to reluctantly return her polite gesture with a bow, hence forcing him to finally acknowledge her as queen of England, something he had steadfastly avoided doing for the past three years out of loyalty to Katherine. In fact, he and Anne had never met in all his years at court. But despite this having now gone down in history as the stuff of Tudor legend, as Chapuys explains in his original sixteenth-century report in the *Calendar of State Papers, Spain*, that's not quite how the moment unfolded.

Firstly, it appears both Anne and the king passed him in the doorway, where Chapuys tells us first-hand that he was already bowing in respect – something, we might wonder, that would allow those present to interpret as being meant only for the king? But as Chapuys tells us, Anne simply 'turned round to return the reverence I made to her when she passed',[500] meaning she was responding to and accepting his voluntary submission.

In all the accounts of Anne's life so much has been made of this 'tricking Chapuys to acknowledge her as queen', as though it was seen as a major and somewhat smug victory for her. But in reality, Anne was suspicious that Chapuys went on to dine with George and Jane Seymour's brother Edward, rather than with her and the king.[501] Henry, in turn, was concerned that Chapuys was still hostile to Anne, having refused to kiss her hand and bowing only when he thought he should. All this must have led them to worry that Chapuys's boss, old Charles V, couldn't have been that keen on accepting their marriage after all.

The king had already been having doubts about the imperial alliance. Henry was adamant that he wouldn't budge on the clause recognising Mary as his legal heir – a concern he had already expressed to Chapuys at Christmas – as he felt it would inadvertently validate his marriage to Katherine.

All in all, the imperial alliance seemed decidedly one-sided in favour of the Holy Roman Emperor, and it appears Henry chose this moment to tell Cromwell just how unhappy he was with the deal. Chapuys reports that this caused Cromwell and Henry to have a heated debate. So heated, in fact, that Cromwell had to excuse himself and sit alone to regain his composure before he really lost his shit with the king of England.

Forgive the clichés, but the pressure was really starting to get to Cromwell, the cracks clearly beginning to show.

But just when the king thought international relations couldn't get any worse, England learned that Francis I had a devastating papal decree that denied Henry's right to the throne – the contents of which the king of France was threatening to publish, hoping that by doing so he would win kudos with the pope, who would then back him in the war. This is what the Tudors had feared all along – someone questioning their claim to the throne.

Luckily, Charles V was using all his power to stop Francis from actioning his papal decree – a nifty little blackmail attempt to sway Henry VIII to side with him and the Holy Roman Empire.[502] Henry, and indeed England, were backed into a corner. The king's council met every day in April 1536, desperately trying to decide how to play the situation. And so, *this* was Henry's main concern in the few weeks leading up to Anne's arrest – not, it should be pointed out, his love life.

Of course, this vital information is rarely included in Anne's more commercial biographies nor in the countless media portrayals of the 'six wives', let alone the historical fiction based on her life. But why on earth not? After all, it changes the climax to Henry and Anne's 'love story' somewhat, dramatically moving it away from love and passion to war and politics – or have I just hit the nail on the head?

Could it be that the more commercial historians and producers of Anne Boleyn's story believe their audiences to be predominantly female? We can't deny that this is certainly how most Boleyn–six wives biographies and period dramas are packaged and sold to the public at large[503]– and we ladies aren't meant to be interested in war, are we? We want love triangles and seduction presented in the outmoded style of a 1970s novella. Do you know what I'm told when I challenge the status quo on this? 'It's not what the audience want to hear!'

Do you want to tell them, or should I? That this is the twenty-first century and we're here for the truth, not the fantasy.

Don't decide for us what we do and don't want to see; like a parent putting childproof settings on the internet!

This is why all these media depictions of historical women's stories – fiction and non-fiction – presented to us *only* in the style of a whimsical romance minus the serious work and politics, are not so innocent and easily dismissed. With each one, they seep into the subconscious of readers and viewers, telling them over and over that women should only be interested in fluff and frivolity.

But I've said it before, and I'll say it again: Henry and Anne's story was not about love. It never was. Not in the beginning and certainly not now it was nearing the end. Because one thing Henry's war game proves is that up until just two days before Anne's arrest, he was using his marriage to her as a political tool, not plotting how to get rid of her. Indeed, six days before her arrest the king sent a powerful message to the ambassador of Rome, Richard Pate, boldly affirming the 'likelihood God will send us heirs male' with 'our most dear and most beloved wife, the queen'.[504]

So, what on earth happened in that one week to cause him to order his wife's arrest? Whimsical writers, rejoice – we've arrived at the affairs!

With Anne's increasing power in Parliament, convincing the king to use money from the monasteries to help the poor rather than the war effort, and now her marriage to Henry being a key make-or-break reason this reconciliation with the Holy Roman Empire was collapsing, Cromwell panicked.

He made the drastic decision to defect from the Boleyn faction to the opposition – something he managed to do pretty quickly through his connection with Chapuys, by giving the impression he would endeavour to reinstate Mary as the imperial reconciliation negotiations lumbered on. Of course, this wasn't quite how things would eventually pan out – with Cromwell arresting most of Mary's faction soon after Anne's death in order to push her into accepting her own illegitimacy. Not that her faction suspected his double-dealing at the time of his defection; the former lawyer was skilled in the art of deception.

We know Cromwell was behind the plot to bring down the queen thanks to not one but two admissions of guilt, as recorded by his new pal Chapuys.

In a letter to Charles V on 6 June 1536, Chapuys writes that '[Cromwell] himself had been authorised and commissioned by the King to prosecute and bring to an end [Anne's] trial, to do which he had taken considerable trouble.'[505]

This statement should not be misunderstood to mean that Henry told him to concoct a reason to arrest Anne but rather that, upon hearing Cromwell's 'evidence' against her, the king instructed him to destroy his wife. Chapuys backs this up with a second incriminatory admission that 'It was [Cromwell] who . . . had planned and brought about the whole affair,' meaning the charges against Anne that he presented to the king.[506]

But before we feel inclined to sympathise on the basis that the minister was merely backed into a corner, that he couldn't have taken any joy in plotting Anne's murder, even for political reasons, may I draw your attention to a horrifying moment during a later conversation. Chapuys describes how Cromwell stifled laughter when discussing Henry and Anne's disintegrating marriage the very day before Anne was arrested: Cromwell 'leaned against the window in which we were, putting his hand before his mouth to avoid smiling'.[507] This account gives us a deeply disturbing insight into how Cromwell truly felt about framing Anne and sending an innocent woman to her death.

But considering that defecting to the other side is exactly what got his predecessor Wolsey arrested, Cromwell had to make sure there was no room for Anne to outmanoeuvre him. He needed all hands on deck, with everyone conspiring together, looking for anything they could turn into evidence against her. Luckily for him, there were more than enough people ready to hatch a plan to kill the queen.

Everyone had a role to play.

Stephen Gardiner, once a supporter of the king's marriage to Anne yet one who had always held on to his traditional religious beliefs, started rumours as far afield as the French court, where he was working as ambassador, that she was having an affair.[508] Letters containing this salacious gossip were to find their way back to England, where Cromwell could show the king and overwhelm him with suspicion.

Hey, there's no smoke without fire.

Unless, as in this case when there *was* no fire, we start the fire ourselves.

Key members of Anne's household were cornered by Cromwell's newly adopted faction and instructed to be on the hunt for anything they could turn into incriminating evidence, and on 29 April they got their first piece. To be fair, it was pretty damning.

Anne and Henry Norris had a 'furious altercation'[509] in which she accused the king's long-standing and closest companion of having feelings for her. Surely, we've all heard her infamous line by now: 'You look for dead man's shoes; for if ought came to the king but good you would look to have me.'

Following which, she demanded Norris go to her almoner the next morning and swear on oath that she was 'a gud woman'.[510]

Now where would this have come from? What triggered such an intimate argument? I've witnessed academics and popular historians alike explaining Anne's 'dead man's shoes' comment as flirtatious banter; courtly love gone too far before she comes to her senses, realising she has just committed treason by imagining the king's death.

But Anne was not stupid. At this most dangerous time, while waiting for some catastrophe to befall her, why would she publicly flirt with her husband's closest companion, accusing him of wanting to marry her should the king die?

However, when put into context of what had been happening with Norris at court, it starts to make a lot more sense. While poised for disaster to strike, Anne was given the news that Norris was backing out of a long-arranged marriage match between himself and Anne's cousin Margaret Shelton.[511]

Why the sudden change? Who had got to him? Was Norris being advised to distance himself from the Boleyn faction? What did he know?

You immediately get a sense of Anne's panic and paranoia that would have led to this uncontrolled outburst where she went too far and once again said the wrong thing. But that's the old Boleyn foot-in-mouth syndrome for you – her badly phrased comment not ringing of excessive flirting but of suspicion and hot-headed anger. Anne wasn't teasing him at all; she was goading him into telling her the truth, a sort of '*Why else would you delay marriage arrangements with a member of my family? Is it because you truly love me? Because that's what it looks like to the court.*' She's almost saying it to provoke him into confessing the real reason and perhaps revealing what plot was going on behind the scenes, which would be less damaging to him than the accusation that he'd fallen for the king's wife.

But why would Anne even think of accusing Norris of wanting her instead?

It appears to have come from an earlier conversation in which she had warned off courtier Francis Weston from flirting with Margaret Shelton because she was intended for Norris, at which point Weston hit back with the claim that Norris went into the queen's chambers more for Anne than Margaret. So underneath it all, Anne was aware that Norris might have harboured inappropriate feelings for her, and on the spur of the moment it seems she used this to try and embarrass him into revealing the truth.

Of course, it was because this argument got out of hand that Anne asked Norris to go to her almoner to swear she was 'a gud woman'[512] – not, I hasten to add, because there had been suspicions of an affair circulating.

Yet time and time again, historians report that this conversation was merely risqué flirting on Anne's part because she was feeling unloved, and was testing her powers of attraction to see if they had survived the years. In fact, this is how some academics have explained away the possibility that Anne actually had full-blown affairs with several men and it not being a set-up at all. I guess they do have a point; there is no better way for a woman to feel more desirable than to have an affair that would undoubtedly lead to her own gruesome execution. Personally, when I want to test if I've *still got it* I like to try something equally as dangerous, like bear-baiting.

Of course, this 'testing of her prowess' theory is seemingly backed up by the much-repeated notion that Anne 'liked to surround herself at court with men'.

Well, firstly, that's simply not true. She was surrounded at all times by her ladies. But the reason Anne was encircled by men in her political work was the same reason that any woman in modern politics is surrounded by men: not because we are all sultry seductresses wanting to test our sexual prowess but due to a gender imbalance that is beyond our personal control.

Alas, to those who still insist that Anne's interaction with Norris was flirting gone too far, I say this cannot be the case because of one final, and vital, piece of evidence: this story is provided by one source only – Anne Boleyn herself. She recounted her argument with Norris during her time in the Tower, after being arrested on suspicion of adultery with several men.

In the past, when hearing of how Anne spilled so much incriminating information knowing full well her every word was being recorded by spies, I wondered what on earth she was thinking by speaking so unguardedly about such a delicate issue. But the minute you read the original letters from William Kingston, the constable of the Tower, which detail Anne's so-called 'confession', it suddenly becomes clear that her words weren't incriminating at all. In fact, she was going out of her way to talk about the only interactions she'd had recently with the opposite sex to prove just how innocent they were – how there was no part of them that warranted her arrest.

Think about it logically: if Anne was being charged with adultery, why would she tell several stories to her captors about flirting with men only a few days before? She wouldn't! Cromwell had to work extremely hard to make her stories sound salacious and worthy of condemnation.[513]

Anne's interaction with Norris was undoubtedly based on anger, which we can fully understand given her growing paranoia.

But how did Francis Weston get dragged into all this and become a suspect himself? Well, it goes back to when Anne accused him of not loving his wife (yes, he was married) and flirting with Margaret Shelton instead, subsequently distracting her from Norris. Making a joke of the situation, Weston told Anne that he loved someone in her household more than his wife or Margaret. When Anne enquired who, Weston replied, 'Yourself.'

Now *this* sounds like a bit of courtly love banter. See the difference?

Once in prison, Anne recounted this story, so keen was she to illustrate that it wasn't *her* fault the men fancied her, and that in actual fact she had been telling them off for flirting with other women.[514] However, it's safe to say that her plan backfired, and her words went on to be used as proof she had committed adultery with both Norris and Weston.

It's left for us to presume that it was Anne's argument with Norris that triggered the scene we've seen played out so many times in her story, where she and Henry are spotted arguing at Greenwich the next day, Sunday 30 April, by Alexander Alesius – who was to later relay this story to Elizabeth I in 1559. Alesius explains how Anne was holding Elizabeth in her arms as she approached Henry, who was looking out of an open window. The Scottish reformer reports that the king was angry and it was obvious some 'deep and difficult question was being discussed'.[515]

As it turns out, Cromwell managed to frame two of his five male victims with evidence from the same day. Yes, 29 April turned out to be quite eventful, as that was the day Anne noticed the young musician Mark Smeaton looking lonely and made the mistake of trying to cheer him up. Granted, her words of comfort left much to be desired, as by her own admission she told him, 'You may not look to have me speak to you as I should do to a noble man, because you be an inferior person.'[516]

But before we leap to the conclusion that Anne was a rude and raging snob, we have to understand that this was, again, relayed by her while in prison, and reeks of a desperate attempt to get across just how professional her relationships with her courtiers were; she knew her place as queen and would not interact with the 'lowly' staff.

Eager to drum this message home, Anne insisted Smeaton was never in her chambers, and that she only asked him to play for her once, at Winchester, as her rooms were directly above the king's. The letter cuts out here (the originals were, rather devastatingly, damaged in a fire) but the implication seems to be that she merely asked Smeaton to play for her so the king would hear some music through the ceiling.

Alas, that innocent interaction with Smeaton was all it took for the nervous young man to be the first suspect singled out for interrogation.

But before we go any further past the events of 29 April, it must be pointed out that five days earlier, on the 24th, Cromwell commissioned an 'oyer and terminer' – a small council tasked with trying the accused. A lot of historians over the years have wrongly presumed that this was Henry VIII giving the go-ahead to launch an investigation into Anne, as he would have had to sign off on it. But that is not quite the case, because Henry VIII did *not* sign that commission. As his minister, Cromwell actually had the power to do this alone, and it appears he did so, in secret, with the presumed help of his close ally the Lord Chancellor Audley.[517]

But as an oyer and terminer didn't run an investigation itself – it was their job only to try the accused – they were usually commissioned *after* an investigation had been conducted. So why would Cromwell feel the need to secretly issue one without the king's knowledge or consent, and most importantly, without anyone to try yet?

Because it takes approximately eleven days between the commission and the trial being set up. Cromwell wanted everything in place so there would be no delay, and vitally, no time for Henry to back out of his decision – that is, once Cromwell had managed to convince the king Anne was guilty of whatever crimes he had manage to concoct.[518]

While we're on the subject of the oyer and terminer, there is no better time to clear up the lie that just won't stop resurfacing – that Anne's father, Thomas Boleyn, was part of the team that condemned his daughter to death. This was a rumour that began when Anne was arrested; but as Thomas's biographer informs us, her father was not part of either the Middlesex or Kent-based oyer and terminer used to try Anne and her fellow prisoners. He was originally listed for Middlesex, but by the time it was used to try Anne, her father had been scrapped from the list, for obvious reasons.[519]

It was around this point that Cromwell ran into a problem. If he was going to try the queen of England then this was a parliamentary matter. The only thing was, Parliament had been dissolved just two weeks earlier, shortly after the attempt to pass the Poor Law, meaning an emergency Parliament would need to be summoned.[520] This time, Cromwell definitely needed the king's consent and signature, and so created the pretence of fixing a loophole in a current law whereby defending the pope was not a criminal act. If anything was going to get Henry to leap into action, this would do it. So, on 27 April Parliament was summoned, Cromwell knowing full well that it could then be used against Anne at a moment's notice.[521]

Now everything was in place, and most of it without the king or queen's knowledge.

Three days later, on 30 April, Smeaton was invited to dine at Cromwell's house, where he was apparently seized by six men upon arrival and held in unofficial questioning for twenty-four hours.[522]

An important bit of backstory to know about Mark Smeaton is that he was just a young lad, not much older than twenty. A low-ranking musician at court, Cavendish says he was the son of a carpenter – in other words, an easy first target. Smeaton didn't have the confidence or authority that come from a lifetime of privilege to help him hold his nerve. If they could scare a false confession out of anyone, it would be him.[523] So, while Smeaton wasn't an important or influential courtier to dispose of, he was a vital element in creating the devastating domino effect that Cromwell needed to frame Anne.

It's presumed Smeaton must have been offered a plea bargain or tortured until he confessed to a crime he hadn't committed. Over the years there were rumours that he was stretched on the rack, but as he was still at Cromwell's house and only taken to the Tower upon confession, this couldn't have been the case. However, it *was* reported the poor lad was held in irons for the whole twenty-four-hour interrogation period, which might lead one to ask what kind of person has iron shackles casually waiting for use at home. The fact that de Carles goes out of his way to tell us Smeaton gave his confession 'without being tortured' shows there were suggestions at the time that he was.[524] One method they spoke of was tightening a knotted rope around his head – although Eric Ives points out that this may not have happened as 'such a course would have been illegal'.

Yeah, I'm thinking the whole 'creating false evidence to kill six people including the queen of England' was also illegal, so I'm not entirely convinced that working within the confines of the law was Cromwell's main concern.

But whether it was via intimidation or battery, the offer of a plea bargain or a deal for a less gruesome death, Smeaton would have felt the situation to be hopeless: he was trapped, with no way out other than to confess to a crime that, as we are about to discover, was impossible for him to have committed. Cromwell himself must have been in slight shock that after twenty-four hours of exhaustive interrogation it actually worked, and they finally got a fake confession out of him.

Smeaton arrived at the Tower at 6 p.m. on 1 May 1536.[525]

Smeaton's confession was a start, but Cromwell's case against Anne couldn't rest upon the testimony of one fragile and unreliable boy. However, now that he had a confession from one man to convince Henry his powerful wife had committed the ultimate crime, he saw a unique opportunity to get rid of all the key members of the Boleyn faction in one fell swoop.

Later that afternoon, after receiving the shocking news of Smeaton's confession during the May Day celebrations at court, possibly on Cromwell's recommendation the king decided to confront and interrogate Norris about his suspicious altercation with Anne. As they rode to Whitehall, Henry reassured Norris that even if he was guilty his life would be spared if he simply admitted his affair with Anne. However, Norris had nothing to admit, and wasn't as gullible as Smeaton; but despite his ardent denial, he was arrested the next day and sent to the Tower.[526] And yet the lawyer in Cromwell felt it was still a weak case. He could not fail. Anne could not come back from this. They needed more. They needed statements from the queen's most loyal and trusted ladies who would swear on oath that they had witnessed these imaginary affairs taking place. This is where history credits Cromwell with the work of one other key player in the framing of Anne Boleyn, a player who, until now, has been astonishingly overlooked, and whose connection and influence over every single key witness in the case against Anne has been bafflingly ignored. Well, not any more.

Charles Brandon, it's time to take the stand.

You may have heard Cromwell's officially approved story[527] of how investigations into Anne's alleged affairs began, when one of her ladies-in-waiting, Elizabeth Browne, was reprimanded for her rather dubious conduct at court; at which point she threw Anne under the bus by saying that her own actions were *nothing* compared to those of the queen.

This admission is all the more incriminating for Anne when we learn that Elizabeth Browne was not only her lady but a close and supposedly loyal friend who was by her side at her coronation, and that

Anne had even lent her money for a private matter. So it didn't bode well for the queen that this admission of debauchery came from such a reliable source. That is, until you learn that Elizabeth Browne's sister was once married to Anne's arch-enemy Charles Brandon.

In 1503 Brandon had a romance with Elizabeth's sister Anne Browne, and the couple were contracted to marry. However, true to form, he abandoned her while she was heavily pregnant with their first child to marry her rich aunt Dame Margaret Mortimer. Browne's family were horrified at the abandonment and took Brandon to court,[528] where he was forced to annul his new marriage on account of now having a child with his wife's niece. So, Brandon cut his losses – not before the old charmer sold Margaret's manor house in Devon for £260,[529] I hasten to add – and went back to Anne Browne, marrying her in 1508. However, she died within two weeks of giving birth to Brandon's second daughter, Mary, in 1510, freeing Charles to move on to Margaret of Austria in Anne Boleyn's early days in France, where the duo's lifelong feud began.

Given that Brandon had put the Browne family through intense emotional turmoil, we might be tempted to presume he wasn't on the most affectionate terms with Elizabeth, but he was still the father of her nieces and worked closely in the king's privy chamber with her brother, Anthony Browne, who himself was a huge supporter of Princess Mary. So when we consider that Elizabeth's 'statement' was first given to her brother, it looks increasingly suspicious, and smacks of intimidation from both men.

At this point, I probably don't even need to inform you that Elizabeth Browne was also the stepsister of Sir William Fitzwilliam, treasurer of the household, who was one of the men who arrested Anne. So, as far as reliable witnesses go, her evidence would hardly hold up in a non-corrupt court of law.[530]

Ironically, while Elizabeth – among other women – was helping to create false evidence to condemn her queen and friend, Anne was in prison worrying about the health of Elizabeth's unborn baby, which she hadn't felt move in a while.[531]

Next up, scraping the barrel of reliable witnesses, was Lady Bridget Wingfield, who had been dead for two years by the time of Anne's trial; and yet evidence was provided on her behalf against the queen. Bridget was Anne's former lady of the bedchamber, who, after her death in 1534, had left in her belongings a personal letter from Anne Boleyn. Bridget's family then produced the letter as evidence of Anne having had an affair not long before she married Henry.

OK, so this must have been pretty serious. Written evidence: just what Cromwell needed. So what incriminating admission of adultery did Anne write in the letter? 'I pray you leave your indiscrete trouble, both for displeasing of God and also for displeasing of me.'[532]

That was it. The sole offending line. No context. No suggestion as to what this 'indiscrete trouble' had been. Anne literally could have been referring to anything, and yet this one line was interpreted by Cromwell as, *'Your indiscrete trouble [regarding the fact I'm having an affair] is upsetting God and upsetting me.'*

A slight stretch of the imagination. Particularly when we take into account that this letter was written in 1532, the year before Anne married Henry, when she wouldn't have risked the crown for an affair with anyone, let alone commit an admission of guilt to paper.

But why would Lady Bridget Wingfield's family try to incriminate Anne? Perhaps it was because Bridget was once married to Charles Brandon's cousin Sir Richard Wingfield.[533] Brandon's biographer, Steven Gunn, goes on to report that the whole Wingfield family often asked Brandon for help in advancing their various causes to the king, and so it's safe to say the family owed him.[534] But when Bridget's husband died in 1525, she and Anne fell out over her choice of new husband, Robert of Kettleby – who was a close friend of . . . guess who?

That's right: Charles Brandon.

Not that this was Anne's main cause for concern. The real problem she had with Robert was that he was fighting for that old Tudor classic, stamping out Lutheranism; his own father went on to have close links to the later Catholic rebellion, the Pilgrimage of Grace.[535] He, in turn, did not appear to be a huge fan of the Boleyn family, having been an envoy with Anne's father at the beginning of his career, where Thomas repeatedly upstaged him during their missions.[536] And suddenly we have plenty of motives for the family to have handed Anne's letter over to Cromwell to be twisted into evidence.

It was Henry VIII himself who admitted, almost ten years after Anne's murder, that no prisoner in the Tower stood a chance against false evidence.[537]

Alexander Alesius gave further insight into how they convinced Anne's household to work against her: tempting her ladies with bribes, while reassuring them that the king hated Anne for her failure to provide an heir. 'There is nothing which they do not promise the ladies of her bedchamber.'[538]

The one thing these false statements from Anne's disloyal ladies highlights is why she and George became so close, her brother being the only person she felt she could completely trust and confide in. So it's easy to see why George's wife, Jane Rochford, would have grown to resent the amount of time he spent with his sister, especially following her own banishment from court in 1534. This incident, two years earlier, would have illustrated to Jane that being on Anne's side did her no favours. There was no protection or preferential treatment that came with being sister-in-law to the queen of England – aside from being let out of prison without charge when arrested for protesting in favour of the opposition.

It has long been suspected that Jane was recruited in the framing of Anne Boleyn and was eager to chip in with lurid accusations of incest between Anne and her brother, George. Even Wyatt believed the accusations stemmed from George's wife wanting to be rid of her husband, rather than from any real fact.[539] It will also come as no surprise that it's been suggested Charles Brandon had influence over this witness too, apparently encouraging the incest claims as payback for Anne's own accusations of Brandon's alleged incestuous abuse of his daughter.

It is his wife we presume George is talking about when he stated at his trial that 'on the evidence of only one woman you are willing to believe this great evil of me, and on the basis of her allegations you are deciding my judgement'.[540]

Some argue that this 'one woman' could have been one of Anne's ladies, given that John Husse speculated it was 'Nan Cobham and another maid'[541] who had given evidence and, as historians have rightly pointed out, Jane Rochford was no maid. However, this doesn't rule out her involvement; and indeed, the situation appears increasingly suspicious when we discover that Jane's own father, Henry Parker, sat on the jury at George's trial.[542]

Not only that, but it is considered that only Jane could have provided the private letter written by Anne to George that further condemned the siblings. This letter was said to have proved beyond reasonable doubt that brother and sister had been having an incestuous relationship, because in it Anne wrote to George informing him she was pregnant.

No, you're not missing anything. Anne sharing the happy news of her pregnancy with her closest family member was successfully interpreted by Cromwell to mean 'SISTER TELLS BROTHER SHE IS PREGNANT . . . WITH HIS BABY!'[543]

Hard to argue with that kind of irrefutable evidence. Case closed. We can all go home.

But would Charles Brandon really want Anne and her faction dead? He had already bounced back from the incest slur, so was murder really called for? Divorce, perhaps, but death?

Though it's said he didn't care much for the reformist movement, he was apparently tolerant of it. So, religion doesn't appear to be at the heart of his hatred. We know that Brandon served in the powerful role of high steward and constable at Anne's coronation in 1533, but almost immediately he was ousted by her family, with Norfolk requesting Brandon give up the office of earl marshal to him – something he was said to have done reluctantly and with ill grace.[544] Not only that, but he was increasingly eclipsed in the king's inner circle by Anne's faction, with the king only visiting his 'friend' three times between 1531 and 1535, their jolly jousts becoming few and far between. Therefore, we can perhaps start to understand why Brandon had no qualms about the men who replaced him becoming collateral damage in his takedown of Anne.

But if you're still in need of a more convincing reason as to why Brandon would want to conspire to kill the queen and in turn bastardise her innocent daughter, then look no further than this: with both the king's children deemed illegitimate, Brandon's children with Henry VIII's sister Mary Tudor would have a stronger claim to the throne. No, his own daughters were never going to take the crown themselves, but that wasn't his end game. As his biographer, Professor Steven Gunn of Oxford University points out, the closer they were in line to the throne, the greater chance they had of a diplomatic marriage, hence the higher the dowry Brandon could demand.[545]

Kerrr-ching! You can almost hear the cash rolling in.

And so it starts to make sense as to why the ever financially unstable Brandon would want to permanently delete Anne Boleyn. It also explains why, for all those years, he was so heavy-handed and keen in helping the king to get Princess Mary to accept her own illegitimacy.[546]

Yes, it seems money motivated his entire co-conspiracy with Cromwell, because not only did Brandon benefit directly from Anne's death – he was given three manors from her estate, which brought him an income of £100 (just under £50,000 in today's currency[547]) – but he also sued for a share in the lesser monasteries. Oh yes, the very same smaller monasteries that Anne was fighting to save at the time of her arrest.[548] And when you consider that the money raised from only the first phase of the dissolution of the monasteries was the equivalent of £32 million, as well as an additional £10.3 million in annual income, it's suddenly all too clear why Cromwell and Brandon were willing to kill Anne for a slice of that pie.[549]

Lo and behold, after Anne's death, Brandon's attendance at court started to pick up again, and he became a regular fixture at Parliament, frequently sitting in council.[550]

◆ ◆ ◆

Cromwell sent what became the official version of events to the English ambassadors Stephen Gardiner and John Wallop in France on 14 May 1536. He revealed that the queen was living such a debauched lifestyle, her offences towards the king were so 'rank and common' that her ladies of the privy chamber could no longer cover for their depraved and sinful queen . . . but that he wouldn't go into details because it was 'so abominable' that he couldn't bring himself to repeat it[551] (i.e., he was making the whole thing up).

But if it was all an invention, why couldn't the king see through it? Surely it wouldn't have taken much to realise it was a set-up?

Anne was the love of his life . . . so she must have done something pretty devastating for him to order her death. It couldn't all have been fabricated. There must be at least some truth in the rumours . . . Right?

So, now we are out of the murky waters of 'When a man cheats, what did the woman do to cause it?' and wading into the oil slick of 'When a man murders his wife, what did she do to deserve it?'

Sounds ridiculous and mildly disturbing, but this is pretty much what I have found repeatedly during my research: the view that there must have been more to it, to drive a man to kill his wife. Not so for a sociopath, but psychological analysis aside for a moment – could any of the affairs actually have taken place?

Well, firstly, the time frame given for these affairs makes it completely unrealistic that Anne had been able to keep every one of them a secret until all five were exposed at once – conveniently, just at the time when her enemies needed incriminating evidence against her. Anne knew that the imperial faction at court were constantly spying on her, looking for anything to accuse her of – Chapuys's constant stream of tell-tale letters to Charles V is proof of that. As we've seen, any little phrase she said that could be taken out of turn, any action that could be misconstrued, was jumped on with the schadenfreude of a tabloid editor. Anne would not have dared attempt an affair for fear of being found out.[552] Even Wyatt points out that it would have been 'impossible' for Anne to conduct one affair, let alone several, given that she was surrounded at all times by 'the necessary and no small attendance of ladies'.[553]

Which brings us to another obvious point: if Anne had conducted just one of these alleged affairs, she would have needed the help of her ladies to get away with it. Case in point – when Henry VIII's later wife Katherine Howard was caught cheating, George Boleyn's widow, Jane Rochford, was executed along with her new mistress for helping her get away with it. Yet not one of Anne's ladies went down with their queen. Each of them who provided statements of having apparently witnessed and concealed Anne having these illicit affairs escaped any charges of aiding and abetting, and went on to serve her replacement, Jane Seymour.[554]

Yet why Anne would risk having sex with anyone other than Henry is beyond me. No one could help her cause better than the king; certainly no one was more powerful than him, and it's not as if she hadn't proved she could go for years without having her personal needs satisfied – lest we forget, with the lack of pregnancies before her marriage, it appears she was a virgin until the age of thirty-one. And if that male heir came out and he wasn't a redhead like his dad . . . Awkward!

But couldn't there have been a good reason for Anne to have an affair? Perhaps more out of desperation than wanton sexual desire?

Oh, you mean the rumour that she wanted to get pregnant by her brother, the only man she trusted, in order to save herself and pretend it was Henry's?

I'll admit that in a warped way this accusation seems vaguely plausible. If Anne's life rested upon her giving birth to a male heir, and if the king seemed unable to get her pregnant, then she might have taken drastic action to get pregnant by another man. But the crucial evidence ruining this theory is that the king *was* getting her pregnant. It was *she* who was struggling to carry to full term, so she could have been equally laying the blame on her own health, rather than Henry's. In which case, what would make her think she could carry another man's baby more successfully to make such a dangerous strategy worth the risk? As for sleeping with her brother, like we've already discussed, George and his wife never had a child in all their years together – hardly a ringing endorsement for his virility. And do I really need to point out that for a deeply religious woman like Anne, even if her husband never discovered her adultery, God would have been deathly aware of her sins. If Leviticus condemned you to the fiery pits of purgatory for 'laying with your brother's wife', then I imagine *laying with your brother* would result in eternal damnation – and there's not one piece of evidence to suggest that Anne valued the fleeting cheap thrills of life on earth over salvation and God's grace in the afterlife.

And so, I'll leave the final word on Anne's false charges to, of all people, Chapuys. For the mere fact that it came from the man who hated her the most accentuates just how ridiculous the charges were. Chapuys said Anne was 'condemned upon presumption and certain indications without valid proof or confession'.[555]

Of course, this may seem somewhat rich, considering Chapuys had fought so hard to get rid of Anne for years. But he was only ever pushing for an annulment. That Anne should be set up on such extreme false charges that resulted in her murder must have left a bad taste for the Spanish ambassador. Chapuys only wanted to ruin Anne's life, not end it.

This is evident when he repeated the age-old accusation that Anne had indeed married Henry Percy years earlier and the two had consummated their relationship, an accusation that would conveniently render Anne's subsequent marriage to the king invalid. However, Percy continued to strenuously deny these accusations. As we've already seen, there was no evidence of a pre-contract, no former admission of guilt they could draw on from Percy or Anne, hence the attempt now to interrogate and bully him into a false confession. But the fact that in the end, not only was Percy not one of the men arrested or accused but was asked to sit in on Anne's trial and pass judgement on her is really all the evidence we need to close the lid on this once and for all.[556]

When George Boleyn was arrested at Whitehall following the May Day jousts, historians believe he was there having gone to find his brother-in-law the king and talk some sense into the man who had become a close and trusted family member. But all access to Henry was denied.[557] This has been repeatedly blamed on Cromwell, yet for all his scheming, I don't think we can pin this particular incident on him. If we've learned anything by now, it's that no one tells Henry Tudor what to do, and, more to the point, who he can and can't see.

What we have here is the archetypal sociopathic response of cutting everyone off once it's been decided they are out. Henry didn't want to see any weeping or begging. (All these people with their boring emotions.) Cromwell had presented him with the 'facts' and Henry had made up his mind: they were all guilty. *Now can we move on?*

If Henry truly loved Anne in the way those who sell us '*The Most Tragic Love Story of all Time*' say he did, then he could have stopped her murder at any point. He was sitting beside her at the May Day jousts when he was delivered news of Smeaton's confession.

So did he question her?

Did he demand an explanation?

Did he ask her how she could possibly break his heart in such a cruel and flippant way?

He did not. He stood and left without a word, never to see her again. He froze her out, erasing his wife and partner of ten years from his mind with chilling ease. This was the final stage in Henry's socio-pathic relationship with Anne: *discard.* This is why he was able to accept her guilt without challenge. Even his pal of the privy chamber, Henry Norris, got the privilege of an interrogation as they rode from the joust to Whitehall. Yet Anne, the supposed love of his life, got nothing.

What do we make, then, of Chapuys's story about the following night? That after Anne's arrest, Henry apparently sobbed to his illegitimate son, the duke of Richmond, after hearing that Anne had planned to poison Richmond and Mary so that her daughter, Elizabeth, would take the throne. Aside from the fact that both Richmond and Mary were illegitimate and not a threat anyway, with Henry lacking the capacity to feel this kind of emotion and Chapuys's obsession with poison, alarm bells start ringing immediately. However, not to dismiss the report, it could easily have been a case of Henry taking every and any ridiculous accusation about Anne seriously, in order to create a compelling case against her and rationalise his disposal of her to the people around him – paired, once again, with him mimicking the right emotions for those who expected him to be distraught.

Indeed, according to Chapuys, Henry wrote down all his apparent heartbreak at being deceived by Anne in a little book that he would show to anyone and everyone who would stop and read it. Chapuys, then, seems to confirm Henry's actions as being sociopathic by stating, 'You never saw prince nor man who made greater show of his [misfortune] or bore them more pleasantly.'[558]

That's putting it mildly.

Chapuys was appalled to hear further reports of Henry partying through the night in the days following Anne's arrest and later her death sentence. One evening he even filled a royal barge with women and minstrels for a boat party on the Thames.[559] This may be how a man might react after breaking up with his troublesome girlfriend, but not after condemning his wife to death.

So, if Henry's sociopathy allowed him to cut Anne off without a second thought, what then politically justified this sudden change? How did he go from using their marriage as a bargaining tool with the leaders of Europe to disposing of her within days?

Scottish reformer Alexander Alesius provides the answer.

Remember how Anne had been pushing the king to pursue an alliance with the Lutheran princes of Germany? Crucially, in autumn 1535 her chaplains Nicholas Heath and Edward Foxe went on a royal envoy to Wittenberg to meet them. The German princes had been building a defensive Protestant union called the Schmalkaldic League, with its own officials, treasury and troops; this made them an increasingly powerful alliance, which Henry proposed that England should now join.[560] Foxe and Heath finally came to a preliminary agreement between England and the princes on their differing religious beliefs and how their faith should be practised, this being a deal-breaker for the alliance.[561]

But, as Alesius explained to Elizabeth I years later, Henry was infuriated that not only did the princes suddenly want more money than he had offered, but they still refused to send Martin Luther's right-hand man, Melanchthon, over to England to meet him.

Cromwell has always been credited as the one pushing for an alliance with the princes, but as we've seen, he was working with Chapuys and pushing Henry towards a reconciliation with Charles V at that time. Logically, Cromwell would only have been backing an alliance with one ruler, given they were at odds with each other; so it seems more likely that Cromwell wanted an alliance with Charles V via Chapuys, while Anne was pushing the king to pursue an alliance with the Lutheran princes. We can't overlook the possibility, however, that Cromwell was hedging his bets and romancing both leaders at the same time, which his biographer Diarmaid MacCulloch does not put past the slick minister.[562]

However, once word of the Lutheran negotiations got back to Charles V in the midst of his blackmailing Henry VIII, it's safe to say he was not best pleased at being two-timed. He subsequently threatened the German princes and prepared to retaliate with his brother, various nobles of Europe and the pope.[563] You see, the princes were a bit of a sore point for Charles, as back in 1530 he too had tried and failed to settle the dust with them at the Diet of Augsburg.

So, we can suddenly understand how Henry would have been horrified at the thought of angering Charles at this most crucial and precarious time, when the emperor was the only one standing in the way of the papal decree that could remove Henry from the throne.

Did this mean he held Anne responsible for giving him bad advice and pushing such a controversial alliance? Was this yet another reason for Cromwell to want Anne gone, her political interests clashing once again with his own? That's certainly how it looked to courtiers, with sixteenth-century sources John Foxe and Alexander Alesius stating it was Anne's involvement in the attempted alliance with the German princes that triggered Henry's decision to kill her.

This claim becomes all the more conclusive when we discover Alesius was no mere outsider commenting on events from afar, but was a vital part of the German negotiations. He had in fact come to the Tudor court on envoy from the very man Henry was trying to woo: Melanchthon.[564] So, his is an insider account of Anne's final political work that confirms, at last, her involvement in the Lutheran alliance and pinpoints it as the final straw that killed the queen of England. An account that has been brushed over for centuries in favour of tales of sex scandals and flirting as being at the root of Anne's murder.

Of course, even if Cromwell *had* been double-dealing by supporting Anne's Lutheran alliance as well his own imperial partnership, once it became clear that the former had angered Charles V, it seems he was quick to pass all blame on to Anne.

This suited Henry, because he needed someone to blame for this new threat of war, and it most definitely could not be himself. As Dr Kevin Dutton explains:

> One of the few things sociopaths can experience is something called Blame Externalisation, where they don't believe they are ever to blame; everyone else is. People are against you and out to get you. This paranoia isn't an emotion, it's faulty reasoning; you've got to get them before they get you.

So it was while Henry was trapped in the midst of this threat of potentially losing the throne, all because of Anne Boleyn's political and religious agenda, that Cromwell chose to present him with the 'evidence' that she had cheated on him.[565] With nerves frayed and tensions high, it suddenly makes sense that this was why Henry made the sociopathically impulsive decision that Anne was a liability and no longer worth the fight. This is why he asked no questions, and is yet another reason he accepted her guilt without challenge. It was an easy way out for him. Indeed, it was. Before Anne's men returned from negotiations in Wittenberg, she was dead.

◆ ◆ ◆

So as the evidence mounts up, it looks increasingly likely that no one individual killed Anne Boleyn. Instead, it was the result of a spectacular group effort, timed to perfection.

Hey, teamwork makes the dream work.

But there is one person we have overlooked. One person whose unforgiving and relentless work triggered this whole plot, and we can no longer brush over it. That is Anne Boleyn herself. Knowing just how perilous her situation was in those final months, she could have scaled things back. Toed the line on controversial government policies. Not challenged the Dissolution Act until she was safely pregnant again. But time was of the essence, and Anne was a woman on a mission. So, let me end this chapter by asking one question – and know that I don't ask it to make a martyr of Anne Boleyn, but only to understand her psyche. Were her final missions of 1536 in fact suicide missions?

The fact that only days before her arrest, she was making plans for her daughter's care tells us that she knew her political activism was putting her life in danger. But had she already come to accept the possible consequences? After all, Anne had grown up watching men and women die for the greater good. She knew she couldn't cause shockwaves in the Church, Parliament and royal courts of Europe without making real enemies. The title of queen protected her to some degree, but did she realise that fighting as strongly as she did could end up getting her killed?

During Anne's imprisonment, the constable of the Tower of London reported that 'this lady hath much joy and pleasure in death',[566] almost as if a part of her had made peace with the inevitable outcome some time before. Which leads me to suspect that the real cause for her shock and horror at her arrest was more due to the fact that, when it came down to it, unlike those whose amnesty she herself had campaigned for, she wasn't actually imprisoned for her political work or religious cause. The reasons given for her eventual condemnation were so underhand that the people of England would never know she had been taken down for fighting for their human rights and religious freedom.

Instead, her name was being blackened, her character systematically ruined and her memory soiled. The cause was not even a talking point, and I fear *this* may have been the hardest part of all for Anne to come to terms with.

CHAPTER 13

THE MURDER OF A QUEEN:
WHY ANNE BOLEYN HAD TO DIE

It's the question everyone asks.

Not just what went wrong, but why Anne Boleyn had to die. Why was she not simply imprisoned, sent to a nunnery or divorced and banished like Katherine of Aragon before her?

Sadly, there were too many inescapable reasons as to why Anne's fate was sealed before her crimes had even been fabricated. Firstly, as this all began with Cromwell, it wasn't simply a case of appeasing the king and finding him an escape route, in which case another annulment would have been the obvious option – especially now they were in full control of the law. Alas, the current situation was unique in that Cromwell had to convince the king to get rid of his wife at a time when this wasn't something he was actively pursuing himself. In order to achieve this spectacular feat, Cromwell had to present Henry with shocking evidence that would play on his paranoia, trigger his well-known explosive anger and push him to make the kind of irrational and catastrophic decisions his minister had now come to know him for.

Of course, once Cromwell had taken this underhand route, he knew that while Anne lived there was always a chance she could make a comeback, just as Wolsey had done. The fight she had unleashed in recent months was all the proof he needed that she would not go quietly and accept her fate. While there was breath in her body, she would conspire for revenge against the man who ruined her. Who knows, maybe one of those damn poison plots might have finally come to fruition. So, the lawyer in him knew he couldn't risk her survival; he needed to tie up all loose ends, and with Anne having been an English commoner, Cromwell knew they could kill her off without starting the kind of war that would have followed any attempt on Katherine of Aragon's life.

But what about Henry?

Once he realised the evidence Cromwell had provided him with had given him a sudden and unplanned escape route, the king understood what needed to be done. Anne was as strong-willed as Katherine. Henry knew she would fight him for years, as his first wife had done, and in the process cast doubts over the legitimacy of his next queen and subsequent heir.

But that was not the only practical factor for Henry. He had been warned before that any annulment from Anne could be interpreted as acceptance of the pope's long-standing belief that Katherine of Aragon was the true queen – something England could never back down on after all they had sacrificed for it.[567]

So, as soon as it was decided that Anne was no longer to be queen, Henry would have realised the urgent need for her to die; and unfortunately for Anne, her husband had no conscience urging him not to kill her.

◆ ◆ ◆

When Henry abruptly left the May Day celebrations without a word of explanation to Anne and rode to Whitehall Palace, she knew something was happening. She wouldn't have known of Smeaton's confession and arrest, or of Henry interrogating Norris on their journey to Whitehall.

Instead, she was left at Greenwich Palace with her toddler, Elizabeth, her anxiety building and eating away at her.

The following day, 2 May, Anne tried to distract herself by watching a tennis match with her ladies. And that was when they came for her. Three men: Master Treasurer Fitzwilliam, Master Controller William Paulet, and most galling of all, Anne's own uncle the duke of Norfolk – a man with zero moral compass, yet with the innate ability to sense whose team he needed to be on for his own self-serving interest; to hell with any notions of loyalty or family ties. Norfolk knew that if he were to escape going down with his sister's family, he needed to convey to the king his disgust at the unfolding situation. Indeed, he displayed an impressive willingness that bordered on eagerness to bring his niece to justice. Never having been a fan of Anne's power when it was teamed with her increasingly strong-minded independence, Norfolk's patronising show of horror at her supposed misconduct was a role he played to convincing perfection.

As Norfolk took control of Anne's capture, she describes how she was 'cruelly handled' when told of her alleged offences by the council and that she was to be arrested and sent to the Tower of London. It sounds like Paulet was playing good cop and acted like a gentleman, and Fitzwilliam was quiet, apparently in a world of his own; but it was Norfolk, as Anne told her jailers in the Tower, who was the most antagonistic, passive-aggressively tutting and shaking his head at her.[568] The sheer condescension of his mock disappointment would have made the whole scene that much more infuriating for her.

And so this is what it came to. Of all the doomsday scenarios she might have tortured herself with, could she ever have imagined it would end like this? She must have been experiencing such confusion as to where this had come from . . . Was this even Cromwell's doing? It had nothing to do with their politics, so was it a plot by Mary? But there were no allegations of being a heretic, so was it Henry's accusation?

There would have been no answers. They were here to take her away. But fate gave Anne one small respite. As they were to travel by barge to the Tower, they had to wait for the tide to turn, so she was taken to her queen's quarters within Greenwich Palace – essentially under house arrest – until they could set off.[569] Did this give Anne a chance to say one last goodbye to her daughter, Elizabeth? Would they have allowed her the privilege? Is this what she alluded to when she said she was cruelly handled? Either way, those few hours alone before she had to face the horror of the Tower would have given her essential time to regain her composure and come to terms with what was happening. Indeed, when the men finally escorted her aboard the barge, she is said to have stayed silent for the hour-long journey down the Thames.

Anne arrived at the Tower at 5 p.m., but contrary to popular legend she didn't make her entrance through the infamous Traitors' Gate. Surprisingly, as queen she was still afforded the luxury of using the royals' private entrance at Court Gate, a few hundred yards along – the one she had passed through for her coronation celebrations only three years earlier. From there she crossed the bridge over the moat and was escorted through the Byward entrance into the Tower, where a cannon was fired, as was customary to mark the arrival of all nobility into the fortress.[570] Here, Anne was greeted by the prison's own grim reaper, William Kingston, the constable of the Tower. It's at this point that Anne's composure is said to have crumbled. Wyatt reports her as having prayed before them all, 'O Lord, help me, as I am guiltless of this whereof I am accused.'[571]

Then she asked if she would be taken to a dungeon. When Kingston replied that she was to stay in the same lodgings as for her coronation, it's claimed Anne said, 'It is too good for me.'[572] Some historians have taken this to be an accidental admission of guilt; what else could she have possibly meant by such a statement? But we cannot presume to know Anne's inner turmoil at that terrifying moment, or indeed what harrowing thoughts she was torturing herself with. Could her desire for self-punishment have been the result of a mother's guilt at leaving her daughter in the hands of the monsters responsible for this horrific turn of events? Did she believe she deserved this fate, having gone too far and now placed everyone she loved in dire jeopardy?

Anne had held it together stoically until this moment; but now, as Kingston reported to Cromwell, she broke down as reality set in, dropping to her knees on the cobblestones, weeping. Then overcome with a sudden hysteria, 'in the same sorrow fell into a great laughing, and she hath done so many times since'.[573]

Anne was put with four female attendants but none of her own ladies, which she told Kingston she thought 'very unkind'.[574] Little did she realise her own ladies had been spying on her just as much as these new women had now been instructed to, going out of their way to interact with Anne in order to get incriminating stories out of her.[575] But in the first moments of her incarceration, Kingston reported back to Cromwell that she only had scattered and fragmented thoughts, asking, 'Do you know why I am here? When saw you the king? I pray you to tell me where my Lord Rochford is? Oh where is my sweet brother?'[576]

Kingston pleaded ignorance as to the reasons for her imprisonment, claiming that he hadn't seen Henry since the celebrations the day before, and that at this point George was still at Whitehall. Anne concluded sadly, 'O my mother, though will die for sorrow.'[577]

Then, fully aware that she was at the mercy of a corrupt system, she asked Kingston, 'Shall I die without justice?'

His response? 'The poorest subject the king hath, had justice,' to which Anne laughed – the only appropriate response to such a false claim.[578]

It was here that Kingston wrote how he had 'seen many men and women executed and they have been in great sorrow, and to my knowledge, this lady hath much joy and pleasure in death'.[579] Indeed, while Anne was in prison she would go on to display many erratic actions that were out of character, not least prophesying they would have no rain until she was delivered out of the Tower and that a disaster from heaven would follow her execution.[580]

It was on her first night in prison that she asked for the sacrament in her chamber 'that she might pray for mercy', as Kingston put it.[581] Now, while we have already discussed how this does not prove a lack of true evangelical faith or motivation on Anne's part, merely that she was a moderate reformer, Kingston did also report her as saying, 'I shall be in heaven, for I have done many good deeds.' This seemingly goes against the core values of evangelism; but it was Melanchthon of the German Lutheran Schmalkaldic League, a friend and pupil of Martin Luther, who insisted that justification and salvation by good deeds was less important than being justified by faith alone. *Less* important. Alas, still important, and arguably the basis for most religious schools of thought. So not, I must point out, the last grains of evidence history provided us with that Anne was a selfish, faithless, morally corrupt adulteress with only her own self-serving interest at heart.

By his third written report to Cromwell, Kingston noted that 'one hour she is determined to die, the next much contrary to that'.[582]

Once again, while musing over what possible events of the past few days could have led her to here, Anne asked Kingston, 'Shall I have justice?' But so confident was she that the silly encounters she detailed with Norris, Smeaton and Weston were not worthy of imprisonment, she declared, 'If any man accuse me I can say but nay and they can bring no witness.'[583]

Little did she realise that it was around this point that they were bribing and bullying her ladies into giving false witness accounts.

◆ ◆ ◆

Though Anne's brother, George, had been arrested mere hours before her on 2 May when he rode to see the king at Whitehall, Anne herself did not hear of him being at the Tower with her until much later. When she did, clearly unaware of the accusations levied against him, she found it strangely comforting to know she wasn't in this harrowing situation alone, telling Kingston she was very glad they were both together.[584]

In fact, Anne's only comfort and familiarity during this entire terrifying and isolating experience were the regular visits from her chaplain and sermon partner in crime, John Skippe.[585] At last, she had someone who knew the full story and could bring her news from the outside, as well as discuss the truth of why she was being targeted, and by whom. This is surely when the plot against her must have fallen into place, particularly as she then asked Kingston to pass a letter on to Cromwell. However, he offered her the opportunity only to pass on a verbal message, to which she said, 'I have much marvelled that the king's council come not to me.'[586] But unbeknown to her, Cromwell had come to the Tower several times by this point, he had just been too scared to face Anne himself – no doubt not wanting to weaken his resolve to kill her.[587]

It's a miracle they actually granted Skippe access to such a high-risk prisoner, as it would appear all other close family members and friends were banned from visiting the Tower. Kingston reported that Anne complained her female attendants couldn't provide any news on her father – this, of course, leading to one of history's most notorious lies about Thomas Boleyn.

Second only to the notion that he pimped out his daughters to the king is the idea that he left his children to die in the Tower and made no attempt to save them. Even if you are unconvinced of his moral integrity, let's logically assess the situation from a self-preservation viewpoint: surely any skilled diplomat of Thomas's pedigree, trained to defuse high-tension incidents exactly like these, would have fought to save his children – if only because their demise would result in his own. If we overlook for a moment every protective, fatherly instinct he had displayed throughout Anne's life, from securing her a nobility-level education to sheltering her away from Henry's early bombardment and discouraging this whole dangerous marriage, we realise there is not one plausible reason for Thomas Boleyn to have stayed silent, leaving his children to die and his own reputation to be inevitably ruined.

Historians are well within their rights to argue that there is no evidence that he fought to save them. Indeed, no evidence survives. But it seems illogical to presume it never existed. If Cromwell was as smart and calculating as he appears to have been, he would have destroyed any begging letters appealing for amnesty so as not to risk Thomas wrangling his family out of this almighty set-up.

We also have to realise, though, there was a limit to how hard Thomas could fight for his children without putting the rest of his family in grave danger. He knew Cromwell was baying for all Boleyn blood, and as he himself was a powerful and key member of the king's inner circle, if Thomas took a public stance against the monarch's decision to execute Anne and George he risked becoming a target himself. And if Thomas was wiped out too, who would protect and provide for his wife, his remaining daughter and three grandchildren?

As his biographer concludes, 'Just because Thomas's grief was not officially recorded does not mean he and his wife did not suffer over the loss of their children.'[588]

And yet Anne's father wasn't the only person criticised for not doing enough to save her from her fate.

The day after her incarceration, Anne's closest confidant and ally, Thomas Cranmer, wrote what has now become an infamous letter to the king. With limited information on exactly why she had been arrested, the archbishop knew he had to walk a tightrope; one false step and the entire evangelical cause that he and Anne had been championing in England could come crashing down with her. Which more than explains his lacklustre attempt at defending her innocence in the way we might have hoped.

But before we condemn him as a traitor to his patron, it must be pointed out that by the time Cranmer came to send his letter to Henry, he had been given full details of the lurid claims against Anne; but instead of rewriting the letter to further safeguard and distance himself from her, he sent the original, in which he attested that, 'I never had better opinion in woman, than I had in her; which maketh me think, that she should not be culpable.'

Of course, he quickly threw in that surely Henry would never have reacted in such an extreme way had she not been guilty and, if so, she should suffer the full extent of the law. Yet, even after this safe acknowledgement that the king was right, Cranmer still put his neck on the line and declared his alliance and love for the queen by telling him that 'next unto your Grace I was most bound unto her of all creatures living . . .'[589]

Alas, this might give us pause to consider that if a letter clearly accepting the possibility of Anne's guilt was allowed to reach the king, why a more impassioned letter from her father arguing only the irrefutable evidence of Anne's innocence might have been destroyed, for fear it would change Henry's mind.

◆ ◆ ◆

As Anne became more desperate and desolate in prison, cut off from all communication, it's said she penned a heartfelt and somewhat cutting letter to the one man who could make all of this stop: her husband, the king. Yes, a letter exists that is said to have been written by Anne on 6 May, during her first week in prison. This letter's authenticity has gone from hotly debated to downright dismissed, with persuasive arguments for and against it being genuine.

Indeed, upon first inspection the letter is convincing. The fact that it was found among Cromwell's papers after his own arrest in 1540, along with the letters from William Kingston, the constable of the Tower, makes a very good case for authenticity.[590] However, why would Cromwell not destroy a letter like this that could run the risk of being discovered and change the king's mind? Or, worse, that could bring about Cromwell's arrest for concealing vital evidence regarding the execution of the queen? Henry was impulsive; what if he changed his mind about Anne and blamed Cromwell for withholding information?

It is said that stylistically, in language and penmanship, this intriguing letter doesn't match any of Anne's other writings. In it, she repeatedly refers to herself in the third person, something she had never done before, as well as signing off as simply *Anne Boleyn*, not her usual *Anne the Quene*. But this has been explained away as either Anne writing under extreme stress or having dictated the letter to a scribe – and yes, both are plausible.[591]

There is also a lot of truth in the content of the letter. If this is a forgery, it is clear the writer knew certain things about Anne's situation and was angered at the negative propaganda following her death. So for this reason I still believe it's an important document that we should pay attention to, but there are also some vital oversights in the detail that the writer couldn't have realised, and these straight away call the letter out as fake.

Firstly, it opens with, 'Your displeasure and my imprisonment are things so strange unto me, as to what to write or what to excuse, I am altogether ignorant.' But she wasn't ignorant. She was told upon arrest exactly why the king was displeased with her and why she was being arrested. Surely, she would have used this one chance to defend herself eloquently against the lurid and outrageous claims, rather than play dumb to make a point?[592]

The fact that the letter then goes on to entirely blame Jane Seymour for her imprisonment 'for whose sake I am now as I am' is another warning sign. That might be how it appeared to an outsider dreaming up a letter from Anne, but she herself knew, as we do now, that the real reason for the plot against her was her political interference and not Henry taking a new mistress – an affair which, for all Anne knew at this stage, could have blown over in a couple of months like all the others.

Another thing historians have called into question is the fact Anne tears into Henry with the line 'I desire of God, that he will pardon your great Sin . . . and that he will not call you unto a strict Account of your unprincely and cruel usage of me.'[593] I agree with some that if anyone would have dared speak to Henry in this way it would have been Anne, particularly given that her emotions were so erratic during her imprisonment. However, as letters are a more measured form of expression, I'm unconvinced she would take this stance at such a delicate time. It wasn't just her own life at risk here; after all, it was for the sake of her daughter that Anne sugar-coated her execution speech and practically celebrated the king. She knew better than anyone how Henry reacted to goading comments like this. So why would she have risked angering him when she and her family's lives were in his hands?

There is another unrealistic moment in the final paragraph, where Anne pleads for the lives of the men accused with her. But by the date of this letter, she knew she had been joined in prison by her brother, so it seems odd that she wouldn't specifically plead her brother's innocence over those of the court staff.

Finally, a postscript written in the third person on the reverse side of the letter, seemingly by an assistant, has a suspiciously retrospective tone; here, Anne thanks the king for making her a marquess, then queen, and 'now, seeing he could bestow no further honour upon her on earth, for purposing to make her, by martyrdom, a saint in heaven'.

But when Anne supposedly wrote this letter, she didn't know she was going to die. Also, her being seen as a 'Protestant martyr' was an idea that would grow in time, when her supporters felt safe to talk about her again. Not only that but she had been arrested for adultery, not heresy. Her name was being dragged through the mud; there was no martyrdom in what was happening to her, which, disappointingly, renders this bold letter unlikely to have been written by Anne.

As the days went on, Cromwell got a little gung-ho with the arrests. Not content with Smeaton, Norris, Weston and Anne's own brother, he also brought in for questioning Thomas Wyatt, Richard Page and William Brereton.

Wyatt we know well from his pursuit of Anne in the early days, and so may seem an obvious target. But during Cromwell's initial years at court the two became good friends, which makes his arrest seem even more cold-hearted. Or was this the very reason he was allowed to leave, free of charge? Did his release conveniently add more weight to those who were convicted – for if some were found to be not guilty upon interrogation, wouldn't this imply they found real evidence for those they condemned?[594] That would certainly seem to be the case, for they also released Page without charge. Unfortunately, Brereton was not so lucky. A past run-in with Cromwell – he had rigged the trial of a man Cromwell tried and failed to save from execution[595] – sealed his fate. Vitally, Brereton also dominated the monasteries in Cheshire and had blocked Cromwell from dissolving them. And so, suddenly, the list of men accused reads like a personal vendetta against all those who had ever wronged Master Thomas Cromwell.[596]

Finally, on Friday 12 May, it was time for the first of the men to stand trial at Westminster Hall. For Smeaton, Norris, Weston and Brereton, Cromwell selected a suitably biased jury that included Edward Willoughby, who owed Brereton money, William Askew, a supporter of Princess Mary, Walter Hungerford, a dependant of Cromwell's, and Giles Alington, who was married to Thomas More's stepdaughter. The remaining jurors were members of the anti-Boleyn faction or Cromwell's own allies.[597] The accused didn't stand a chance.

Though all the men pleaded not guilty – apart from Smeaton, for whom it was too late to back out of his original confession – you'll not be surprised to hear there was no room for a fair defence and they were quickly found guilty, sentenced to the horrifying prospect of being hanged, drawn and quartered. Thankfully, this was later downgraded to only a beheading by axe as a 'royal favour' – something that was more likely to have come from a potentially guilt-ridden Cromwell than the king, who didn't possess the capacity to feel guilt or sympathy. Though it's an interesting thought that if Henry truly believed these men to be guilty, surely he would have wanted them to suffer as much as possible?[598] The fact that he signed off on such simple beheadings speaks volumes as to how emotionally invested he really was in this supposedly heartbreaking trial of adultery and treachery.

Because the men's trials took place on the Friday, this meant Anne and George, who were being tried separately at the Tower of London, had to wait the weekend before their own trials on Monday 15 May.

Though George's fate still hung in the balance, the guilty verdicts for the men on the Friday meant only one thing for Anne. If they were guilty, so was she, and this is why they called for her executioner before she had stood trial. This also explains why Henry would tell Jane Seymour of Anne's condemnation before she had even set foot in the courtroom. It sounds like a set-up to us, but even Anne would have realised that her trial was merely a formality; if her so-called lovers had already been convicted, it could only go one way for her.

So really, Friday 12 May was the day Anne Boleyn discovered she had been found guilty of adultery. This meant that when she stepped into the courtroom on Monday she was prepared. She knew the inevitability of what was coming. It was no longer a case of fighting to prove her innocence, but of defending her name with as much dignity as possible.

Anne and George's trials took place in the King's Hall within the Tower of London, where special stands were built to hold an audience of two thousand. The siblings' uncle the duke of Norfolk had the galling nerve to sit as lord steward, with his son deputising as earl marshal.[599] And as a needlessly spiteful finishing touch, Henry Percy was made to sit on the jury and condemn Anne to death.

As queen, she was tried first, and made her entrance accompanied by the constable's wife, Lady Kingston, and one of her aunts, Lady Boleyn.

For someone so hot-headed, the fact that Anne managed to stay calm and composed as the most ludicrous accusations were thrown at her says so much about the towering strength of character that had got her this far and intimidated all who opposed her. She was poised, focused and fully in control as she confirmed that no, she hadn't been unfaithful, and no, she hadn't wished or plotted the king's death. Nor Katherine's. Nor Mary's.

While on the stand, it was also put to Anne that she had conspired to poison the king and promised to marry one of her lovers because, *of course*, it's easy for us to see that any one of them were more powerful and more important than the *King of England!* That such a notion could stand up in court would be laughable had it not contributed to the deaths of six innocent people. If Henry had died for any reason whatsoever, Anne would have remarried one of the highest-born noblemen in Europe, not one of the king's privy chamber staff members.[600]

De Carles reports that Anne 'defended herself soberly against the charges . . . She said little but no one to look at her would have thought her guilty.' Funny, that.[601] It was also he who reported what Anne was meant to have said in her defence on the stand: 'I do not say I have always borne the king the humility which I owed him, considering his kindness and the great honour he showed me . . .' Quite true; he made her queen of England, after all. '. . . and the great respect he always paid me.' Not so accurate. He did cheat on her multiple times and sacrificed her life for the Holy Roman Emperor. But this was her last chance at a lenient sentence, so she had to lay it on thick. 'I admit, too, that often I have taken it into my head to be jealous of him . . . But God be my witness if I have done him any other wrong.'[602]

Even Thomas Wriothesley of Princess Mary's faction conceded Anne was incredibly believable. But that could not save her from the inevitable. The jury gave their guilty verdict one by one. Norfolk, fickle as ever, wept as he concluded she had been found guilty.[603] This much Anne expected. But what of her fate? Was she to be banished to a European nunnery? Divorced? Exiled . . . ?

It was Norfolk who announced her death sentence. She was to be 'burned or beheaded as shall please the king'.[604]

According to Alexander Alesius, Anne was said to have 'raised her eyes to heaven', but only de Carles reports that she turned to the judges and 'said she would not dispute them, but believed there was some other reason for which she was condemned than the cause alleged'.[605] Whether or not she did indeed say this, the fact that de Carles reports it confirms that people at the time were aware that she was no adulterer but, rather, the victim of a set-up. Although the reason for this would remain a secret for centuries to come.

He says Anne went on to insist that 'she did not say this to preserve her life, for she was quite prepared to die'. To which de Carles, a hostile source and strong supporter of Mary, admitted 'her speech made even her bitterest enemies pity her'.[606]

And so, as the shock of her death sentence sank in, Anne was escorted out of the oppressive King's Hall and back to her prison lodgings, for it was now her brother's turn.

Formal charges Cromwell brought against George were that he once stayed too long in Anne's chambers, and joked that Elizabeth might not be the king's child. George was then handed a piece of paper on which was written a delicate question they didn't want to ask aloud. At this point, you get a real sense of his rebellion and contempt at the attack on his family – daring and defiant, he read the question aloud to the court of two thousand people: 'Had George ever said that the king couldn't have sex with women and had neither virtue or staying power?'[607]

Under the circumstances, I feel we can forgive him this one last dig and not deem it antagonistic or reckless. His sister, the queen, had just been sentenced to death, which not only sealed his own fate but tells us this was no courtroom banter from George. He was in pain. He was angry. He wanted to hurt and humiliate the man who was doing the same to those he loved. But the mere fact that Cromwell felt the need to ask such a question in a court of law illustrates that rumours of this nature had been circulating among courtiers – indeed, it was Chapuys who had repeated them some weeks before[608] – and that he was determined to pin their source as Anne Boleyn.

As the jury of peers started to deliver their sentencing it all became too much for Henry Percy, who collapsed and had to be helped out of the courtroom. Fellow jury member Charles Brandon suffered no such guilt and was happy to push on with the proceedings.

George's guilty verdict and death sentence were delivered with the speed and flippancy that only a Tudor court could muster. Just like that, another life was to end.

◆ ◆ ◆

Though Anne was initially sentenced to death by burning or beheading, in the end Henry opted for the unusual method of execution by sword. And here we arrive at one of the biggest misconceptions surrounding Anne's execution: that Henry displayed spontaneous compassion by opting out of the traditional beheading by axe, which regularly went disastrously wrong, and chose instead swift decapitation by sword. One final act of mercy for the woman he still loved, but who had betrayed him so deeply.

However, in situations like this, acts of mercy for someone you were supposedly once hopelessly in love with might include hearing their defence against the accusations, giving them a lesser sentence, letting them live. Not once during the investigation was Anne Boleyn herself ever questioned or asked to explain what had happened, so we can't now turn round and claim that the manner in which she was to be brutally murdered was a sign of Henry's everlasting love for her. Death by sword was no act of mercy. As a sociopath, he was devoid of any feelings of compassion, remorse or conscience. The fact that he was betrothed to Jane Seymour the very day after Anne's death should tell you just how much her fate was playing on his mind.

It's not that Henry consciously chose to be as cold and evil as possible – *the tyrant who just loved to hurt people*. This was the science of how his brain functioned. Yes, it's heartless and inhumane, but this is the devastating reality of living with a severe mental illness such as sociopathy. This also renders somewhat questionable the claim by the French priest André Thevet that Henry repented on his deathbed for the 'injustices done to Queen Anne Boleyn'.[609]

So, if not an act of mercy, then what could explain this unprecedented move with Anne's execution?

Henry may have felt indifferent to his wife at the time of her murder, but that's not how he could allow it to look to his subjects. As we have witnessed, sociopaths have an innate ability to mimic the emotions they lack, and a death by sword would enable the king to appear merciful. More importantly, this was the first time a reigning queen had been executed – in fact, this would have been one of the main reasons Henry needed to annul his marriage to Anne before she died, ensuring she wasn't technically a queen when killed. Not that this dulled the impact of her death. To the outside world, Anne still represented the monarchy, and so a noble death by sword would appear more dignified than burning her like a witch at the stake. Even Wyatt describes her death by sword as 'honourable'.[610]

Of course, as the years went on and Henry's mental health deteriorated further, the act of killing a queen evidently lost its shock value. And with Cromwell no longer around to oversee damage limitation for the monarchy, Henry was later to kill his fifth wife, Katherine Howard, employing a standard axeman.

But back in 1536, this was a royal precedent.[611] The Tudor monarchy needed to appear merciful and chivalric; so death by sword was simply the first step in the royal propaganda machine saving Henry from the PR disaster of executing the woman for whom, in the public's eyes, he broke from the Catholic Church. The fact that it is still referenced by historians today to illustrate the king's mercy shows just how effective it was.[612]

◆ ◆ ◆

After her trial, Anne's chaplain John Skippe was on hand to comfort her, staying with her until 2 a.m. the following day.[613] Though she tried to focus her mind with prayer, in the hours and days following her death sentence her thoughts in prison became more and more fragmented and disconnected from reality. Kingston reported that she wondered if Henry was doing all this to test her, and proposed that she should be sent to a nunnery in Antwerp, a move that might have allowed him to marry again. At other times, she was determined to die, and mused darkly that she would come to be known as 'Queen Anne the Headless'. Her mind drifted back to her childhood with Margaret of Austria, and even to whether she'd won the bet she placed on the tennis match she was watching when arrested.[614]

However, on 16 May, the day after Anne's trial, everyone else's minds were focused on the business of killing the condemned. Kingston reports he met with the king himself, who told him all the men should die the following day, on the 17th, and that Archbishop Cranmer would be Anne's confessor – a move that would coincidentally allow the two a chance to say a heartbreaking goodbye and, dare we imagine, perhaps a chance for Anne to pass on a final message to her parents. Yet no news on the date of Anne's own death, with Kingston actively pushing Cromwell for the details of her execution so he could put her mind at rest and prepare the scaffold.[615]

However, Kingston was able to inform George Boleyn that he was to die the next day; George was said to have accepted this, but was deeply worried about the effect his death would have on those around him. The previous day in court, he had even read out a list of people he owed money to, so they wouldn't be left wanting. We might note that this is rather telling of his true personality – that his main concerns were for others and not himself as his final hours passed.[616] Not that this should come as such a great surprise, for in his lifetime George had become governor of the mental asylum Bethlehem, or Bedlam as it is better known – proving that, like his sister, he didn't waste his days indulging solely in the fleeting frivolities of court life.

When the awful day rolled round, it was said that Anne witnessed her brother's beheading from a window in her prison quarters. However, given the location, it would have been impossible to see the scaffold on Tower Hill beyond the north-west walls of the prison. Whether she requested to be moved and whether they would have complied, we will never know.

The only record of Anne's reaction to the men's deaths comes from de Carles. Upon hearing that Smeaton pleaded his guilt on the scaffold with the conventional phrase, 'Masters, I pray you all pray for me for I have deserved the death,' Anne supposedly replied, 'Alas! I fear that his soul will suffer punishment for his false confession.'[617] But does this simply illustrate once again just how scared young Smeaton was of doing the wrong thing? Or was this part of his plea deal with Cromwell? '*Plead guilty and you will have a swift death.*' Might this be why the men's punishment was downgraded from being hanged, drawn and quartered to a quick beheading?

On that very same day, 17 May, something else was to die, and that was Anne's marriage to the king. Thomas Cranmer was forced to declare it annulled on the grounds of Henry's earlier affair with her sister, Mary. Of course, this didn't stop rumours circulating over the centuries that it was in fact due to a pre-contract between Anne and Henry Percy. With no firm evidence either way – Chapuys confirms he heard rumours that it was because of Mary Boleyn, but also ridiculous gossip that it was down to Elizabeth being Norris's child, not the king's[618] – we are left to make our own rational conclusions in light of everything we've learned thus far.

It's also important to note that the marriage annulment wasn't in relation to the crimes that Anne was charged with, and therefore should not be misread as yet another treacherous move from Cranmer, confirming he believed in the guilt of his patron.[619] Stripping Anne of the title of queen wasn't one final insult before the grave, but a necessity to fix a major issue regarding Anne's daughter, Elizabeth. If Anne died as Henry's wife and queen, her daughter would remain heir to the kingdom. Annulling their marriage was simply Henry's way of lining everything up so that his next child with Jane Seymour would have no legal heir to challenge it.

The fear and worry this must have instilled in Anne over the uncertainty of Elizabeth's future is unfathomable. Having seen how Henry had treated Mary after disinheriting her, Anne's anxieties for her daughter must have been tormenting her at this point.[620]

But she had run out of time. She was to die the next day.

At 2 a.m. on 18 May, Anne was still awake with her almoner. She requested that Kingston hear Mass with her shortly after dawn, so he would witness her swearing on the sacrament that she had never been unfaithful to the king. This was the sixteenth-century equivalent of a lie detector test, and not something anyone took lightly; you were risking the eternal damnation of your soul if you lied before the sacrament. This was essential to Anne in order to prove to those present that she was genuine in her declarations of innocence.[621] There was nothing more she could say or do. She was now prepared to die.

But that's when she heard news that she wasn't to be killed until the afternoon. Kingston tells how she called for him, panicking: 'I hear

I shall not die afore noon, and I am sorry there for, for I thought to be dead by this time and past my pain.'[622]

However, as Kingston explains, the date of her execution had still not been set.

Anne had mentally prepared herself for her moment of reckoning and now the emotional rollercoaster dropped her into the abyss of another torturous day of imagining the horrors that were to come.

Kingston reassured her that he would forewarn her on the morning of her death and that she should not fear the execution itself, as the fatal blow wasn't painful but, in his own words, 'so subtle'. Anne's haunting reply to his attempt to soothe and calm her nerves has gone down in history. She said, 'I heard say the executioner was very good, and I have a little neck,' putting her hands around her neck to double-check. At which point, the grim ridiculousness of measuring her own neck for decapitation hit her, and she dissolved into a disturbing fit of laughter.[623]

◆ ◆ ◆

The following day, 19 May 1536, the time had finally come.

Witnesses say Anne was serene and calm as she faced the scaffold. Religious supporters put her seemingly bold and courageous attitude down to unwavering faith. And while I have no doubt that this would have certainly come into play for such a devout evangelical, the more likely reason for her lack of tears and show of emotion come judgement day was that her nerves had been torn to shreds. She would have been dazed, drained and sleep-deprived. Mentally and emotionally exhausted. Are we really surprised an unnatural calm enveloped her at the sheer relief that the suffering was almost over?

An anonymous hostile source reported that Anne walked to the scaffold 'feeble and half stupefied'. I'm sure this was intended as an insult, by someone unaware that future readers aren't in need of Anne the Stoic Martyr and are merely striving to comprehend how Anne Boleyn the human being would have felt at the stark reality of her execution; but her appearing 'half stupefed' strikes me as a completely normal human reaction to this final surreal moment.[624]

However, upon further analysis with Dr Kevin Dutton, we believe we may have identified what Anne was experiencing in the days, hours and indeed minutes leading up to her death. The fact that she knew the inevitability of the verdict of her trial a full week before her execution suggests she may have been displaying symptoms of post-traumatic stress disorder days before she even stepped on to the scaffold: these are the emotional highs and lows, the poor sleep patterns, lack of concentration, the mind whirring with scattered thoughts and an emotional detachment from the situation, which explains her jests about being decapitated.[625] It may seem a bizarre notion to consider, yet seemingly not impossible within the complex labyrinth of the human mind.

And so now, after weeks of isolation, as Anne was led out through a crowd of a thousand spectators packed within the tower walls, her mind and emotions would have been numb to the terrifying scene that surrounded her. Kingston led the way, followed by the four wardresses, as Anne walked the short journey from the queen's quarters, through Coldharbour Gate, to the scaffold awaiting her directly behind the north face of the White Tower.[626] This would have been her last sight on earth, its northern wall dripping with excrement where the toilet drainage poured out. Quite apt, methinks, that Anne should see a wall of human filth before she died. A fitting representation of the corrupt world she was leaving behind.

Kingston led her up the steps, leaving her to face the silent crowd on the four-foot-high scaffold draped in black. We don't know if Anne managed to pick out the faces of the men who were responsible for her death, Cromwell and Brandon, who came to witness the result of their weeks of scheming and plotting. Could Anne even have imagined their level of involvement in her murder at that point? Could anyone?

Reports that she kept looking behind her, nervous of the executioner striking before she was ready, have been misinterpreted as her desperately looking for any sign of a last-minute pardon from the king, and are in contrast to all other reports that she was calm and at peace.

And with that, Anne stepped forward and addressed the crowd.

From the multiple and varying reports of what she said that day, the words that were corroborated by a number of sources were roughly as follows:

> Good Christian people, I have not come here to preach a sermon; I have come here to die. For according to the law and by the law I am judged to die, and therefore will speak nothing against it. I am come hither to accuse no man, nor to speak of that whereof I am accused and condemned to die, but I pray God save the king and send him long to reign over you, for a gentler nor a more merciful prince was there never, and to me he was ever a good, a gentle, and sovereign lord. And if any person will meddle of my cause, I require thee to judge the best. And thus I take my leave of the world and of you all, and I heartily desire you all to pray for me.[627]

Her final words of kindness towards the king may appear to the modern reader to be steeped in sarcasm and irony, but it's clear at this stage that she was being overly gracious for the simple aim of protecting her daughter. If Anne had defended her name and publicly torn into the king, it was only her remaining family members who would have suffered the repercussions. In warning that 'If any person will meddle of my cause, I require thee to judge the best,' she knew any support for her would be seen as treason against the king, and she didn't want any more innocent people to die in her name.

But what we can be sure Anne *didn't* say, as reported by a Portuguese gentleman, is 'Alas, poor head! In a very brief space thou wilt roll in the dust on this scaffold; and as in life thou didst not merit to wear the crown of a queen, so in death, thou deservest not a better doom than this.' How do we know she didn't say this? Firstly, because no foreigners were allowed to witness the execution. Secondly, because the reporter has her saying in the very next breath, 'And ye, my damsels, who, whilst I lived, ever showed yourself so diligent in my service.' And as we well know, the ladies at her execution were not the ladies who had served her in life; she had only known these women for the seventeen days she'd been in the Tower.[628]

In reality, Anne was said to have spoken with 'an untroubled countenance',[629] and sensationalism aside, when her speech ended she turned to say goodbye to her four wardresses, only to find them now in tears. Yes, these were the same women who had been spying on her for the past few weeks in the Tower, providing her own words to be twisted into a case to condemn her to this death over which they were weeping. But their hypocrisy was of no matter to Anne now.

Her ermine mantle was removed, revealing a grey damask gown lined with fur. She took off her gable hood and replaced it with a cap provided by the women. She turned back to the crowd, knelt down and prepared to die. One of the ladies stepped forward to secure a blindfold over her eyes as she started to pray:

'To God I commend my soul. To Christ I commend my soul. Jesu, receive my soul.'[630]

Then the swordsman decapitated Anne with one blow. It was over. She was gone.

◆　◆　◆

One woman had the horrific experience of having to pick up Anne's severed head and wrap it in a cloth. The other ladies wrapped her body in a sheet, and together carried her to the chapel a few hundred yards away. There, she shared the indignity of all victims of the Tower, and was stripped of her clothing. Her body was then placed not in a coffin but an elm chest and buried next to her brother, George, where Anne could finally rest in peace after, let's face it, one almighty fight in this formidable lifetime of hers.[631]

◆ ◆ ◆

ANNE BOLEYN 1501–1536

They say few mourned her, but that's not true. Many mourned Anne Boleyn.

The evangelical reformists knew Anne was the only one in England fighting their cause from a genuine position of power, and now she was gone. And if *she* could be killed, what about them? So, when historians state that few mourned Anne, perhaps what they should say is that few were *allowed* to mourn her. To support the former queen was considered treason, and meant they must automatically be against the king. Hence, few dared risk their life to defend the name of a woman who was now dead and could no longer be hurt, whereas they and their cause still could be.

But make no mistake, Anne was mourned:[632] by the youths whose education she relentlessly championed, by the underprivileged families for whom she fought so hard, by those who could not live in the freedom of their religious beliefs – they would all have mourned the loss of Anne Boleyn; now that we know the full story of her work, it's impossible to think otherwise.

So, there you have it. The whole truth. Nothing left out for convenience. An honest analysis that takes into account the fact that Anne Boleyn was a real person who wasn't reading from a script, whose shortcomings made her human, whose fight should be an inspiration to us all. Like for Anne, now is not a time to sleepwalk through life turning a blind eye, believing if it's not affecting us, then it's not our responsibility. Take note from what you've just read, for history has a nasty habit of repeating itself. This is why it's so important we know the truth about what really happened, in order to make damn sure it never happens again. History is watching you.

BIBLIOGRAPHY

PRIMARY SOURCES

Baroni, Victor. *La Contre-Réforme devant la Bible*. Slatkine Reprints, 1986.

Calendar of State Papers, Spain. British History Online.

De Carles, Lancelot, in George Ascoli, *La Grande-Bretagne Devant L'opinion Française Depuis La Guerre de Cent Ans Jusqu'à La Fin Du XVIe Siècle*, 233–34. Paris: Gamber, 1927.

Cavendish, George. *The Life of Cardinal Wolsey*. Ed. S. W. Singer, second edition. Thomas Davison for Harding and Lepard, 1827.

Cherbury, Edward, Lord Herbert of. *The Life and Raigne of King Henry VIII*, E.G. for T. Whittaker, 1649.

Colwell, Thomas. In *The Manuscripts of His Grace the Duke of Rutland*, Volume I, 1888.

Dowling, Maria, ed. 'William Latymer's *Chronickille of Anne Bulleyne*'. In *Camden Miscellany Vol XXXIX*. Butler & Tanner, 1990.

Hall, Edward. *Hall's Chronicle*. AMS Press, 1965.

Leti, Gregorio. *Historia o vero vita di Elisabetta, regina d'Inghilterra*. *Apreſſo Abramo Wolfgang 1693*.

Letters and Papers, Foreign and Domestic, Henry VIII. British History Online.

Norton, Elizabeth. *The Anne Boleyn Papers*. Amberley Publishing, 2013.

Sander, Nicholas. *The Rise and Growth of the Anglican Schism*, edited by David Lewis. Burns and Oates, 1877.

Thevet, André. *La Cosmographie universelle*. Guillaume Chaudiere, 1575.

Wriothesley, Charles. *A chronicle of England during the reigns of the Tudors, from A.D. 1485 to 1559*. London, Longmans, 1838–1901.

SECONDARY SOURCES

Please note: This is intended solely as a bibliography for the works referenced within the endnotes. It is not to be taken as a recommended reading list approved by the author.

Bernard, G. W. *The King's Reformation: Henry VIII and the Remaking of the English Church*. Yale University Press, 2005.

Borman, Tracy. *Thomas Cromwell: The untold story of Henry VIII's most faithful servant*. Hodder and Stoughton, 2015.

Bragg, Melvin. *William Tyndale: A Very Brief History*. Society for Promoting Christian Knowledge, 2017.

Clinton, Hillary Rodham. *What Happened*. Simon and Schuster, 2017.

Cholakian, Patricia F. and Rouben C. *Marguerite de Navarre (1492–1549): Mother of the Renaissance*. Columbia University Press, 2006.

Dowling, Maria. 'Anne Boleyn and Reform.' *The Journal of Ecclesiastical History*, Vol. 35, issue 1, Cambridge University Press, 1984.

Dunn, Sarah. 'The mark of the Devil: medical proof in witchcraft trials.' Electronic theses and dissertations, University of Louisville, 2014.

Elton, G. R. *Reform and Renewal: Thomas Cromwell and the Common Weal*. Cambridge University Press, 1973.

Elton, G. R. 'An Early Tudor Poor Law.' *The Economic History Review*, Vol. 6, No. 1, 1953.

Erickson, Carolly. *Great Harry: A Biography of Henry VIII*. St Martin's Press, 2007.

Fraser, Antonia. *The Six Wives of Henry VIII*. Phoenix, 2003.

Freeman, Thomas S. 'Research, Rumour and Propaganda: Anne Boleyn in Foxe's "Book of Martyrs".' *The Historical Journal*, Vol. 38, Issue 4, 2009.

Friedmann, Paul. *Anne Boleyn*. Ed. Josephine Wilkinson. Amberley Publishing, 2010.

Gordon, Peter and Denis Lawton. *Royal Education: Past Present and Future*. Frank Cass, 2003.

Gunn, Steven. *Charles Brandon*. Amberley Publishing, 2016.

Hayward, Maria. *Dress at the Court of King Henry VIII*. Routledge, 2017.

Hibbert, Christopher. *The Virgin Queen: A Personal History of Elizabeth I*. Penguin Books, 2010.

Ives, Eric. *The Life and Death of Anne Boleyn*. Blackwell Publishing, 2005.

Ives, Eric. 'Anne Boleyn and the "Entente Évangélique".' OpenEdition.org.

Lipscomb, Suzannah. *1536: The Year that Changed Henry VIII*. Lion Hudson, 2009.

Loades, David. *Henry VIII*. Amberley Publishing, 2011.

MacCulloch, Diarmaid. *Thomas Cranmer: A Life*. Revised Edition. Yale University Press, 2016.

MacCulloch, Diarmaid. *Thomas Cromwell: A Life*. Allen Lane, 2018.

Mackay, Lauren. 'The Life and Career of Thomas Boleyn (1477–1539): Courtier, Ambassador and Statesman.' Unpublished PhD thesis, University of Newcastle, Australia, 2018.

Mackay, Lauren. *Among the Wolves of Court*. I. B. Tauris, 2018.

Mackay, Lauren. *Inside the Tudor Court*. Amberley Publishing, 2014.

Marshall, Peter. *1517: Martin Luther and the Invention of the Reformation*. Oxford University Press, 2017.

Marshall, Peter. *Heretics and Believers: A History of the English Reformation*. Yale University Press, 2017.

Matusiak, John. *Henry VIII: The Life and Rule of England's Nero*. The History Press, 2014.

Morley, Henry. *Clement Marot and Other Studies*. Chapman and Hall, 1871.

National Archives of the UK Government. Trial records, viewed by private appointment.

National Institute of Mental Health. nimh.nih.gov.

Nichols, John Gough, ed. *Narratives of the days of the Reformation, chiefly from the manuscripts of John Foxe the martyrologist*. Camden Society, 1838–1901.

Norton, Elizabeth. *The Anne Boleyn Papers*. Amberley Publishing, 2013.

Norton, Elizabeth. *Jane Seymour: Henry VIII's True Love*. Amberley Publishing, 2010.

Parker, Matthew. *The Correspondence of Matthew Parker, D.D., Archbishop of Canterbury*. Edited for the Parker Society by John Bruce and Thomas Thomason Perowne, 1853.

Russell, Gareth. *Young and Damned and Fair*. Simon and Schuster, 2016.

Robinson, Mary F. *Margaret of Angoulême, queen of Navarre*. Roberts Brothers, 1887.

Scarisbrick, J. J. *English Monarchs: Henry VIII*. Methuen, 1990.

Sharpe Hume, Martin Andrew. *Chronicle of Henry VIII of England*. G. Bell and Sons, 1889.

Starkey, David. *Six Wives: The Queens of Henry VIII*. Vintage, 2004.

Warnicke, Retha M. *The Rise and Fall of Anne Boleyn: Family Politics at the Court of Henry VIII*. Cambridge University Press, 2003.

Weir, Alison. *The Six Wives of Henry VIII*. Vintage, 1991.

Weir, Alison. *The Lady in the Tower: The Fall of Anne Boleyn*. Jonathan Cape, 2009.

ACKNOWLEDGMENTS

Dear Reader,

You would not be holding this book were it not for the following people. Pray, be standing for those who have served history and the truth with diligence and generosity . . .

Anna Hogarty, my literary agent at Madeleine Milburn Literary, TV & Film Agency, who was the first person not only to believe in me and this book, but to be equally as passionate as I am about getting the truth out there. I will be forever grateful and indebted to you. Indeed, huge thanks go out to the whole team at MMLA for their enthusiasm and support.

Alex Carr, who was the first editor at Amazon Publishing to propose that this powerhouse company publish my research. Victoria Pepe, who took over the helm as editor and reminded me that history is written by the winners, so no wonder we've only had a twisted version of Anne. Of course, so much love, respect and gratitude must be sent to the entire team at Amazon and publishing imprint Little A. Anne's true story deserved nothing less than the all-conquering, global giants that you are!

Richard Collins, with whom it has been an absolute joy to edit this book. I am so very grateful to have had someone of your calibre and expertise to debate counter-arguments with while perfecting the finer detail of this extensive analysis. A huge thank you for your time and work.

Richard Rex, professor of Reformation history at the University of Cambridge, thank you for the invaluable theology lessons, for taking the time to advise me on the complex issues of the Reformation and first-generation evangelicals. You've been so generous with your time and knowledge from the very start, and I will always be grateful for that.

Dr Kevin Dutton, research psychologist at the University of Oxford, for being the superstar psychologist that you are. It was as much a pleasure as it was absolutely fascinating to have conversations with you about the psyche of the Tudors. The world will finally understand Henry VIII that much better thanks to your contribution. I also would like to extend my gratitude to Professor James Fallon; thank you for taking the time to add to the debate. I dedicate Chapter Three to both of you.

Diarmaid MacCulloch, with whom it has been an honour to discuss the intricacies of sixteenth-century politics! A huge thank you must also be said for allowing me an advance copy of your Cromwell biography.

Thanks must also be extended to the late Eric Ives, whose decades of research have served as a vital reference and starting point for my own work. I doff my cap to you, sir, for your services to Anne Boleyn and help in inching closer to the truth.

Lauren Mackay, thank you for sharing your extensive research on Thomas and George Boleyn. It's been essential in helping piece together and complete this mammoth Boleyn family puzzle.

Thanks also goes to Alison Palmer and Owen Emmerson at Hever Castle for your help in confirming Anne's time back at her childhood home.

Judith E. Lewis, your expertise in midwifery has been so greatly appreciated in relation to the sensitive topic of Anne's pregnancies. It's pure serendipity that you also happen to have an immense love of the Tudors!

Of course, thanks to G & The Team for alerting me to the censorship of Anne Boleyn and giving me the fight and inspiration to expose the truth. It's been a weird old journey that I never saw coming.

Sophia Raja, thank you for the endless support over the (many) years; you've been a wonderful and loyal friend in this modern-day Tudor court of ours! Also, huge thanks for advising on my #TudorRants in that first draft, then nit-picking with me on the last night of the final rewrite!

Thank you to my whole family for your individual support in many different ways, but special mentions must of course go to my parents JNK and PB for being the best cheerleaders a reclusive writer could wish for. Finally, thank you to my darling OG, whose face pulls me out of the isolation and despair every time. You are truly *The Most Happy* and I love you for it.

Most gratefully,
Hayley Nolan

ABOUT THE AUTHOR

Photo © 2018 Dawn Bowery

Hayley Nolan is the historical researcher, writer and presenter of hit social media mini-series *The History Review*, which reached 3 million viewers in its first year. She also produces and fronts the spin-off iTunes podcast of the same name.

Hayley's work has led her to partner with some of the country's most respected historical organisations, including the Houses of Parliament for the 2017 General Election, the National Archives of the UK Government, Historic Royal Palaces including the Tower of London and Hampton Court Palace, Royal Museums Greenwich, the English Heritage site of Henry VIII's home, Eltham Palace, and Anne Boleyn's childhood homes of Hever Castle and the Château Royal de Blois.

A graduate of London's prestigious Royal Court Theatre Young Writers Programme, Hayley further trained in scriptwriting at the Royal Academy of Dramatic Art (RADA).

Hayley was born on the edge of England's Peak District, and at the age of twelve moved to France, where she grew up in Bordeaux and Chamonix. She now lives in London.

ENDNOTES

Introduction

1   Hillary Rodham Clinton, *What Happened*, p.9.

Chapter 1

2   Elizabeth Norton, *The Anne Boleyn Papers*, Intro, p.9.

3   Mackay, 'The Life and Career of Thomas Boleyn (1477–1539)', p.32.

4   Lauren Mackay, *Among the Wolves of Court*, p.26.

5   Tracy Borman, *Thomas Cromwell: The Untold Story of Henry VIII's Most Faithful Servant*, p.50.

6   Norton, *Anne Boleyn Papers*, p.32.

7   Lauren Mackay, 'The Life and Career of Thomas Boleyn (1477–1539): Courtier, Ambassador and Statesman', pp.32–33.

8   Steven Gunn, *Charles Brandon: Henry VIII's Closest Friend*, p.43.

9   Ibid., pp.42–4; Eric Ives, *The Life and Death of Anne Boleyn*, p.6.

10   Mackay, 'The Life and Career of Thomas Boleyn (1477–1539)', p.76.

11   Ives, *Life and Death of Anne Boleyn*; Norton, *Anne Boleyn Papers*, Intro, p.9.

12   Mackay, 'The Life and Career of Thomas Boleyn (1477–1539)', p.34.

13   Christopher Hibbert, *The Virgin Queen: A Personal History of Elizabeth I*, p.6. The quote is: 'Rarely or never did any maid or wife leave the court still chaste.'

14   Patricia and Rouben Cholakian, *Marguerite de Navarre (1492–1549): Mother of the Renaissance*, p.39.

15   Ibid.

16   Norton, *Anne Boleyn Papers*, Intro, p.9.

17   Cholakian, *Marguerite de Navarre*, p.43.

18   Ives, *Life and Death of Anne Boleyn*, p.33.

19   Mary F. Robinson, *Margaret of Angoulême: Queen of Navarre*, p.29.

20   Ives, *Life and Death of Anne Boleyn*, p.32.

21   Robinson, *Queen of Navarre*, p.29.

22   Mackay, 'The Life and Career of Thomas Boleyn (1477–1539)', p.182.

23   Henry Morley, *Clement Marot and Other Studies*, p.102, p.111.

24   Cholakian, *Marguerite de Navarre (1492–1549)*, p.66–67.

25   Ibid., pp.48-50.

26   Robinson, *Margaret of Angoulême*, p.56.

27   Ibid., pp.53–54.

28   The line is *'per una grandissima ribalda et infame sopre tutte.'* Pio the Bishop of Faenza in a letter to Prothonotary Ambrogio, *Letters and Papers, Foreign and Domestic, Henry VIII*, Vol. 10, 10 March.

29   Bishop of Faenza to Mons. Ambrogio, *Letters and Papers*, Vol.10, 10 May.

30   Cholakian, *Marguerite de Navarre (1492–1549)*, pp.43-44.

31   John Matusiak, *Henry VIII: The Life and Rule of England's Nero*, pp.122–123.

32   Ibid., pp.119–120.

33   Ibid., p.120.

34   Ibid., p.119.

35   Ibid.

36   Peter Marshall, *1517: Martin Luther and the Invention of the Reformation*, p.38.

37   Ibid., p.19.

38   Ibid., p.20.

39   Ibid., p.22.

40   Ibid., p.31.

41   Ibid., p.58.

42   Ibid., pp.46–47.

43   Ibid., p.51.

44   Ibid., p.52.

Chapter 2

45   Henry Morley, *Clement Marot and other Studies*, p.132.

46   J. J. Scarisbrick, *Henry VIII*, p.148.

47   *Letters and Papers, Foreign and Domestic, Henry VIII*, Vol. 3, 1762, Nov 1521.

48   Tracey Borman, *Thomas Cromwell: The Untold Story of Henry VIII's Most Faithful Servant*, p.66.

49   George Cavendish, *The Life of Cardinal Wolsey*, p.120.

50   Scarisbrick, *Henry VIII*, pp.67, 79.

51   Wyatt in Elizabeth Norton, *The Anne Boleyn Papers*, p.22.

52   Ives discusses in detail the various debates over the years regarding these poems. Eric Ives, *The Life and Death of Anne Boleyn*, pp.72–76.

53   Wyatt in Norton, *Anne Boleyn Papers*, p.26.

54   Nicholas Sander, *The Rise and Growth of the Anglican Schism* (1571), p.35.

55   Sarah Dunn, 'The mark of the Devil: medical proof in witchcraft trials,' pp.57–59.

56   John Matusiak, *Henry VIII: The Life and Rule of England's Nero*, p.118.

57   Wyatt in Norton, *Anne Boleyn Papers*, p.21.

58   Borman, *Thomas Cromwell*, p.66.

59   Sander, *Anglican Schism*, p.35.

60   de Carles in Norton, *Anne Boleyn Papers*, pp.354–358.

61 In 1534, Margaret Chanseler called Anne a 'goggle-eyed whore'. Peter Marshall, *Heretics and Believers: A History of the English Reformation*, p.214.

62 Anne Boleyn's cleric John Barlow called her 'reasonably good-looking'. Maria Hayward, *Dress at the Court of King Henry VIII*, p.180.

63 Wyatt in Norton, *Anne Boleyn Papers*, pp.21–22.

64 Maria Dowling, *Camden Miscellany XXXIX*, p.35.

65 Scarisbrick, *Henry VIII*, p.110.

66 Cavendish, *Cardinal Wolsey*, pp.119–121.

67 Lauren Mackay, 'The Life and Career of Thomas Boleyn (1477–1539): Courtier, Ambassador and Statesman,' p.122.

68 Norton, *Anne Boleyn Papers*, Intro, p.8; Mackay, 'The Life and Career of Thomas Boleyn (1477–1539)', p.27.

69 Scarisbrick, *Henry VIII*, p.149.

70 Cavendish, *Cardinal Wolsey*, pp.119–121.

71 Ibid., pp.122–123, 129.

72 Ibid., p.129.

73 Mackay, 'The Life and Career of Thomas Boleyn (1477-1539)', p.122.

74 Scarisbrick, *Henry VIII*, p.149.

75 Cavendish, *Cardinal Wolsey*, pp.122-123.

76 Ibid., p.129.

77 Ibid., p.129.

78 Ibid., p.129.

79 Eric Ives, *The Life and Death of Anne Boleyn*, p.44.

80 Ibid., p.44.

81 Ibid., pp.269, 270, 271.

82 Thomas S. Freeman, 'Research, Rumour and Propaganda: Anne Boleyn in Foxe's "Book of Martyrs",' pp.800–801.

83 Ives, *Life and Death of Anne Boleyn*, p.273.

84 Lauren Mackay, *Among the Wolves of Court*.

85 Victor Baroni, *La Contre-Réforme devant la Bible*, p.57.

86   *Calendars and State Papers, Spain*, Vol. 5, 2, p.85; *Letters and Papers*, Vol. 10, p.601.

87   Mackay, *Among the Wolves of Court*, p.156.

88   Eric Ives, 'Anne Boleyn and the Entente Évangélique.'

89   Dowling, *Camden Miscellany XXXIX*, p.42.

90   Freeman, 'Research, Rumour and Propaganda'.

91   Wyatt in Norton, *Anne Boleyn Papers*, p.19.

92   'William Latymer's *Chronikille of Anne Bulleyne*,' in Dowling, *Camden Miscenally Vol. XXXIX*, p.60.

93   Ives, *Life and Death of Anne Boleyn*, p.264.

94   Wyatt in Norton, *Anne Boleyn Papers*, pp.19–20.

95   Ives, *Life and Death of Anne Boleyn*, p.36.

Chapter 3

96   In conversation with Kevin Dutton, PhD, research psychologist at the University of Oxford.

97   John Matusiak, *Henry VIII: The Life and Rule of England's Nero*, pp.15, 18.

98   Ibid., p.16.

99   Scarisbrick says Skelton probably stopped tutoring Henry in 1502, J.J. Scarisbrick, *Henry VIII*, p.27. Loades says his successor was John Holt, David Loades, *Henry VIII*, p.39. He was followed by William Hone in 1504, Scarisbrick, *Henry VIII*, p.27; Matusiak, *Henry VIII*, pp.23–24.

100   Matusiak, *Henry VIII*, p.25.

101   Ibid., p.48.

102   Ibid., p.35.

103   Scarisbrick, *Henry VIII*, p.28.

104   Ibid., p.29; Matusiak, *Henry VIII*, p.41.

105   Scarisbrick, *Henry VIII*, p.6.

106   Ibid., p.7.

107   Loades, *Henry VIII*, pp.40–41.

108 Steven Gunn, *Charles Brandon: Henry VIII's Closest Friend*, p.24.

109 Ibid., pp.27, 86, 118.

110 Matusiak, *Henry VIII*, p.14.

111 Ibid., p.32.

112 Scarisbrick, *Henry VIII*, p.28.

113 Matusiak, *Henry VIII*, p.50.

114 Ibid., p.54.

115 Scarisbrick, *Henry VIII*, pp.11–12.

116 Matusiak, *Henry VIII*, pp.50–54.

117 Suzannah Lipscomb, *1536: The Year That Changed Henry VIII*, pp.28–33.

118 Scarisbrick, *Henry VIII*, p.163.

119 Ibid., p.165.

120 Ibid., p.42.

121 George Cavendish, *The Life of Cardinal Wolsey*, pp.176, 182.

122 Scarisbrick, *Henry VIII*, p.154.

123 Ibid., p.37.

124 Matusiak, *Henry VIII*, pp.70–71.

125 National Institute of Mental Health, nimh.nih.gov

126 In conversation with Dr James Fallon.

127 National Institute of Mental Health, nimh.nih.gov

128 Tracy Borman, *Thomas Cromwell: The Untold Story of Henry VIII's Most Faithful Servant*, pp.245–246.

129 With Katherine of Aragon he married his older brother's beautiful and exotic widow (idealise) but he began to realise she was doomed to never give him a son, their marriage being 'cursed' by God (devalue), so he fought to divorce her for seven years, then sent her away to live in exile (discard). With Jane Seymour, he held her up as his escape from 'evil' Anne Boleyn, a calm and placid alternative (idealise); however, she failed to get pregnant for almost a year, during which time he kept delaying her coronation (first signs of devalue). Alas, she died two weeks after childbirth and before devalue and discard could

really kick in. He brought Anne of Cleves to England to marry him after only seeing her portrait (idealise), but he failed to 'perform' and consummate the marriage on their wedding night, blaming her ugliness (devalue), so he divorced her, bribing her with several properties so she would go quietly (discard). Henry next obsessed over the youth and beauty of Katherine Howard (diealise); however, he was told his new bride was 'spoiled' having conducted affairs before and even during their marriage (devalue), so he had her executed (discard). Which brings us finally to Catherine Parr who was in love with another man when the king decided he wanted her as his own, forcing them to break up (idealise); then he secretly plotted to have her arrested for pushing her religion on him (devalue), but she was tipped off and managed to backtrack, saving herself some time, at which point Henry himself died before he could reach the discard phase.

Chapter 4

130 Lauren Mackay, 'The Life and Career of Thomas Boleyn (1477-1539): Courtier, Ambassador and Statesman,' p.35.

131 Lauren Mackay, *Among the Wolves of Court*, p.149.

132 Eric Ives, *The Life and Death of Anne Boleyn*, p.263.

133 George Cavendish, *The Life of Cardinal Wolsey*, pp.204–205.

134 Mackay, 'The Life and Career of Thomas Boleyn', p.6.

135 Ibid., pp.6, 28, 29, 48–50, 52, 59, 67, 75, 79, 81, 101, 116, 119, 120, 148, 160.

136 A theory brought to light in Mackay's doctoral study, 'The Life and Career of Thomas Boleyn'.

137 Mackay, 'The Life and Career of Thomas Boleyn', pp..6, 28, 29, 48–50, 52, 59, 67, 75, 79, 81, 101, 116, 119, 120, 148, 160.

138 Ibid.

139 Again, not you, Mackay! ;)

140 Cavendish, *Cardinal Wolsey*, p.130.

141 J. J. Scarisbrick, *Henry VIII*, p.148, endnote 2.

142 Wyatt in Elizabeth Norton, *The Anne Boleyn Papers*, pp.23–24.

143 Ibid., p.23.

144 Although Luther accused Henry of having a ghostwriter for his now infamous *Assertio Septem Sacramentorum adversus Martinum Lutherum (or Defence of the Seven Sacraments)*, it seems Henry's work was a group effort; written by Henry, edited by Dr Edward Lee and revised by John Fisher and Thomas More.

145 John Matusiak, *Henry VIII: The Life and Rule of England's Nero*, pp.129–133.

146 Ives, *The Life and Death of Anne Boleyn*, p.90.

147 Wyatt in Norton, *The Anne Boleyn Papers*, p.24.

148 Antonia Fraser, *The Six Wives of Henry VIII*, p.187.

149 In conversation with historian Elizabeth Norton.

150 Wyatt in Norton, *Anne Boleyn Papers*, pp.23–24.

151 Ibid., p.22.

152 Ibid., pp.22–23.

153 Both stories of the game of cards and bowls come from Wyatt (the younger) who doesn't date them, but he does put them together in the same time frame. The only reason I place them after the February joust is because bowls is an outdoor game that I doubt they would have played in the dead of winter any time before February.

154 Norton, *Anne Boleyn Papers*, p.55.

155 We have two letters written by Anne's father on 17 July and 8 August 1526 that confirm he himself was back living at Hever Castle, overseeing official works at nearby Tonbridge. This was after completing his work at court as treasurer of the household in around February 1526. *Letters and Papers, Foreign and Domestic, Henry VIII*, Vols 3 and 4.

156 *Letters and Papers*, Vol. 3, 1628; Vol. 4, 1279, 2433.

157 Scarisbrick, *Henry VIII*, p.160.

158 Norton, *Anne Boleyn Papers*, pp.54–61.

159 Fraser, *Six Wives*, p.295.

160   Norton, *The Anne Boleyn Papers*, p.55.

161   Ibid., p.56.

162   Norton, *The Anne Boleyn Papers*, pp.54–61.

163   Ibid.

164   Ibid.

165   Tracy Borman, *Thomas Cromwell: The Untold Story of Henry VIII's Most Faithful Servant*, p.150.

166   Matusiak, *Henry VIII*, p.171.

167   John Foxe, *Acts and Monuments*, IV, pp.656–658.

168   Melvin Bragg, *William Tyndale: A Very Brief History*, p.4.

169   We know these were her plans due to the evidence presented throughout the remainder of this book.

170   Ives, *Life and Death of Anne Boleyn*, p.84.

171   Ibid., p.83; Scarisbrick, *Henry VIII*, p.154.

172   Herbert of Cherbury, *Henry VIII*, p.393.

173   Available to view in the British Library.

174   *British Library, Shelfmark: Kings Ms. 9, f.231v & f.66*

175   *British Library, Shelfmark: Kings Ms. 9, f.231v & f.66*

176   Borman, *Thomas Cromwell*, p.28.

177   Ives, *Life and Death of Anne Boleyn*, p.196.

178   Diarmaid MacCulloch, *Thomas Cromwell: A Life*, p.23.

179   Elizabeth's surname was either Wykes or Prior; MacCulloch, *Thomas Cromwell*, p.35.

180   *Calendar of State Papers, Spain*, Vol. 5, Part 2, 29 January 1536.

181   Borman, *Thomas Cromwell*, pp.23, 33.

182   David Starkey interview conducted by Laura Fitzpatrick, 'Historians need to have loved and lost to understand the past,' Telegraph.co.uk, 6 Oct 2018; David Starkey interview conducted by Caroline Lintott at thirteen.org for 'The Six Wives of Henry VIII' website.

183   David Starkey for 'The Six Wives of Henry VIII' website.

184   One example comes from *Vulture.com* interview with Hilary Mantel, 'Wolf Hall Author Hilary Mantel on Thomas Cromwell, and Why

Henry VIII Was The Ultimate Romantic', 3 April 2015, where Mantel states 'King Henry VIII was a romantic, and he truly believed each relationship would work out.' Another example comes from *Radio Times* interview with Lucy Worsley, 'The Truth About Henry VIII's Six Wives', 7 December 2016. She called him romantic in relation to Henry VIII being seen to publicly mourn the death of Jane Seymour, the mother of his only legitimate living son.

185 Fraser, *The Six Wives of Henry VIII*, p.160.

186 Suzannah Lipscomb, *Henry and Anne: The Lovers Who Changed History*, Channel 5, Lion Television, 2014.

187 Du Bellay in Norton, *The Anne Boleyn Files*, p.105.

188 Norton, *The Anne Boleyn Papers*, p.55.

189 Mackay, *Among the Wolves of Court*, p.125.

190 Mackay, 'The Life and Career of Thomas Boleyn', pp.130–131.

191 Norton, *The Anne Boleyn Papers*, p.59.

192 Scarisbrick, *Henry VIII*, pp.210–211.

Chapter 5

193 G. W. Bernard, *The King's Reformation: Henry VIII and the Remaking of the English Church*, p.534.

194 Ibid.

195 Diarmaid MacCulloch, *Thomas Cromwell: A Life*, pp.79–80.

196 Bernard, *The King's Reformation*, p.539.

197 Diarmaid MacCulloch, *Thomas Cranmer: A Life*, p.74.

198 Ibid., pp.106–113.

199 Bernard, *The King's Reformation*, p.533.

200 MacCulloch, *Thomas Cromwell*, p.261.

201 MacCulloch, *Thomas Cromwell*, p.120; *Letters and Papers, Foreign and Domestic, Henry VIII*, Vol. 4, 17 May 1530, Cromwell to Wolsey.

202 Tracy Borman, *Thomas Cromwell: The Untold Story of Henry VIII's Most Faithful Servant*, p.25.

203 Ibid., pp.24–26.

204 MacCulloch, *Thomas Cromwell*, p.140.

205 Eric Ives, *The Life and Death of Anne Boleyn*, p.99.

206 Ibid.

207 Ibid., p.111.

208 David Starkey, *Six Wives: The Queens of Henry VIII*, pp.372–375.

209 Ives, *Life and Death of Anne Boleyn*, p.134; Foxe, *Acts and Monuments*, Edition 4, pp.656–658.

210 Thomas S. Freeman, 'Research, Rumour and Propaganda: Anne Boleyn in Foxe's "Book of Martyrs",' p.802.

211 Ibid., pp.797–819.

212 Ives, *Life and Death of Anne Boleyn*, p.117.

213 Ibid., p.114–115.

214 Ibid., p.114; *Letters and Papers*, Vol. 4, 5519, 5481.

215 Ives, *Life and Death of Anne Boleyn*, p.133.

216 George Wyatt in George Cavendish, *Cardinal Wolsey*, pp.422, 439 (Wyatt is related to Gainsford and heard the story directly from her.); *Narratives of the Days of the Reformation*, pp.57–58.

217 Ives, *Life and Death of Anne Boleyn*, p.134.

218 In conversation with Kevin Dutton, PhD.

219 Wyatt in Norton, *Anne Boleyn Papers*, p.28.

220 Ibid., p.24.

221 Cavendish, *Cardinal Wolsey*, p.132.

222 Steven Gunn, *Charles Brandon: Henry VIII's Closest Friend*, p.124.

223 MacCulloch, *Thomas Cromwell*, p.95.

224 Gunn, *Charles Brandon*, p.41.

225 *Calendar of State Papers, Spain*, Vol. 4, Part 2, 29 May 1533, Chapuys.

226 Lauren Mackay, *Among the Wolves of Court*, p.183.

227 Mackay, *Among the Wolves of Court*, p.178; *Calendar of State Papers, Spain*, Vol. 4, Part 2, 15 February 1533.

228 Ibid., Chapuys, 29 May 1533.

229 Ibid.

230   Ibid.

231   Ives, *Life and Death of Anne Boleyn*, p.116.

232   Ibid., p.117.

233   Cavendish, *Cardinal Wolsey*, p.210.

234   Ibid., p.220.

235   Ibid., p.230.

236   MacCulloch, *Thomas Cromwell*, p.84.

237   As the king was preparing to go on summer progress with Anne on 31 July 1529, the anti-Wolsey faction presented him with thirty-four charges against the cardinal that proved to them he was guilty of praemunire, but Henry didn't act on these accusations. There were long talks and confrontations between Wolsey and the king on 19 September 1529 at Grafton Hunting Lodge, which again didn't result in any action against Wolsey.

238   Cavendish, *Cardinal Wolsey*, pp.246–251.

239   Ibid., pp.270–278.

240   Ibid., pp.277–286.

241   Ives, *Life and Death of Anne Boleyn*, pp.273–275.

242   Ibid., p.131.

243   J. J. Scarisbrick, *Henry VIII*, p.239; Mackay, *Among the Wolves of Court*, p.158.

244   Cavendish, *Cardinal Wolsey*, pp.238–239.

245   Ives, *Life and Death of Anne Boleyn*, p.131.

246   Cavendish, *Cardinal Wolsey*, p.388.

247   Ibid., p.343.

248   Ibid., p.360.

249   Norton, *Anne Boleyn Papers*, Intro, p.12.

250   Cavendish, *Cardinal Wolsey*, p.312.

251   Ibid., p.362.

252   Ibid., p.367.

253   Ibid., p.378.

254   Ibid., p.376.

255 Ibid., p.367.

256 Ibid., p.378.

257 Ibid., pp.378, 393.

Chapter 6

258 For an example of Anne depicted as still serving Katherine in biographies see: Antonia Fraser, *The Six Wives of Henry VIII*, p.160. For examples of Anne being smarmy and having catty confrontations with Katherine in TV documentaries, see *Six Wives with Lucy Worsley*, BBC1, 2016; *Henry and Anne: The Lovers Who Changed History*, Lion Television, Channel 5, 2014. In film, see *The Other Boleyn Girl*, Sony Pictures 2008.

259 *Letters and Papers, Foreign and Domestic, Henry VIII*, Vol .3 & 4, 1519–1530.

260 Eric Ives, *The Life and Death of Anne Boleyn*, pp.127–128.

261 Ibid., p.128.

262 *Calendar of State Papers, Spain*, 1529–30, pp.708–709.

263 Steven Gunn, *Charles Brandon: Henry VIII's Closest Friend*, p.134; *Calendar of State Papers, Spain*, Vol. 4, Part 2, 1531–1533, 17 July 1531.

264 Gunn, *Charles Brandon*, p.44.

265 Ives, *Life and Death of Anne Boleyn*, p.140–141.

266 J. J. Scarisbrick, *Henry VIII*, p.255.

267 Ives, *Life and Death of Anne Boleyn*, p.132.

268 Diarmaid MacCulloch, *Thomas Cranmer: A Life*, p.75.

269 Ibid., p.82.

270 Ibid., pp.94–96, 98.

271 Lauren Mackay's doctoral study, 'The Life and Career of Thomas Boleyn (1477–1539): Courtier, Ambassador and Statesman,' p.157. George Boleyn was first tasked with collecting the opinions of the universities in 1529, but his father took over in order to push the universities into making their stance official by stamping it with their seal on 2 June.

272   Herbert of Cherbury, *Henry VIII*, pp.446–451; Ives, *The Life and Death of Anne Boleyn*, pp.134–135.

273   Ives, *Life and Death of Anne Boleyn*, p.135.

274   MacCulloch, *Cranmer*, p.55; Ives, *Life and Death of Anne Boleyn*, p.21.

275   Ives, *Life and Death of Anne Boleyn*, p.138.

276   Ibid., p.136.

277   Scarisbrick, *Henry VIII*, p.280.

278   *Calendar of State Papers, Spain*, 1531–33, p.63.

279   Ives, *Life and Death of Anne Boleyn*, p.139.

280   Elizabeth Norton, *Anne Boleyn Papers*, p.107. (Most historians have taken this view.)

281   Lauren Mackay, *Among the Wolves of Court*, p.181.

282   Ibid., p.187.

283   Alison Weir, *The Six Wives of Henry VIII*, p.219.

284   In conversation with registered midwife Judith E. Lewis: owing to the unpredictable nature of due dates and the fact that a full-term pregnancy can be anywhere between thirty-seven weeks (when Elizabeth actually arrived) and forty weeks (when Anne expected to give birth), it makes sense for us to go by Anne's calculations and not Elizabeth's actual birth when trying to work out when she was conceived. So if Anne went into confinement on 26 August (traditionally one month before her due date) that means she would have calculated back from 26 September that it was nine months prior, on 26 December, that she conceived. However, if Anne knew the classic full term was forty weeks exactly, then that specifically calculates conception back to 20 December. Either way, it looks likely conception was during the Christmas festivities, which might lead us to make a connection with the religious symbolism of the birth of Christ and Henry and Anne finally conceiving what they believed to be the savior of their kingdom.

285   Anne's elevation to the peerage: British Library, Harley MS303, fol.1; further explanation in Ives, *The Life and Death of Anne Boleyn*, p.167. Also in conversation with Tudor historian Elizabeth Norton, who says,

'The suggestion that Anne and Henry started having sex in Calais is based . . . on the wording of the patent creating her marquess of Pembroke. This ensures that the title will pass to any children born to her (not just legitimate ones), suggesting that she and Henry were at least contemplating a sexual relationship before marriage.' The patent making Anne marquess of Pembroke refers to the title being passed down to any 'heirs male' – it did not include the standard provision of being passed down to 'lawfully begotten heirs male', meaning legitimate children born in wedlock. This was unusual, so the message was clear: Anne's title would pass to any children she had with the king, including ones born outside marriage. This was the couple acknowledging that they might have children out of wedlock – logically, after seven years of fighting, they didn't know what other obstacles might be thrown at them, and they had to *accept that something else could prevent them from being legally married.*

286   Edward Hall, *Hall's Chronicle, p.794.*

287   Wyatt in Norton, *The Anne Boleyn Papers*, p.28.

288   John Foxe, *Foxe's Book of Martyrs*, p.243; Chapuys in Norton, *Anne Boleyn Papers*, p.208 (though note Chapuys misinforms readers that Cranmer married Henry and Anne, while Diarmaid MacCulloch informs us it was reported to be Rowland Lee. Diarmaid MacCulloch, *Thomas Cranmer: A Life*, p.125).

289   MacCulloch, *Thomas Cranmer*, p.86.

290   John Matusiak, *Henry VIII: The Life and Rule of England's Nero*, p.211.

291   Ibid., p.213.

292   Ives, *Life and Death of Anne Boleyn*, pp.172–182.

Chapter 7

293   George Cavendish, *The Life of Cardinal Wolsey*, p.316.

294   'William Latymer's *Chronickille of Anne Bulleyne*,' in Dowling, *Camden Miscellany Vol. XXXIX*, p.57.

295 Thomas S. Freeman, 'Research, Rumour and Propaganda: Anne Boleyn in Foxe's "Book of Martyrs", pp.797–819.

296 Ibid.

297 Latymer's *Chronickille* in Dowling, p.56.

298 Maria Dowling, *Camden Miscellany* Vol. XXXIX, p.36.

299 Eric Ives, *The Life and Death of Anne Boleyn*, p.284.

300 Ibid., p.286.

301 Ibid., pp.286–287.

302 Ibid., pp.286–287.

303 *Letters and Papers, Foreign and Domestic, Henry VIII*, Vol. 4, 1524–1530, 5366.

304 Tracy Borman, *Thomas Cromwell: The Untold Story of Henry VIII's Most Faithful Servant*, p.98.

305 Ives, *Life and Death of Anne Boleyn*, p.185.

306 Borman, *Thomas Cromwell*, p.3.

307 Diarmaid MacCulloch, *Thomas Cromwell: A Life*, p.292.

308 *Letters and Papers, Foreign and Domestic, Henry VIII*, 478, Michaelmas 25–27; Ives, *The Life and Death of Anne Boleyn*, p.207.

309 Ives, *The Life and Death of Anne Boleyn*, pp.208–209.

310 Borman, *Thomas Cromwell*, p.109.

311 Maria Dowling, *Anne Boleyn and Reform*, The Journal of Ecclesiastical History.

312 Retha M. Warnicke, *The Rise and Fall of Anne Boleyn: Family Politics at the Court of Henry VIII*, p.111; Freeman, 'Research, Rumour and Propaganda', pp.813–815.

313 Ives, *Life and Death of Anne Boleyn*, p.269.

314 MacCulloch, *Thomas Cromwell*, p.117.

315 Latymer's *Cronickille* in Dowling, p.56.

316 Ives, *Life and Death of Anne Boleyn*, p.275.

317 Maria Dowling, *Camden Miscellany* Vol. XXXIX, p.36.

318 Ives, *Life and Death of Anne Boleyn*, pp.274–275.

319 Dowling footnotes, *Camden Miscellany* Vol. XXXIX, p.56.

320   Latymer's *Cronickille* in Dowling, p.56.

321   Ives, *Life and Death of Anne Boleyn*, p.263.

322   MacCulloch, *Thomas Cranmer*, pp.149–150.

323   Latymer's *Cronickille* in Dowling, p.61.

324   Lauren Mackay, *Among the Wolves of Court*, p.179.

325   Latymer's *Cronickille* in Dowling, p.61.

326   Ibid., p.51.

327   Freeman, 'Research, Rumour and Propaganda', pp.797–819.

328   Latymer's *Cronickille* in Dowling, p.54; Wyatt in Elizabeth Norton, *The Anne Boleyn Papers*, p.29.

329   Norton, *Anne Boleyn Papers*, p.198.

330   As estimated by the currency converter of the National Archives of the UK government.

331   Ives, *Life and Death of Anne Boleyn*, pp.214–215.

332   Latymer's *Cronickille* in Dowling, p 55.

333   Freeman, 'Research, Rumour and Propaganda', pp.797–819.

334   Ibid.

335   Latymer's *Cronickille* in Dowling, p.53.

336   Ives, *Life and Death of Anne Boleyn*, p.284.

337   Freeman, 'Research, Rumour and Propaganda', pp.797–819.

338   George Cavendish, *The Life of Cardinal Wolsey*, pp.248–250.

339   Many do this; for an example see Antonia Fraser, *The Six Wives of Henry VIII*, p.214.

340   Freeman, 'Research, Rumour and Propaganda', pp.815–819.

341   Ibid., pp.797–819.

342   Henry Clifford, *Life of Jane Dormer*, in Norton, *Anne Boleyn Papers*, p.201.

343   Latymer's *Cronickille* in Dowling.

344   Clifford, *Life of Jane Dormer* in *Anne Boleyn Papers*, p.199; Nicholas Sander, *The Rise and Growth of Anglican Schism, 1585*.

345   Gareth Russell, *Young and Damned and Fair*, p.147.

346   Latymer, *Cronickille*, p.52.

347 Ibid., p.62.

348 Ibid., p.51.

349 Maria Dowling, Camden Miscellany Vol. XXXIX, p.36.

350 Latymer's *Cronickille* in Dowling, p.53.

351 Kingston in Norton, *Anne Boleyn Papers*, pp.333–337.

Chapter 8

352 In conversation with registered midwife Judith E. Lewis.

353 Eric Ives, *The Life and Death of Anne Boleyn*, p.193.

354 John Matusiak, *Henry VIII: The Life and Rule of England's Nero*, p.59.

355 Gregorio Leti, *Historia o vero vita di Elisabetta, regina d'Inghilterra*.

356 Martin Andrew Sharp Hume, *Chronicle of King Henry VIII of England*, p.42.

357 'William Latymer's *Cronickille of Anne Bulleyne*' in Maria Dowling, *Camden Miscellany Vol. XXXIX*, p.63.

358 Elizabeth Norton, *The Anne Boleyn Papers*, Intro, p.14.

359 *Letters and Papers, Foreign and Domestic, Henry VIII*, Vol. 7, 7 March 1534.

360 Ibid., 18 April 1534.

361 *Calendar of State Papers, Spain*, Vol. 5, Part 1, 24 October 1534–1535.

362 *Letters and Papers*, Vol. 8, January–July, 25 March 1535.

363 Ibid., Vol. 10, January–June 1536.

364 Ives, *Life and Death of Anne Boleyn*, p.191.

365 *Calendar of State Papers, Spain*, Vol. 5 Part 1, 1534–1535; *Letters and Papers*, Vol. 7, 1534.

366 Ibid.

367 Ibid.

368 *Calendar of State Papers, Spain*, Vol. 5, Part 1, 1534–1535, 13 October.

369 *Letters and Papers*, Vol. 8, 4 July 1535, bishop of Faenza to M. Ambrosio.

370 *Calendar of State Papers, Spain*, Vol. 5, Part 1, 1534–1535, 13 October.

371 *Letters and Papers*, Vol. 8, January–July 1535, 25 February.

372 Norton, *Anne Boleyn Papers*, pp.49–50; letter 14 January 1535 (DeGayangos 1886:376; Hulme says it was Jane Seymour p.261).

373 *Letters and Papers*, Vol. 8, 4 May, p.661.

374 Ibid., Vol. 8, 30 April, Cranmer to Cromwell.

375 Ibid., Vol. 8, 4 May, p.663.

376 Without wanting to jump ahead, in terms of Anne's chaplains preaching her messages, I'm thinking specifically of Skippe's 1536 'sermon war cry', which we will come to later. In the case of the Charterhouse monks, there is no firm evidence to prove Anne was specifically behind this appeal (as with the sermons, historians can provide no physical evidence, only highlight an obvious connection), so I am opening the idea for debate and consideration rather than making any irrefutable assertions.

377 Elizabeth Norton, *Jane Seymour: Henry VIII's True Love*, p.18.

378 Ives, *Life and Death of Anne Boleyn*, p.293.

379 Tracy Borman, *Thomas Cromwell: The Untold Story of Henry VIII's Most Faithful Servant*, pp.59–60.

380 Ibid., pp.113–114.

381 Ibid., p.65.

382 Latymer's *Cronickille* in Dowling, p.61.

383 Ibid.

Chapter 9

384 Lauren Mackay, *Among the Wolves of Court*, p.170.

385 *Letters and Papers, Foreign and Domestic, Henry VIII*, Vol. 5, Chapuys to Granville, 11 July 1532.

386 Mackay, *Among the Wolves of Court*, p.197.

387 Tracy Borman, *Thomas Cromwell: The Untold Story of Henry VIII's Most Faithful Servant*, p.176. Borman ends her story about Mary and Anne's falling-out by stating, 'Mary was obliged to stay away from court.' We

then have to follow the citation to the endnotes of the book, on p.425, if we want to read the hidden truth that 'Mary was eventually forgiven by Anne and attended Anne during her final ill-fated pregnancy in 1536.'

388 Elizabeth Norton, *The Anne Boleyn Papers*, pp.203–205.

389 Mackay, *Among the Wolves of Court*, p.126.

390 Lauren Mackay, 'The Life and Career of Thomas Boleyn (1477–1539): Courtier, Ambassador and Statesman,' pp.128–130.

391 Norton, *Anne Boleyn Papers*, Intro, p.16; Eric Ives, *Life and Death of Anne Boleyn*, p.349.

392 Maria Dowling, Camden Miscellany XXXIX, p.31.

393 Norton, *Anne Boleyn Papers*, Intro, p.13.

394 *Calendar of State Papers, Spain*, Vol. 5, Part 1, October, 1534–1535.

395 *Letters and Papers, Foreign and Domestic, Henry VIII*, Vol. 10, January–June, 21 January 1536.

396 Ibid.

397 Mackay, *Among the Wolves of Court*, p.205.

398 *Letters and Papers*, Vol. 10, January–June, 21 January 1536.

399 Edward Hall, *Chronicle*, p.818.

400 *Letters and Papers*, Vol. 10, January–June, 21 January 1536.

401 *Calendar of State Papers, Spain*, Vol. 5, Part 2, 29 January, 1536–1538.

402 In conversation with Kevin Dutton, PhD.

403 Borman, *Thomas Cromwell*, pp.210–212; Antonia Fraser, *The Six Wives of Henry VIII*, p.282.

404 *Letters and Papers*, Vol. 10, January–June, 21 January 1536.

405 Diarmaid MacCulloch, *Thomas Cranmer: A Life*, p.124.

406 Peter Gordon and Denis Lawton, *Royal Education: Past Present and Future*, p.34.

407 Alison Weir, *The Six Wives of Henry VIII*, p.262.

408 *Letters and Papers*, Vol. 7, 7 March, 1534.

409 Ibid.

410 Norton, *Anne Boleyn Papers*, p.202.

411 *Calendar of State Papers, Spain*, Vol. 5, Part 1, 1534–1535.

412   Norton, *Anne Boleyn Files*, p.203.

413   Henry Clifford, *The Life of Jane Dormer* in Norton, *Anne Boleyn Papers*, p.202–203.

414   Norton, *Anne Boleyn Papers*, p.284.

415   *Calendar of State Papers, Spain*, Vol. 4, Part 2, 10 April 1533, Chapuys.

416   Fraser, *Six Wives*, p.248.

417   Interview with Tudor historian and expert Elizabeth Norton; for detailed reference see Elizabeth Norton, *The Lives of Tudor Women*.

418   Ives, *Life and Death of Anne Boleyn*, pp.137–138.

419   Ibid., p.198.

420   *Letters and Papers*, Vol. 9, 22 November 1535.

421   Ives, *Life and Death of Anne Boleyn*, p.361.

422   Thomas Colwell in *The Manuscripts of His Grace the Duke of Rutland*, Vol. I (1888).

423   Fraser, *Six Wives,* p.248.

424   Chapuys wrote that he personally told Cromwell: 'I could not but wish him a more gracious mistress, and one more grateful for the inestimable services he had done the King . . .' *Letters and Papers*, Vol. 10, 1 April 1536, Chapuys to Charles V.

Chapter 10

425   George Ascoli, La Grande-Bretagne Devant L'opinion Française Depuis La Guerre de Cent Ans Jusqu'à La Fin Du XVIe Siècle, 233–34, De la Royne d'Angleterre, Lancelot de Carles, lines 303–312. (He places the fire as after Katherine's death but before Henry's jousting accident.)

426   *Letters and Papers, Foreign and Domestic, Henry VIII*, Vol. 10, January–June 1536, Chapuys 29 Jan 1536.

427   Charles Wriothesley, *A Chronicle of England during the Reigns of the Tudors, from A.D. 1485 to 1559*, p.33.

428   *Letters and Papers*, Vol. 10, 6 March, to Empress.

429   Ibid., Vol. 10, January–June 1536, Chapuys, 29 January 1536.

430   Ibid., Vol. 10, 10 February 1536.

431   Wyatt in Elizabeth Norton, *The Anne Boleyn Papers*, p.30.

432   Eric Ives, *The Life and Death of Anne Boleyn*, p.299.

433   Ibid., p.296.

434   Wyatt in Norton, *Anne Boleyn Papers*, p.30.

435   Camden Miscellany Vol. XXXIX, p.28.

436   A good breakdown of the situation is provided by Diarmaid MacCulloch, *Thomas Cranmer: A Life*, p.145.

437   MacCulloch, *Thomas Cranmer*, p.147.

438   This converts to £88,255.40 in today's currency according to the National Archives of the UK government.

439   G. R. Elton, 'An Early Tudor Poor Law,' pp.55–67; Ives, *The Life and Death of Anne Boleyn*, p.284.

440   Maria Dowling, *Humanism in the Age of Henry VIII*, p.239; Ives, *Life and Death of Anne Boleyn*, pp.284–285.

441   Elton, 'An Early Tudor Poor Law,' p.56.

442   Ibid., p.60.

443   Ibid., p.59.

444   Ibid., p.58.

445   Ibid., p.58.

446   Ibid., p.58.

447   Ibid., p.59; G. R. Elton, *Reform and Renewal, Thomas Cromwell and the Common Wealth*, p.123.

448   G. R. Elton, *Reform and Renewal, Thomas Cromwell and the Common Wealth*, p.124.

449   Tracy Borman, *Thomas Cromwell: The Untold Story of Henry VIII's Most Faithful Servant*, p.173.

450   Elton, 'An Early Tudor Poor Law', p.66.

451   Ives, *Life and Death of Anne Boleyn*, p.285; Potentially the Vagabonds Act 1535 c. 25 1535 (27 Hen. VIII).

452   Elton, 'An Early Tudor Poor Law', pp.64–65.

453   Elton, *Reform and Renewal*, p.124. Here it has been confused, where Elton states 'All commissions of the peace were to be renewed before 24th June 1536.' Diarmaid MacCulloch has confirmed this was an error (he was citing Tudor Royal Proclamations I no.138) and should be March 1538 where The Poor Law scheme was renewed; however, it was not renewed again in 1539, and that's where it ended until Elizabeth I revived it in its originally intended form. Elton, 'An Early Tudor Poor Law', p.60.

454   Elton, 'An Early Tudor Poor Law', p.63.

455   'William Latymer's *Cronickille of Anne Bulleyne*', in Maria Dowling, *Camden Miscellany Vol. XXXIX*, p.57.

456   Ives, *Life and Death of Anne Boleyn*, p.311.

457   Latymer's *Cronickille* in Dowling, p.57.

458   Ives, *Life and Death of Anne Boleyn*, p.310.

459   Ibid., p.307–308.

460   Both Ives and MacCulloch have independently identified the link between the story of Haman and Cromwell. MacCulloch, *Thomas Cranmer*, pp.154–155.

461   Latymer's *Cronickille* in Dowling, p.57.

462   Ibid., p.57.

463   Ives, *Life and Death of Anne Boleyn*, p.311.

464   Latymer's *Cronickille* in Dowling, p.58.

465   Ibid., p.58.

466   Ibid., p.59.

467   Ibid., p.59.

468   MacCulloch, *Thomas Cranmer*, p.139.

469   Latymer's *Cronickille* in Dowling, footnote 26, p.60.

470   Ibid., p.59.

Chapter 11

471   Elizabeth Norton, *Jane Seymour: Henry VIII's True Love*, p.75.

472   Ibid., p.81.

473   Ibid., p.12.

474   Ibid., p.14.

475   Ibid., p.18.

476   *Letters and Papers, Foreign and Domestic, Henry VIII*, Vol. 10, 18 May 1536, Chapuys to Antoine Perrenot.

477   Norton, *Jane Seymour*, p.35.

478   Ibid., p.45.

479   Ibid., p.46.

480   *Letters and Papers*, Vol. 10, 1 April 1536, Chapuys.

481   Norton, *Jane Seymour*, pp.61–62.

482   *Letters and Papers*, Vol. 10, 1 April 1536, Chapuys.

483   Ibid.

484   George Cavendish, *The Life of Cardinal Wolsey*, pp.130–132.

485   *Letters and Papers*, Vol. 10, 1 April 1536, Chapuys.

486   Anne has been quoted by various sources as saying: 'How well I must be since the day I caught that abandoned woman Jane sitting on your knees.' (Nicolas Sander, *The Rise and Growth of the Anglican Schism*, p.132) and 'I saw this harlot Jane sitting on your knees while my belly was doing its duty!' (Ives, *The Life and Death of Anne Boleyn*, p.304; Wyatt in Cavendish, *Life of Wolsey*, p.443).

487   Ives, *Life and Death of Anne Boleyn*, p.304.

488   Henry Clifford, *The Life of Jane Dormer*; Norton, *Jane Seymour*, p.52–53.

Chapter 12

489   Matthew Parker, *The Correspondence of Matthew Parker, D.D., Archbishop of Canterbury*, pp.59, 391.

490   Eric Ives, *The Life and Death of Anne Boleyn*, p.316.

491   Lauren Mackay, 'The Life and Career of Thomas Boleyn (1477–1539): Courtier, Ambassador and Statesman,' p.162.

492   Ives, *The Life and Death of Anne Boleyn*, p.313.

493   Ibid., p.312.

494 Ibid., p.314.

495 Diarmaid MacCulloch, *Thomas Cromwell: A Life*, p.292.

496 *Letters and Papers, Foreign and Domestic, Henry VIII*, Vol. 10, 1 April 1536, Chapuys to Charles V.

497 Lauren Mackay, *Inside the Tudor Court*, p.227.

498 *Letters and Papers*, Vol. 10, 21 April 1536.

499 Ives, *Life and Death of Anne Boleyn*, p.313; Antonia Fraser, *The Six Wives of Henry VIII*, p.298.

500 *Calendar of State Papers, Spain*, Vol. 5, Part 2, 21 April 1536; Mackay, *Inside the Tudor Court*, p.228. Also see a mistranslation of Chapuys's quote, likely to be the cause of confusion for it can be easily misunderstood to mean Anne bowed first, in *Letters and Papers*, Vol. 10, 21 April 1536.

501 Mackay, *Inside the Tudor Court*, p.229.

502 Ives, *Life and Death of Anne Boleyn*, p.315.

503 This is not exclusive to Anne Boleyn's story. The majority of historical non-fiction and fiction that has women at its centre are sold to female audiences with romance, sex and whimsy (think *The Other Boleyn Girl*, any Jane Austen book or adaptation, *Anna Karenina*, *Marie Antoinette*, *Young Victoria*, etc.), while stories with men at the centre can be action-packed, political and focus on the intricacies of war for the supposedly male audience (think *Braveheart*, *Darkest Hour*, *The King's Speech*, *Dunkirk* etc.). Only now that we are in an exciting era of change are we starting to see movies like *Elizabeth: The Golden Age* and *Mary Queen of Scots*, and indeed, a non-fiction book like this being published, all of which are daring to show the truth of these women's stories: powerful women embroiled in politics. There will always be exceptions to this rule but my point is the glaringly obvious way the stories of historical women are told to what is largely a female audience.

504 Ives, *Life and Death of Anne Boleyn*, p.320.

505 *Calendar of State Papers, Spain*, Vol. 5 Part 2, 6 June 1536, Chapuys to Emperor Charles V.

506 Ibid.; Diarmaid MacCulloch, *Thomas Cranmer: A Life*, p.155.

507 *Letters and Papers*, Vol. 10, 1 April 1536, Chapuys to Charles V.

508 Elizabeth Norton, *The Anne Boleyn Papers*, p.325.

509 Ives, *Life and Death of Anne Boleyn*, p.325.

510 Kingston in Norton, *Anne Boleyn Papers*, p.333.

511 Ibid., p.333.

512 Ibid.

513 Ibid., pp.333–334.

514 Ibid., p.334.

515 Ives, *Life and Death of Anne Boleyn*, p.335.

516 Kingston in Norton, *Anne Boleyn Papers*, p.334–335.

517 Ives, *Life and Death of Anne Boleyn*, pp.319–323.

518 Ibid., p.323.

519 In conversation with Lauren Mackay, PhD, Thomas Boleyn expert.

520 Ives, *Life and Death of Anne Boleyn*, p.320.

521 Ibid., p.319–324.

522 Ibid., pp.319, 326.

523 Ibid., p.336.

524 de Carles in Norton, *Anne Boleyn Papers*, p.354–358.

525 Ives, *Life and Death of Anne Boleyn*, pp.319, 326, 327.

526 de Carles in Norton, *Anne Boleyn Papers*, p.354–358.

527 Cromwell's 'official' version of Anne's downfall and arrest as detailed in the letter he sent to the English ambassadors in France. Cromwell in Norton, *The Anne Boleyn Papers*, p.345–346.

528 John Matusiak, *Henry VIII: The Life and Rule of England's Nero*, p.46.

529 Approximately £114,000 in today's currency, according to the currency converter of the National Archives of the UK government.

530 Ives, *Life and Death of Anne Boleyn*, p.332.

531 Kingston in Norton, *Anne Boleyn Papers*, p.333–334; Ives, *Life and Death of Anne Boleyn*, p.333.

532 Norton, *Anne Boleyn Papers*, pp.341–342.

533 Steven Gunn, *Charles Brandon: Henry VIII's Closest Friend*, p.44.

534   Ibid., p.46.

535   Ives, *Life and Death of Anne Boleyn*, p.331.

536   Lauren Mackay, 'The Life and Career of Thomas Boleyn (1477–1539): Courtier, Ambassador and Statesman,' pp.62, 70, 73.

537   John Gough Nichols, *Narratives of the Days of the Reformation*, p.255.

538   Norton, *Anne Boleyn Papers*, p.326.

539   Wyatt in Norton, *Anne Boleyn Papers*, p.31.

540   De Carles in Ascoli, L'opinion, pp.882–885.

541   Lauren Mackay, *Among the Wolves of Court*, pp.228–229.

542   Mackay, *Among the Wolves of Court*, p.213.

543   Norton, *Anne Boleyn Papers*, p.326.

544   Gunn, *Charles Brandon*, pp.135–136.

545   Ibid., pp.132–133.

546   Ibid.

547   Approximation according to the National Archives of the UK government.

548   Gunn, *Charles Brandon* p.154.

549   Tracy Borman, *Thomas Cromwell: The Untold Story of Henry VIII's Most Faithful Servant*, p.206.

550   Gunn, *Charles Brandon*, p.156.

551   Cromwell in Norton, *Anne Boleyn Papers*, p.345–346.

552   Wyatt in Norton, *Anne Boleyn Papers*, p.31.

553   Ibid.

554   Ives, *Life and Death of Anne Boleyn*, p.348.

555   *Letters and Papers*, Foreign and Domestic, Henry VIII, Vol. 10, January–June 1536, 19 May.

556   Ives, *Life and Death of Anne Boleyn*, p.321.

557   Ibid., p.328.

558   *Letters and Papers*, Vol. 10, January–June, 19 May 1536, 909.

559   Lauren Mackay, *Inside the Tudor Court*, p.235.

560   MacCulloch, *Thomas Cranmer*, p.137.

561   Carolly Erickson, *Great Harry: A Biography of Henry VIII*, p.291.

562   In conversation with Diarmaid MacCulloch.

563   Norton, *Anne Boleyn Papers*, pp.324–325.

564   MacCulloch, *Thomas Cromwell*, p.291.

565   Norton, *Anne Boleyn Papers*, pp.324, 328.

566   Ives, *Life and Death of Anne Boleyn*, pp.344–345.

Chapter 13

567   Eric Ives, *The Life and Death of Anne Boleyn*, p.318.

568   Kingston in Elizabeth Norton, *The Anne Boleyn Papers*, p.335.

569   Paul Friedmann, ed. Josephine Wilkinson, *Anne Boleyn*, p.232.

570   Norton, *Anne Boleyn Papers*, p.327.

571   Ibid., p.30.

572   Kingston in Norton, *Anne Boleyn Papers*, p.333.

573   George Cavendish, *The Life of Cardinal Wolsey*, p.451.

574   Kingston in Norton, *Anne Boleyn Papers*, p.335.

575   Ibid., p.333.

576   Ibid., p.333–337.

577   Ibid., p.333–337.

578   Ibid., p.333–337.

579   Ibid., p.337.

580   Ibid.

581   Ibid., p.333.

582   Ibid., p.335.

583   Ibid.

584   Ibid., p.334.

585   Maria Dowling footnotes, *Camden Miscellany Vol. XXXIX*, p.60.

586   Kingston in Norton, *Anne Boleyn papers*, p.334.

587   Ibid., p.333.

588   Lauren Mackay wrote *Among the Wolves of Court*, Thomas and George Boleyn, but this quote was taken from her doctoral study, 'The Life

and Career of Thomas Boleyn (1477–1539): Courtier, Ambassador and Statesman,' pp.211–212.

589 Diarmaid MacCulloch, *Thomas Cranmer: A Life*, pp.157–158.

590 Norton, *Anne Boleyn Papers*, p.347–348.

591 Ibid., pp.346–348.

592 Ibid., pp.347–348.

593 Ibid., p.348.

594 Tracy Borman, *Thomas Cromwell: The Untold Story of Henry VIII's Most Faithful Servant*, p.43.

595 Ives, *Life and Death of Anne Boleyn*, p.347.

596 Borman, *Thomas Cromwell*, p.241.

597 Ives, *Life and Death of Anne Boleyn*, p.339.

598 Ibid., pp.339–340, 342.

599 Ibid., p.340.

600 Kingston in Norton, *Anne Boleyn Papers*, p.341.

601 Norton, *The Anne Boleyn Papers*, p.328.

602 Ives, *Life and Death of Anne Boleyn*, p.341.

603 Ibid., pp.340–341.

604 *Letters and Papers*, Vol. 10, 876, 15 May, trial of Anne Boleyn and Lord Rochford.

605 Norton, *The Anne Boleyn Papers*, p.328.

606 de Carles in Norton, *Anne Boleyn Papers*, p.357.

607 The rumour Chapuys repeats in a letter prior to Anne's arrest, which prompts this question in court, is 'according to the account given of [the king] by [Anne Boleyn], he has neither vigour nor virtue'. *Letters and Papers*, Vol. 10, 1536, 19 May 1536, Chapuys to Antoine Perrenot; Mackay, *Among the Wolves of Court*, pp.214–215; Ives, *The Life and Death of Anne Boleyn*, p.191.

608 Ibid.

609 André Thevet, *La Cosmographie universelle*.

610 Norton, *The Anne Boleyn Papers*, p.32.

611 Ives, *Life and Death of Anne Boleyn*, p.32.

612   There are too many examples to list individually. For examples in historical biography see: Elizabeth Norton, *Jane Seymour: Henry VIII's True Love*, p.74; Tracy Borman, *Thomas Cromwell*, p.250; Antonia Fraser, *The Six Wives of Henry VIII*, p.312. For an example in TV documentary: Suzannah Lipscomb, *Henry and Anne: The Lovers Who Changed History*, Lion Television, Channel 5, 2014. A simple Google search will provide endless news articles and blogs by historians and researchers in which Anne Boleyn's death by sword is interpreted as an 'act of mercy' by the king.

613   Kingston in Norton, *The Anne Boleyn Papers*, p.337.

614   Ibid., p.335/ 337/ Endnote 90 on p.336 – by Anne stating she should be sent to 'Anvures' (Antwerp) this has been presumed to mean she was indicating a monastery or nunnery in Europe. Anne doesn't explicitly say this would allow the king to remarry but that is what many take the implication of her statement to mean.

615   Ibid., p.336–337.

616   Ives, *Life and Death of Anne Boleyn*, p.342.

617   Ibid., p.343.

618   *Letters and Papers*, Vol. 10, 19 May.

619   Another fascinating thought to digest from Diarmaid MacCulloch is the irony that it was impossible for Anne to have committed adultery now her marriage was deemed never to have existed following the annulment – a technicality that Cromwell and the king both conveniently overlooked at the time. MacCulloch, *Thomas Cranmer*, pp.158–159.

620   Ives, *Life and Death of Anne Boleyn*, p.354.

621   Norton, *The Anne Boleyn Papers*, Intro, p.17.

622   Kingston in Norton, *The Anne Boleyn Papers*, pp.333–337.

623   Ives, *Life and Death of Anne Boleyn*, p.356.

624   Norton, *The Anne Boleyn Papers*, p.362.

625   In conversation with Kevin Dutton, PhD.

626   The scaffold was not where the current monument stands, in front of the chapel. Also, it's sad to note the queen's quarters within the Tower

of London have been long lost; however, the remnants of Coldharbour Gate are still there for us to see.

627   Wyatt in Norton, *The Anne Boleyn Papers*, p.32.

628   *Excerpta Historica* in Norton, *The Anne Boleyn Papers*, pp.360–361.

629   De Carles in Norton, *The Anne Boleyn Papers*, p.357.

630   Wyatt in Norton, *The Anne Boleyn Papers*, p.32.

631   Ives, *Life and Death of Anne Boleyn*, pp.357–359.

632   A few examples of those who dared to admit their grief on record include, but are not limited to, the following: Wyatt declared, 'These bloody days have broken my heart': Wyatt in Norton, *The Anne Boleyn Papers*, p.321; Alexander Ales reported not only his own grief at Anne's murder but also that of Thomas Cranmer, archbishop of Canterbury, who 'burst into tears' when informing Ales that Anne was to die that day. This despite his having to distance himself from her in order to protect their religious mission from going down with her: MacCulloch, *Thomas Cranmer*, p.159; Ales in Norton, *The Anne Boleyn Papers*, p.327.